RUSKINLAND

RUSKINLAND

HOW JOHN RUSKIN
SHAPES OUR WORLD

Andrew Hill

PALLAS ATHENE

For Jimena, Tomás and Ana

Contents

★ When John Ruskin was writing his rambling proto-blog *Fors Clavigera* in
the 1870s and 1880s (described in chapter 8), he paused to offer a 'rough
abstract' of the first letters in the series. I have tried to write these chapter
descriptions in similar style.

R's gift of, joy in, seeing. Neurosis about eyesight. His lifelong habits of observation   2. 1819: birth and childhood idyll. R's overbearing parents: their influence, good and bad. R on the 'gifted and talented' register. What would his school report at 13 predict? R's love of geology.   3. The Big Draw. Author argues for relevance of R's ideas about seeing. R's love of gadgets, cyanometers to daguerreotypes. R's Instagram account. Author shares R's disdain for looking but not seeing. Seeing as antidote to busyness.   4. Ruskin family's travel habits. R's double brougham. Mapping Ruskinland. 1833: R's Alpine epiphany in Schaffhausen.

DRAWING AND PAINTING, P. 53

1. 1837: Oxford. R's oddity and genius as undergraduate. First love, unrequited. First illness. Awarded 'double fourth'. 2. R's facility for drawing, inability to 'invent'. Drawing as 'data'. Author advocates for R as great artist. R's drawing habits. His insights into difficulty of drawing. 'The universal law of obscurity'. 3. R as critic. 1840: First encounters with Turner. *Modern Painters*. R's recipe for great art. Father's insider trading in artworks. Mike Leigh's unfair caricature of R. 4. The Pre-Raphaelites: why did R back them? Author praises R's ability to change his mind. R invents world wide web. 5. R as art teacher. *The Elements of Drawing*. Modern artists' debt to R. Ruskin Prize-winners interviewed. Ruskin School of Art today. Author worries about decline of drawing.

BUILDING, P. 81

1. 1845: Venice. R's first two 'art attacks': tomb of Ilaria di Caretto; Tintoretto's *Crucifixion*. R's concern for war-torn Venice. His tight

focus and wide-angle views.   2. 1848: Marriage to Effie Gray. Ill
omens, myths, pubic hair (or lack of). Emma Thompson's unfair
caricature of R. Author unhappy about persistent obsession with
R's sex life (or lack of).   3. R's Venice notebooks, accuracy of. R's
diligence as 'hero of architecture'. His architectural favourites (and
least favourites) in Venice.   4. Did R save or doom Venice? 'La
Ruskin' pizza. *The Seven Lamps of Architecture. The Stones of Venice.*
R defines architecture. Advises how to design your extension.
Suburban Gothic. R's most hated buildings. The Oxford Museum
and its 'happy carvers'.   6. Author puzzles over R's influence on
Gaudí and Frank Lloyd Wright. Why not stop decluttering and
start decorating?   7. 1852: R and Effie return from Venice. Their
loathing of suburban existence. Glen Finglas: Millais and Effie
thrust together. 1854: Annulment.

LANDSCAPE AND NATURE, P. 117

1. 1858: France, Switzerland and Italy. R's appearance and personality in his late 30s. Turner bequest: two myths busted. R's qualms
about Turner. His 'unconversion'. Art attack #3: Veronese in Turin.
'The Law of Help'.   2. R's love of the Alps, dislike of alpinists. Geology and science. John Muir, differences and similarities.
Charles Darwin, differences and similarities. Matterhorn's impact
on British builders.   3. Beauty of Monsal Dale, destroyed by railway, later restored. National parks. Trains, unexpectedly praised
by R. R as cultural pillar of modern Lake District. Author sits on
Ruskin's Seat, Brantwood.   4. Ruskin Land: rural compromises
and contradictions. Sustainability.   5. R compares Bradford to Pisa.
R's influence on town planning, garden cities, suburbs and villages.
Author speculates about R's view of green belt. R on 'nimbyism'.

5. 1884: 'The Storm-Cloud of the Nineteenth Century'. R and Al Gore compared. R's warnings proved right.   6. Los Angeles. The Ruskin Art Club's 'applied Ruskin'. R-inspired campaigns, from Thirlmere to zipwires. The 'genteel' National Trust.

WORK AND EDUCATION, P. 149

1. Unto This Last, the 21st-century furniture workshop; *Unto This Last*, R's 19th-century polemic. 1860: R switches from art to economic criticism. Controversy, prefigured in earlier works. R's influence on Labour MPs, Gandhi etc. Author's Brantwood epiphany. Parallels with 2008 financial crisis.   2. R's work ethic and workaholism. 'The Nature of Gothic' and the spirit of the worker. 1854: R as teacher at Working Men's College. 'Happy carpenters'.   3. 1858: Rose La Touche: first meeting. 1866: Ill-judged proposal of marriage.   4. Author addresses R's liking for young girls. 1864: 'Of Queen's Gardens': 19th-century progressive influence, 20th-century feminist outrage, paradox explored. Girls' schools inspired.   5. The Ruskin curriculum. R's detestation of the 'three Rs'. Vocational education.   6. Schools that followed R's lead. Integrated education today.   7. The Working Men's College today: life-drawing to English as a Second Language.   8. R's ideas spread to the workplace. Robots: author wonders if R would approve. *Work* by Ford Madox Brown.

CRAFT P. 185

1. John Lewis and the 'Ruskin House' look. R and William Morris not the Simon and Garfunkel of craft. Morris: his R-inspired path,

WEALTH AND WELFARE, P. 223

The Whistler trial. R on opium. Idealism versus pragmatism. 1881: Death of Thomas Carlyle; R's breakdown. 1883: Second, ill-fated stint as Oxford professor. 'Baby-talk' to Joan Severn. 1888: Final trip to Venice.

1. Author visits Ruskin, Florida. McMansions and manatees. 2. How Ruskinites made it to Florida, and why. 3. Impossibility of being a true Ruskinian. The Ruskinland network. Author describes change in his attitude. Basil Fotherington-Thomas and Kenneth Clark evoked. Author makes final case for selective revival of R's legacy. 4. R the man survives in Ruskin the place. 5. Author shares R's difficulty in finishing. Finishes nonetheless.

About this book

This book tells the story of who John Ruskin was, how he lived, and what he was like.

It is not exactly a biography. I have relied on some vastly better-researched recent books about Ruskin's life, which I list at the end of the book.

I have set his work in the context of his astonishing life, though, if only to answer the question most frequently posed when I mention John Ruskin. Grasping for a vague memory of something half-heard in the classroom or lecture theatre or glimpsed in a museum or library, people ask: 'Wasn't he the guy who…?'

At the same time as sketching Ruskin's life and career, I try in this book to open a new and different window onto Ruskinland, through interviews with, visits to and research into the people, places and institutions of the 21st century where Ruskin's influence is still alive, and lively. They range from Brantwood in the Lake District, via Switzerland and Italy, to the Florida community of Ruskin, whose tenuous but real links with Ruskin the man I describe in the last chapter.

In providing an outline of Ruskin's prodigious life, I have tried to follow his guidance to students on drawing a tree. In Exercise VI of his manual *The Elements of Drawing*, he wrote: 'Do not take any trouble about the little twigs, which look like a confused network or mist; leave them all out, drawing only the main branches as far as you can see them distinctly'. That said,

I have occasionally digressed to describe a particularly interesting-looking twig.

The book navigates a rough chronological path through Ruskinland, from Ruskin's birth 200 years ago, via sections named for some of the themes that marked the different phases of his work and thinking.

These were not discrete stages of his career, though. Ruskin built a web of connections over decades. Some parts of the network are visible already in his very early work. To contemporaries, for example, his switch to social criticism from art in the 1860s appeared to be entirely fresh and surprising, but the seeds of his later views on economics and work were present even in the fairy tale *The King of the Golden River,* which he wrote for Effie Gray, his future wife, when he was 22 and she was a teenager. That is why I will occasionally leap forward to pick up a lecture or a piece of writing from later in his career or jump back to refer to something he had already said, written or done.

Ruskin sometimes found himself at odds with his earlier self and struggled to reconcile firm convictions he had laid down in his twenties with the more doubting, better-informed judgments of his middle age. He was, in other words, just like the rest of us, with the crucial difference that his early thinking had been published.

Three tortured emotional relationships, or their shadows, pursue Ruskin through his life and through this book – his unrequited love for sherry heiress Adèle Domecq, his short, dysfunctional marriage to Effie Gray, the annulment of which was the source of most of the myths and rumours about his sexuality, and his obsession with, and ill-fated courtship of, Rose La Touche.

Ruskin was extraordinarily well-read. He was also all too aware of the quantity of ideas lying just beyond the border of the many things he already knew. The realisation that if he could not make the connection between them, others might not even bother, was probably one of the frustrations that drove him mad.

He also suffered the blight of any writer who embarks, inspired, on a project that leads off into a perplexing number of different byways.

In a letter from Venice to a friend in 1859, he grumbled that 'one only feels as one should when one doesn't know much about the matter'. Ten years later, he described the same problem in a letter written in Verona, as he researched different architectural styles:

> I am like a physician who has begun practice as an apothecary's boy, and gone on serenely and not unsuccessfully treating his patients under rough notions, generally applicable enough – as, that cold is caught sitting in a draught, and stomach-ache by eating too many plums, and the like – but who has read, at last, and thought, so much about the mucous membrane and the liver, that he dares not give anybody a dose of salts without a day's reflection on the circumstances of the case.[1]

As I slid deeper and deeper into research for this book, I felt some sympathy with that complaint.

St. Albans, September 2018

The Author of Modern Painters, 1843
Ruskin at 24, in the first flush of celebrity.
Photogravure after watercolour by George Richmond

Chapter I

Celebrity

*There is only one place where a man may be nobly thoughtless –
his death-bed. No thinking should ever be left to be done there.
(The Crown of Wild Olive)*

It was influenza, the signature disease of the connected modern world – which John Ruskin had so often attacked – that finally did for the towering intellect of the 19th century.

The two-year epidemic that had affected the Americas, Australia and much of Europe reached Ruskin's rambling home at Brantwood, overlooking Coniston Water in the English Lake District, in January 1900.

Ruskin had passed the preceding months as a frail invalid, sequestered in his bedroom from which he could enjoy the panoramic views of the mountains. The virus had taken hold in the village of Coniston. Despite the relative isolation of Brantwood's distinguished owner, once a servant introduced it to the house, there was little his devoted staff could do to protect him.

Ruskin ate his last proper meal – sole, pheasant and champagne – on 18 January.[1] He died in his sleep at 3.30 pm on Saturday

20 January, surrounded by paintings by J. M. W. Turner, whose reputation he had helped forge. He was 80 – though with his stoop and Old Testament beard, he could have passed for 100 – and perhaps the most famous living Victorian apart from Queen Victoria herself.

Ruskin's high-profile friends and London society contacts immediately called for his remains to be interred in Westminster Abbey, alongside Britain's great poets and artists. His wishes prevailed, however. He had wanted to be buried in the village graveyard in Coniston, across the lake from Brantwood, next to the simple church erected in 1819, the year of his birth.

'In pitiless weather – driving rain and high winds – the body… was brought from his home' to St Andrew's Church 'in a plain hearse, drawn by two horses', for a lying in state, wrote a special correspondent for *The Standard* – falling into the trap of 'pathetic fallacy', the phrase Ruskin coined for the attribution of human emotions to natural phenomena. Four carriages accompanied the body, one bearing his motto 'To-day, to-day, to-day'.

The sage's stern, bearded face, sketched by an artist for the illustrated weekly, *The Graphic*, was visible through a glass panel in the oak casket. 'It was remarked,' wrote the *Guardian*'s correspondent, 'that Mr Ruskin's hair retained its singular yellow-grey colour.'

By that evening, 'not only was every vestige of the coffin… entirely hidden in a mass of exquisite flowers,' continued *The Standard*, 'but the choir seats, the lectern, and even the front of the pulpit, were similarly covered.' Among them was a wreath sent by the 82-year-old doyen of Victorian artists George Frederic Watts, made of leaves cut from a laurel tree in his garden. It was an honour he had previously afforded to only three other giants of Victorian culture on their passing: the painters Frederic Leighton and Edward Burne-Jones, and the poet Alfred Tennyson. All had known and admired, or been admired by, Ruskin.

The Coniston railway had to lay on additional services to carry the floral tributes and the mourners, who crowded the church and churchyard for Ruskin's funeral on the Thursday following his death. It was an irony that the writer, a regular user of railways but also a violent opponent of their spread into the Lake District, would probably have appreciated. Local hotels, unprepared for midwinter tourism, were overwhelmed.

Spinsters from the district, devoted to Ruskin's principles of craft, made the funeral pall. Over the initials 'JR', it featured a wreath of wild roses and the words 'Unto This Last', the title of the fiery polemic with which, in the 1860s, Ruskin, then best-known as an art critic, had launched himself into political, economic and social criticism.[2]

It was a simple ceremony, including a hymn specially written by Canon Hardwicke Drummond Rawnsley, who, inspired by Ruskin's views on conservation, had helped found the National Trust five years earlier. 'There was no black about his burying, except what we wore for our own sorrow; it was remembered how he hated black,' wrote William Gershom Collingwood, Ruskin's friend, secretary, disciple, biographer and now pall-bearer alongside William Wordsworth's grandson.

Ruskin, who had delighted, informed, harangued and annoyed his fellow Victorians for much of the mid-19th century, in lectures, articles and books that later filled 39 volumes – including one for the index alone – had lived his last decade in near-silence, tortured by what would now probably be diagnosed as bipolar disorder. If anything, though, his reclusiveness and the abrupt curtailment of his public appearances in the 1890s had only increased John Ruskin's celebrity.

It was a strange and contradictory sort of fame. As early as 1858, Ruskin had noticed with grave concern 'the stern impossibility of getting anything understood that required patience to understand' as mass production of books took hold.[3] He had fought to preserve the sanctity (and higher price) of quality editions of his work, making sure they were available only by post from his publisher and protégé George Allen. But Ruskin's later popular reputation rested on the success of cheaper versions, issued from the late 1880s by the canny publisher who expanded his range to include decorative editions, in high demand for presentation as gifts or prizes.

These bestsellers rebuilt his fortune. The great polemicist against 'illth' – his word for misused riches – had assiduously, some said recklessly, given away much of the legacy of his wine-merchant father and spent much of the rest continuing to purchase objects, artworks, and books. Those items he had not in turn donated to schools and museums crammed his rooms at Brantwood.

Ruskin had also suffered the equivalent of two tabloid scandals – and found the taint as hard to expunge as any modern celebrity would. The annulment of his marriage to Effie Gray 'by reason of incurable impotency' – and her subsequent happy, and productive union with John Everett Millais – had led to smears and rumours about the reasons for the non-consummation. It later contributed to the collapse of Ruskin's ill-starred attempts to marry the much younger Rose La Touche, the love of his life.

Ruskin had also fought and lost a court battle with James Abbott McNeill Whistler after libelling the artist with a characteristically pungent – but uncharacteristically out of tune – assessment of his impressionistic work.

The cumulative effect of these humiliations exacerbated his

mental turmoil. His breakdown in 1889 in effect ended his public career.

In spite of his reclusiveness, though – and partly because of his oddness and notoriety – by the end of his life Ruskin had become what he most abhorred: a tourist attraction, bringing visitors to the Lake District on the very railways he had condemned. In the last decade of his life at Brantwood he became in the words of the devoted modern Ruskinian James Dearden 'something of a peep show' as people trekked north to see him.[4] Those travellers who could not get a glimpse, let alone an audience, could choose from an array of postcard images of the man, or his house, peddled locally.

Ruskin had been a target for caricaturists since at least the late 1860s. By now others were happy to appropriate his name for their own purposes, with or without his endorsement. Ruskin ceramics, Ruskin linen and lace products, and Ruskin fireplaces were on the market. La Calcina, the Venetian osteria where Ruskin had taken rooms in the 1870s, started to issue postcards boasting of the association (the hotel that replaced it still subtitles itself 'Ruskin's House'). Most bizarrely, the Lewis Cigar Manufacturing Company of Newark, New Jersey, introduced a premium cigar into its range in 1893 called 'The John Ruskin', despite his vocal opposition to tobacco-smoking.[5]

Queen Victoria's fame owed much to her position; by 1900, Ruskin's was based on his own voluminous pronouncements on art, craft and architecture, on the environment, economics and education.

In the days following his death, telegrams and letters of condolence poured into the sage's Cumbrian retreat. As impressive as the quantity, was the range. The *Times* obituary called Ruskin 'the prophet of Brantwood'. Princess Louise, the Queen's daughter, telegraphed her sympathy. So did the Duchess of Albany, widow of Prince Leopold, Victoria's youngest son, whom Ruskin had taught at Oxford and who had become a trustee of his drawing school. The widow of Burne-Jones, one of the Pre-Raphaelite painters supported by Ruskin, wrote of 'the magic of the master's personality'. At the same time, the village tailor sent a wreath with a card that read, simply, 'There was a man sent from God, and his name was John'.[6]

Ruskin's death sent ripples well beyond Coniston. The news galvanised the network of societies, established in British industrial cities including Manchester, Glasgow, Birmingham and Sheffield during the later years of his life to propagate his thinking.

The Ruskin Union, formed only three weeks after his death to promote the study of his work as 'at once profound, sympathetic, and generous, and nobly used for the benefit of mankind', was presided over by Lord Windsor and Lord May, and included various bishops, deans and university professors on its inaugural committee.

By October of the same year, Hardwicke Rawnsley had raised money for a memorial to Ruskin at one of the writer's childhood haunts overlooking Derwent Water near Keswick – technically the first National Trust property in the Lake District. The memorial also spawned a series of souvenirs, including brassware, toasting forks with the monument as a handle, and miniature replicas of the monument itself.

A campaign to erect a memorial in Westminster Abbey got under way within weeks of his death and a medallion was unveiled in 1902, though Lady Burne-Jones was among those who argued that the critic himself would have condemned a 'continuation of the system which has already defaced the incomparable walls of the Abbey with modern incongruities'.[7]

Across Britain, municipalities and individuals sought to commemorate Ruskin by applying his name to roads, schools, and parks. Ruskin Park, near his childhood home in Denmark Hill, was opened in 1907. In the years immediately after his death, Ruskin's social and economic criticism inspired activists such as Mohandas K. Gandhi, pioneer of non-violent protest and Indian independence. The novelists Marcel Proust and Leo Tolstoy lauded the power and purpose of his prose.

Leather-bound 3- by 4-inch booklets with decorative front- and end-papers, containing the text of lectures or extracts from longer works, were sold as gifts, mainly for young women, a reminder of the writer's strong progressive influence on the education of girls.

Pioneers and disciples of his thinking – perhaps with cheap editions of *Unto This Last* or other favoured works in their backpacks – fanned out during the final years of his life and afterwards to found colonies, claim landmarks and establish townships in his name, from Australia to North America. At Ruskinite co-operative communities set up in the United States, Ruskin food was served and Ruskin music played. The most dedicated members of one ill-fated Ruskinian commune in Tennessee sported Tolstoyan bloomers called 'Ruskin pants'.

Yet the first decade and a half of the 20th century marked the peak of Ruskin's visible influence. By the middle of the century, Ruskin's name had faded.

Visiting the Ruskin Museum, then at Meersbrook Park in Sheffield, for a BBC talk just ahead of the 50th anniversary of the great polymath's death, the writer Lawrence du Garde Peach conducted a vox pop of passers-by: 'Not one knew that Ruskin was a writer. Not one in 50 knew anything that he had written.... Such is fame.'

This once world-famous Victorian thinker had become an encrusted oddity – 'some dreary old has-been with a beard' – unread and largely unknown. Yet, as du Garde Peach, broadcasting in 1950 at the nadir of Ruskin's reputation, pointed out, 'he influenced his age, and he has influenced ours. Things might have been even worse if Ruskin had never lived. Let us remember that.'[8]

Chapter II

Ruskinland

I went mad because nothing came of my work.
(Fors Clavigera)

❋

For much of the 20th century, John Ruskin's reputation seemed as dead and buried as the man himself.

His ideas were quickly overtaken by the industrial, political, economic, military and even artistic forces that ravaged and shaped the century after his death. His contemporary Charles Dickens is often invoked as a writer who would have relished chronicling the 21st century's excesses. But few now call on Ruskin for ideas or inspiration.

Ruskin's long-termist, pre-industrial and ruralist ideals seem to have little connection with our city-centred, technology-fuelled lives of instant gratification. For most people, the Victorian age's best-known, most controversial and most prolific intellectual is still the bearded old has-been referred to in that 1950 BBC broadcast: prudish, aloof, self-righteous, conservative to a fault, and resistant to progress.

Ruskin's personal motto, stamped on later editions of his

books, was, however, powerful, simple, and remains highly relevant: 'To-day'. He rallied followers to take on practical challenges and to do now what they might otherwise put off until tomorrow.

Nobody disputes John Ruskin's importance as a historical figure. I lost count of the number of times I was referred first to archivists, historians or librarians before I made it clear that I was more interested in seeing what was happening now in places that he influenced. Plenty of enthusiasts want to celebrate how Ruskin was then. I want to show why we need Ruskin today.

Ruskin shaped – and still shapes – the world we live in, the way we think and work, the environment, built and natural, that surrounds us, and many of the services we enjoy. Two hundred years since his birth in 1819, we live in 'Ruskinland'.

It becomes obvious that Ruskinland exists as soon as you pick up the trail of Ruskin, say in an art gallery or a museum. Those are the places where his legacy is most obvious, but he is also present in the work of craftspeople and artisans, the thinking of ecologists and scientists, and even in the dry regulatory crevices of modern finance, or the ambitious mission and purpose statements of big companies.

Almost everyone knows at least a little about John Ruskin or his work. Very few people, though, have sight of the whole of Ruskin – which is hardly surprising given the protean, polymathic nature of the man and his thinking.

As a teenager, studying the history of art, I acquired the best-known piece of the patchwork: his role as artist and art critic, a fixture in London artistic circles before he had turned forty. When I revisited Venice for the first time in decades, I found that the places and works that astonished and energised Ruskin in the 19th century – the Tintorettos in the Scuola di San Rocco, the Carpaccios in the Accademia – were on my itinerary in the second half of the 20th, when I first visited his 'paradise of cities', aged 16, with a school art trip. As a regular traveller in the Lake District, with a holiday home not far from Brantwood, I knew about Ruskin's love of the region. I was well aware that Oxford boasted a Ruskin College and a Ruskin School of Art.

But even to those who know a part of Ruskin's legacy, other parts remain obscure. Only relatively recently did I come across his social and economic criticism, and observations on the environment, which seem ever more relevant in an unequal and polluted world. It turned out that people who knew about those corners of Ruskinland were as eager to show me round as I was to explain my journey through other regions of his influence.

The whistlestop tour – which, incidentally, Ruskin, one of the greatest and most leisurely travellers in history, would never deign to join – goes like this.

Ruskin's ideas sowed the seeds of the modern welfare state, universal state education and healthcare free at the point of delivery.

His acute appreciation of natural beauty underpinned the National Trust, while his sensitivity to pollution and environmental change, decades before it was considered other than a local phenomenon, prefigured the modern green movement.

He staked his reputation on Turner and the Pre-Raphaelites when they were under fire, ensuring their reputations have continued to burn brightly even as his has suffered.

His violent critique of free market economics, *Unto This Last,* was the book that most influenced the first intake of Labour MPs in 1906 – more than 40 years after its publication. Those articles, and a series of other writings and lectures in which Ruskin laid into the smug captains of Victorian capitalism, are striking precursors of the current debate about inequality, executive pay, ethical and purposeful business, and the perils and opportunities of greater automation.

Even some elements of Ruskin's personal style could translate to the modern age. After I lectured in 2015 about the lessons for modern business in *Unto This Last*, someone asked me whether Ruskin would have joined Twitter.

He would have struggled with a 280-character limit, that is for sure.

Ruskin wrote a lot: nine million published words by some counts. He was also, according to one delighted correspondent, 'the best letter-writer of his or any age', sending 3,000 to his cousin and later housekeeper Joan Severn alone – and she lived in the same house for much of the final part of his life. Many of the thousands of Ruskin's letters in collections around the world remain unstudied.

Still, it is only one of the fascinating aspects of Ruskin's legacy that erroneous versions of the *kind* of thing he would have said still ripple through our online culture. His many aphorisms are regularly circulated on social media. It turns out, on investigation, that he did not write or say many of the maxims attributed to him. But the fact these misattributions and invented quotations are plausible 'Ruskinisms' even if they are found nowhere in his work, suggests that even those who do not know much about Ruskin, somehow know enough to understand and appreciate the language of Ruskinland.

It is true that Ruskin is hard to read. Where to start, for one thing? Recommending his books can be a quick way to deter people from exploring him further. Not all are available in accessible editions, though the complete 39 volumes can be found, free, online thanks to the Lancaster University, which is custodian of much of his work. It is easy to become bogged down in his fierce, tangly prose, which stretches across page-long paragraphs in multiple volumes: five for *Modern Painters*, three for *The Stones of Venice*, 96 'letters' in his extraordinary blog-like series of pamphlets called *Fors Clavigera*. His long sentences are spiky with Biblical references. His work takes time to digest. Some of what he said and thought, super-charged with a sense of imperial and religious superiority, is, frankly, now indigestible.

It is a pity not to read him at all, though. Once under way, you can become used to his magnificent, orotund style and find it hard to stop, such is the richness of the writing and the striking parallels with modern preoccupations.

Ruskin may have claimed not to enjoy a fight, but as a young man, he was not afraid to provoke and pursue debate, through all contemporary media, including books, magazines, pamphlets and letters to newspapers. He was only 24 when he launched his passionate public advocacy of Turner's work in the first volume of *Modern Painters*. Much of his writing has an exhilarating rudeness. He is entertainingly cruel about bad artists and bad art. This would make him a fine critic and columnist even now. His insights are often strikingly modern. For instance, his withering assessment of the contemporary condition, from the fifth volume of *Modern Painters*, is no less relevant than it was when it was published in 1860. People appear, he wrote, to have 'no other desire or hope but to have large houses and to be able to move fast'.

In his prime, Ruskin was also a hugely popular public speaker, attracting sell-out audiences and lively press criticism with his controversial views and idiosyncratic approach. He would not have been an obvious proponent of the popular TED talk, with its time limit of 20 minutes. His lectures often lasted over an hour. But as a speaker, he had a gift, as one modern biographer has written, for being 'both combative and inspiring'.[1] What is

more, his intense visual sense and interest in early photographic technology would make him a natural enthusiast for today's
image-based social media. Who would not want to follow the
world's most discerning eye for natural and manmade beauty on
Instagram?

'There are few thoughts likely to come across ordinary men,
which have not already been expressed by greater men in the best
possible way,' he wrote in *Modern Painters*; 'and it is a wiser more
generous, more noble thing to remember and point out the perfect words, than to invent poorer ones, wherewith to encumber
temporarily the world'.[2] Ruskin was extra-ordinary, so I make
no apology for quoting him – and for recommending later some
accessible ways of exploring his work.

Another problem with navigating Ruskin is that he is hard
to categorise. 'I am never satisfied that I have handled a subject
properly till I have contradicted myself at least three times,' he
said.[3] He surprised his own fans and enemies with his sudden
swerve into social and political criticism in the 1860s and at different times described himself as a 'violent Tory of the old school'
and 'a Communist of the old school – reddest also of the red',
which always makes me think, that must have been some school.

Where in the bookshop or library should his books be shelved?
Under Art? History? Science? Economics? Politics? Biography?
Different parts of Ruskin's work have a good claim to sit under
any or all of those labels – and more.

I imagine the 39 volumes taking up a whole bank of the 'Smart
Thinking' section of Waterstones. But when I visited the magnificent branch of the bookshop that now occupies Bradford's old
Wool Exchange (a neo-Gothic building whose design Ruskin
himself influenced), I found nothing by Ruskin on its shelves.

Then there is Ruskin's unpalatable darker side. Some of his

reactionary views on race, gender and nationhood are shocking even when viewed in their Victorian context, in part because they seem so clearly at odds with the progressive reforms that his other writings inspired. I will address what informed those views later. But it seems crazy to bury the whole of Ruskin's thinking because of these opinions, let alone to allow the message of his best work to be drowned out by snickering about his sex life, or lack of one.

Lawrence du Garde Peach threw down a gauntlet in that gloomy broadcast from the 1950s when he suggested that 'things might have been worse' if Ruskin had never existed. That is an excessively negative way of thinking about his influence. John Ruskin reminds us of many positive ways to live a better life today:

Seeing and understanding. Ruskin's great lesson to his successors was the vital importance of learning to see clearly in order to understand the world around us. He used to say that such understanding could be achieved through drawing. But the mark on paper was not the point. He wanted people to exercise and refine their powers of observation in a way that fits precisely with today's quest to improve visual literacy.

Reflection. In the same way, Ruskin wanted us to devote time to seeing and thinking. His way of travelling – by horse-drawn carriage, slowly – looks old-fashioned to us and he was wealthy enough, thanks to his father's commercial success and patronage, to be able to take his time. But his leisurely approach chimes with the counsel of monks, mindfulness experts and other advocates of slow food, slow travel and slow living, in our fast-moving world, to live 'in the moment'.

Provenance. Ruskin believed strongly that buildings, work and craft should be rooted in the landscape and communities around them. He urged young artists to start by being true to nature, and artisans to use local materials. As the consequences of globalisation become clearer, it is important to see this not as a prescription to move backwards or stay stuck in the past, but as a more productive, happier and better-balanced way of advancing.

Humans and their environment. It is too tempting to think of Ruskin as an unbending defender of the status quo, or a grumpy crusader for neo-feudalism, cottage life and unattainable rural idylls. He was, rather, someone who thought deeply about how to encourage the fruitful co-existence of people and the places where they lived and worked. He loved wild open spaces, such as the Lakeland fells, but he understood how people related to them. He loathed overbuilt industrial cities – the hellish melting pots of the mid to late 19th century – but he supported ways to make those communities more bearable and more liveable.

One way was through *thoughtful planning and building*. Ruskin fought to conserve buildings and landscapes, not to restore them in new and inauthentic ways, and to preserve a balance of creative architecture, nature, and public amenities. He outlined for the first time, through study of his beloved Venice, among other places, that buildings and cities can have a moral quality, expressed through their art and architecture. There are lessons here for planners, architects and builders, as they strike a balance between pressure to house growing urban populations and to preserve green spaces.

Ethical leadership and meaningful work. Ruskin was rightly criticised in his day for not always being able – or even willing – to put into practice his wild-sounding ideas. He relied on disciples, delegates and the occasional long-suffering employee to do so. It is hard, then, to see why any chief executive, team leader or member of staff should listen to a man who never had a conventional job. Ruskinland is more than ever in need of his principles of ethical leadership, though – what I call rules for the modern merchant. Ruskin was the first great standard-bearer for meaning in work, which he saw shining through the creative impulses of the anonymous builders and decorators of the great Gothic cathedrals.

Finally, *connectedness*. Ruskin was the central weaver of a web of extraordinarily diverse interests. He saw – if not always clearly – how art, science, nature, history, the environment, politics, economics and industry sprang from and relied on each other. We would now describe this linkage using many dull words with the prefix 'inter': interdisciplinary, interconnection, interdependence, the internet itself. John Ruskin's one-man worldwide web had plenty of gaps, patches and oddities (as does its technologically fuelled modern equivalent, for all its claims to comprehensiveness). But in it, Ruskin cultivated myriad hyperlinks to new areas of enlightenment and exploration.

Ruskin was, in other words, a genius at what modish strategists now sometimes call 'joining the dots'. He was much more than that, though. He was also aware that if we did not carefully cultivate the links between these dots, the whole web could collapse. That insight was obvious in his prophetic concern about air pollution and destruction of the natural world and in his pragmatic focus on the education of workers ground down by industrialisation.

To rise to du Garde Peach's implicit challenge, if you had removed Ruskin from the network, it is possible some elements of Ruskinland would still have been built. Ruskin was not, after all, the only 19th-century thinker preoccupied with how his world was changing and how to guide it down the best path. But he was among the most prescient and inspirational. Without him and his more pragmatic and campaigning followers, many of the enlightened ideas of the modern world would have taken longer to evolve, probably developed differently, and in some cases might not have developed at all. John Ruskin, as we shall see, opened eyes.

Chapter III

Seeing

The greatest thing a human soul ever does in this world is to see something,
and tell what it saw in a plain way. Hundreds of people can talk for
one who can think, but thousands think for one who can see.
To see clearly is poetry, prophecy and religion, all in one.
(Modern Painters)

━ *I* ━

To anyone who knows the heavily populated, overbuilt, traffic-
plagued suburbs of South London today, Ruskin's wistful descriptions of the neighbourhood, with its verdant vistas across
the 'beautiful meadows and high avenues' of the 'Dulwich valley' towards 'the plain of Croydon' have an unlikely, even comic
quality.[1]

These days, the roads that lead off down the ridge – near
Ruskin Park, created in his memory close to the site of his south
London homes – are crammed with rows of Victorian semi-
detached and terraced villas. Ruskin's vivid crusade for better
architecture had, to his horror, encouraged this type of building.

When I first moved to London, I lived in such a house on
Frankfurt Road, which descends steeply from near the top of
the ridge, close to the site of the Herne Hill house that Ruskin's

parents bought for him and his wife Effie in 1852. From there, I used to walk down to the station at North Dulwich, to take the commuter train into the City. It is true that you can see the matching ridge of Forest Hill from the top of the road (a parallel road is Ruskin Walk, named in memory of the writer in 1905), but I do not recall celebrating the view.

By the time he was writing his wonderful but unreliable auto-biography *Præterita* in the 1880s, Ruskin believed such railways had ruined the pastoral idyll he lived in as a child. When Ruskin was young, Herne Hill was a semi-rural and wooded area, set apart from central London. If you believe this retrospective ac-count, despite its digressions, omissions and inventions, he once took a stroll with his mother from the family home in Denmark Hill – at a site just opposite what is now Ruskin Park – up to the ridge. After contemplating the panorama across towards Dartford in Kent, he 'frightened my mother out of her wits by saying "the eyes were coming out of my head"'.

Mrs Ruskin, typically, feared her delicate only child was com-ing down with sunstroke. His affliction was both less serious and far more profound. He was demonstrating what he described as 'a sensual faculty of pleasure in sight, as far as I know unparalleled'.[2]

Seeing, for Ruskin, was not just believing, it was understand-ing. His eyes stayed firmly in his head that day. But they remained wide open throughout his life as he drew, painted, lectured about and taught his particular vision of the world. His 'pleasure in sight' was the foundation for his deserved reputation, later in his career, as a visionary – somebody who quite literally saw things before others did.

Ruskin combined his 'sensual faculty' with an acute appreciation for colour – vital in his later mission to describe and save Venice's multi-hued Gothic architecture. He described it as 'a gift, just as definitely granted to one person, and denied to another, as an ear for music'.[3]

Unsurprisingly, the prospect that he might lose this facility could throw him into despair. Ruskin sometimes took 'a quite neurotic interest' in his eyes and measures to protect them.[4] He was known as 'Giglamps' when a student at Oxford because he wore 'blue spectacles', and later had special sunglasses made to shield his eyes from snow-glare when he was climbing and drawing in the Alps.

When only in his late twenties, he wrote to his mother in a characteristic fit of anxiety about his health. He was afraid 'swimming strings and eels' troubling his vision were a sign of that his sight was failing and with it his ability to 'look at things as I used to'. They were almost certainly innocuous 'floaters', semi-transparent shapes caused by collagen filaments that 'float' across the jelly of the eye. The fact he was rarely depicted wearing spectacles was not only down to vanity. He does not seem to have needed vision-correcting glasses until he was in his mid-fifties.

Mostly, though, Ruskin rejoiced in his powers of vision. Throughout his life, he boasted of passing time contemplating nature, paintings or buildings. Aged ten, when at the beach, he would spend 'four or five hours every day in simply staring and wondering at the sea, – an occupation which never failed me till I was forty'.[5] In one of the few self-portraits he painted, he depicts himself in his trademark light-blue stock, a kind of pre-tied cravat, picked out to match his intense blue eyes, which gaze penetratingly back at the viewer.

Even in his later years, Ruskin took pleasure in observation. From the jetty he had built at Brantwood, he would sometimes row his boat, the Jumping Jenny – known to everybody as 'the Jump' – out to the centre of Coniston Water and lie in the bottom of the boat staring at the sky. The turret on the side of his old bedroom at the Lake District house and the distinctive Venetian-style windows in the dining room – seven of them, as in the 'seven lamps of architecture' he laid down in his book of the same name – were eyes onto the panoramas he loved. He could gaze out to Coniston Old Man, the distinctive peak opposite his house, or south down the Lake towards the viewpoints that he had first visited as a boy, probably following the directions of the 18th century pioneer of the picturesque, Thomas West.

From Brantwood, the elderly sage could soak up the views long after he had largely stopped writing, drawing or even speaking. One of the last references to his eyes in his diary – in May 1886 – is a boast about their strength: 'I see everything far and near down to the blue lines on this paper and up to the snow lines on the Old Man – as few men of my age.'[6]

⟩⟩⟩ 2 ⟨⟨⟨

If young John was born with these gifts that served him so well throughout his life, then he owed much to his parents for cultivating them.

Ruskin was an only child. His parents were of the same Scottish stock – in fact, they were first cousins. His father, John James, was a bluff, driven, self-made sherry merchant, who worked tirelessly in partnership with Pedro Domecq of the well-known Spanish sherry dynasty, and a wealthy investor Henry Telford. His mother was born Margaret Cock in Croydon, the pious daughter of a pub landlord who had married up and into the Ruskin family. She was already in her late thirties when she gave birth to John, on 8 February 1819, in a terraced house off Brunswick Square in central London. Like many of the buildings where the Ruskin family lived, it no longer exists. The multi-tiered mid-1960s Brunswick Centre stands on the spot, and the commemorative plaque once attached to the building is an orphan, looked after at Brantwood, one of the few Ruskin houses to have escaped such a fate.[7]

The young boy was coddled and encouraged by his wealthy, doting, and over-protective parents. His father's commercial success allowed them to move to the prosperous comfort of 26 Herne Hill, a house surrounded by gardens that the young Ruskin sketched, described and learnt about in his early childhood and remembered fondly ever after.

John James also had a good eye. If not as acute as his son's, it still played a part in his formation of his son's early prodigious career as an art critic, while he and Margaret, in their different ways, laid the foundations for his admired literary style.

John James took drawing lessons himself, and later arranged them for his son. He was, as we shall see, an active investor in fine art and good books. He invited interesting visitors to the Herne Hill house, to meet John, who was essentially home-schooled until he was 14. John James supplied a literary diet of the classics (Shakespeare, Pope, Johnson), as well as more contemporary writers such as the Scottish novelist Walter Scott and the Romantic poet Byron, both of whom influenced Ruskin profoundly, as well as introducing the boy to popular theatre.

Margaret Ruskin added the Bible. And how. She drummed the rhythm and substance of scripture into her beloved young son every day, reading with him and obliging to him learn tracts by heart. She 'so exercised me in the Scriptures', a grateful Ruskin wrote, 'as to have made every word of them familiar to my ear in habitual music'.[8]

Under such powerful parental stimulus, Ruskin, aged seven, was already writing poems. His first published verse, 'On Skiddaw and Derwent Water' – a significant portent of his later love of the Lakes, appeared when he was only nine. As he turned 12, he produced the 2,000-line *Iteriad*, a lumbering epic poem in the manner of William Wordsworth, the ageing Lakeland poet whom the family had excitedly glimpsed at church during an early trip to the Lakes.

Margaret and John James shielded many of his talents from mundane childhood matters. Ruskin wrote later that he had had no toys, except a box of building bricks. This was an exaggeration. But they were certainly what we would now call helicopter parents. They shaped him, as our parents are bound to do, but – in line with Philip Larkin's poem *This Be The Verse* – they also messed him up. Ruskin put up with, even invited and played to, their hovering ministrations, demands and concerns until he was well into his forties. (The ageing Margaret Ruskin was said to remark 'John, you are talking great nonsense' if the celebrated middle-aged critic banged on too long on subjects with which she disagreed.) 'Get out as early as you can, / And don't have any kids yourself,' advises Larkin. Ruskin may have followed the second part of the poet's counsel, but he inflicted lasting damage on his own psyche by not following the first.

Kept outside the formal school system until he was a teenager, the young Ruskin had few friends of his own age (though an older cousin brought to live with the Ruskins provided a sort of surrogate sister for a while). But he also claimed that being secluded in south London helped him develop ever sharper powers of observation and perception.

At two centuries' distance, knowing what we know about how Ruskin's life and career developed, it is hard to provide an unbiased report on the boy Ruskin. 'Could do better' is not part of it, however. His parents ladled on the praise. 'You may be doomed to enlighten a People by your Wisdom & to adorn an age by your learning,' wrote his father to the ten-year-old genius. Clearly, Ruskin was a prodigy of sorts. In today's school system, he would have jumped straight onto the gifted and talented register. But like many prodigies he was also doomed to suffer a troubled and difficult personal life.

Stop the clock in 1832, when Ruskin was 13, and an observer would probably have predicted a literary future for the precocious boy, based on his production of poetry alone. John James and Margaret thought – and hoped – he would take a path into the clergy. John himself claimed that his first ambition, based on a deep and dedicated lifelong interest in and love of the mineral world, was to become president of the Geological Society, where he was a member until his death.

The obsession with geology is another indication that 'seeing' was Ruskin's greatest gift. His passion for the discipline spurred him to start a mineralogical dictionary before he turned 13. It was just one of the activities he mastered that allows us to classify him as a scientist before he was an artist. But his geological collection – which ultimately amounted to more than 1,500 items stored and displayed in mahogany cabinets at Brantwood – was also for study and description.

'A stone, when it is examined, will be found a mountain in miniature,' he wrote in *Modern Painters*.[9] Throughout his career as an educator, Ruskin used to set his students the apparently simple but highly demanding test of observing and drawing rocks and pebbles. In his 1857 manual, *The Elements of Drawing*, he urged amateur artists to 'look your stone antagonist boldly in the face'.[10]

The book also contains this telling summary of Ruskin's aim:

'The whole technical power of painting depends on our recovery of what may be called *the innocence of the eye*; that is to say, of a sort of childish perception of these flat stains of colour, merely as such, without consciousness of what they signify – as a blind man would see them if suddenly gifted with sight.'

Or, as he told listeners at the opening of the Cambridge School of Art in 1858, 'we shall always do most good by simply endeavouring to enable the student to see natural objects clearly and truly'.[11]

>ɛɛ *3* ◂◂

The opportunity to exploit the gift of Ruskin-like clearsightedness has come down to us in the 21st century by a direct line through the Guild of St George, the idiosyncratic charity that Ruskin himself founded and that flourishes today.

The Guild launched the Campaign for Drawing in 2000, on the centenary of Ruskin's death. It has since evolved into The Big Draw, an annual festival of drawing that stages events but also seeds local drawing activities round a chosen theme every October.

While drawing was the genesis of the campaign, its purpose goes far beyond the application of pencil to paper. The theme of the Big Draw in 2018 was 'Play', chosen with the aim of triggering exploration and experimentation. Drawing is 'a mode of thinking that you can develop. It's like rewiring your brain,' Kate Mason, the charity's director since 2013, told me when I met her at the Big Draw's quirky offices, on an island in the Thames in London's Docklands.

The same spirit animates the John Ruskin Prize for artists,

Kate Mason

inaugurated by the Guild and the Big Draw in 2014. The prize's aim: to uphold Ruskin's belief that drawing 'helps us to see the world more clearly and therefore take greater heed of its fragility'.

British-based artist Kate Genever summed up the importance of seeing in the note accompanying her exquisite pencil and crayon drawing – displayed alongside items from the Ruskin collection in Sheffield in 2017 – of two (glass) eyes. 'To draw the thing that makes this cycle possible is to bring attention to the act of looking and the notion of being seen,' she explained about the work. It is called *I was looking back to see if you were looking back to see if I was looking back at you*. 'I look at the thing that looks, but these eyes are not real,' she writes. 'They are beautifully pretending. Which focuses us onto ideas of honesty and beauty.'

These are all clues to the wider value and endurance of Ruskin's insight about clarity of vision in an era that places emphasis on the importance of visual literacy. The ability, in Mason's words, 'to read the world' as Ruskin did has a vivid importance today, when people are more likely to be looking down at their smartphone screens than out or up at the sea, sky, and mountains, or the buildings around them.

'Sight for us has become omnivorous and largely undiscriminating,' wrote Nichola Johnson, then director of the Sainsbury Centre for Visual Art in 2006, in contrast to Ruskin's highly discriminating sight, and his emphasis on 'depth of looking, not speed of assimilation'.[12] She made that judgment just months before the launch of the first iPhone, and at a point when Evan Spiegel, founder of Snapchat, the application that represents the acme of the smartphone's combination of image-making and connectivity, was still a spoilt teenager in Los Angeles.

It is easy to imagine just how abhorrent John Ruskin would have found Snapchat's self-destructing image-based messages. Yet though he was well aware of how devices could get in the way of an unobstructed appreciation of a scene, he was in his day a regular user of mechanical and optical aids to drawing.

Thomas West, in his *Guide to the Lakes*, which Ruskin may well have used on his childhood visits, advised the use of a 'Claude glass'. This was a tinted convex mirror, which required the would-be landscape painter to turn his or her back on the scene, the better to observe it. Ruskin took with him on his travels a *camera lucida*, a prism that projected an image of a view onto paper for artists. As a teenager, he made a 'cyanometer', a device to measure shades of blue in the sky, based on an invention by Horace-Bénédict de Saussure, the Swiss author and geologist whose *Voyages dans les Alpes* had been a cherished 15th birthday present. (A cyanometer sounds more technical than it is: Ruskin described it simply as a 'sheet of paper gradated from deepest blue to white'.)

Later, Ruskin was himself a pioneer and early adopter of photographic methods. He came across daguerreotypes when still a student and may have been among the first to use the technology. Later, he worked with long-suffering assistants to record images, from the Matterhorn to San Marco in Venice. On his third visit to that city in 1845 he bought some daguerreotypes and enthused about them as 'glorious things'. In an era when laborious engravings were the principal way of transmitting faithful reproductions of paintings, sculptures, buildings and views of nature, these images seemed to him 'very nearly the same thing as carrying off the palace itself; every chip and stone and stain is there'.[13]

But Ruskin also foresaw how photography could become commonplace. He wrote to Julia Margaret Cameron, the Victorian portrait photographer, in 1868 to say that he already 'knew everything that a photograph could and could not do' in the 1850s and had since lost interest in the form.[14] Later, he had a spat with her in which she declared him 'not worthy of photographs'.

I joked in the last chapter that we would all wish to follow Ruskin on Instagram. He was a voracious collector and recorder of scenes that appealed to him, putting a premium on accuracy – which today Instagram users might hashtag #nofilter. (One recent travel feature included his beloved Lake District in a short list of the six 'most Instagram-worthy places in the UK'.)[15] His account would have provided a way of seeing the world through his own eyes, just as his detailed descriptions of works of art and architecture, or geological structures, were a window on his thinking in the 1800s. On the other hand, the contemporary obsession with selecting and snapping excursions, holidays, meals and views, only because they are 'Instagrammable' would have appalled him. The use of images to excite envy and show off 'illth' – riches used for unsavoury or useless purposes – would have been, to Ruskin, complete anathema.

We are these days often guilty of looking but not seeing. On a recent trip to Venice, I watched a couple on the ferry from the airport spend much of the trip setting up a selfie-stick and GoPro action camera to record our arrival, and much of the second part of the journey studying the results on a 3- by 5-inch screen. They were the 21st-century equivalents of the four chattering French tourists a typically judgmental Ruskin spotted in the Simplon Pass in 1876, who 'never moved their heads, nor raised their eyes' to take in the spectacular views around them.

Ruskin was no idle dreamer. He was for most of his career an anxious workaholic, prone to worry excessively about his lapses in concentration or occasional periods of writer's block. But for him, taking the time to see clearly was the first step towards de-cluttering the mind and understanding what was important.

Seeing, for Ruskin, was also an antidote to the busy-ness of the industrial revolution, a way of stepping back from the noisy assault of the day to day, just as it could these days be a solution to the 'always on' culture of the modern city or workplace. He was a century or more ahead of his time in advocating for people to make an active effort to apply their minds. In 1849, he wrote about how he turned a boring hike through 'a monotonous bit of vine-country' in Switzerland into a moment of poetry through a 'possession-taking grasp of the imagination'. By looking more closely and 'putting his mind into the scene… it gilded all the dead walls, and I felt a charm in every vine tendril that hung over them'. He made, as the theologian Alister McGrath has put it, 'an intentional decision to see the world in a new way'.[16]

In *The Stones of Venice*, the fruit of an intense period of observation and analysis of Venice's crumbling buildings in the 1840s,
Ruskin points out that the 'whole function of the artist in the
world is to be a seeing and feeling creature'. 'Nothing must come
between Nature and the artist's sight; nothing between God and
the artist's soul,' he writes, and goes on:

> Neither calculation nor hearsay – be it the most subtle of cal-
> culations, or the wisest of sayings – may be allowed to come
> between the universe, and the witness which art bears to its
> visible nature. The whole value of that witness depends on its
> being *eye*-witness; the whole genuineness, acceptableness, and
> dominion of it depend on the personal assurance of the man
> who utters it. All its victory depends on the veracity of the
> one preceding word, "Vidi."[17]

The Stones of Venice appeared at the beginning of the 1850s,
when Ruskin was still in his early thirties. But while his ideas
changed, and his sprawling works record the changes, 'Vidi' ('I
saw') remained his credo. It would have been as apt a choice for
his motto as 'To-day'.

Ruskin would have known that the 21st-century promotion
of mindfulness and meditation was no fad. As he felt himself slid-
ing into periods of insanity in later life, he may even have used
the discipline of detailed looking and drawing – for example, in
preparing his exquisite studies of peacock and poultry feathers
from the 1870s – as a way of calming himself down.

'He had stared fixedly at details all his life, and, as he grew
older, to look into something intensively was like re-entering a
lost Eden,' the art historian Kenneth Clark wrote.[18]

A telling photograph by Frederick Hollyer, taken in 1894, six
years before Ruskin's death, shows the writer in profile, gazing

Datur hora quieti

left, perhaps out of one of those Brantwood windows. His face, long grey beard and clasped hands are illuminated and the rest of his body and surroundings are in shadow.

A spent force, Ruskin was by this time largely devoted to contemplation and little action. Ruskin's cousin Joan Severn, by then essentially Ruskin's communications director as well as carer, probably masterminded the photo shoot. Looking back, it served Ruskin's reputation poorly. It is certainly the image that springs to many people's mind when they think of him. As a white-bearded sage, his appearance eventually seemed to sum up superannuated Victorian ideals to the younger generation that had survived the first world war.

Even so, the title given to the portrait – *Datur hora quieti* or 'An hour given to quiet' – has a nice relevance for our unreflective lives.

~ 4 ~

Ruskin's father was a traveller by necessity, as the tireless frontman for a thriving sherry trading partnership, and by choice, as a wealthy merchant with the wherewithal to take long tours of Britain and continental Europe. He and Margaret took their son with them. Before he was six, the family had indulged in the then equivalent of a short break – actually several weeks – to France and Belgium, including a side-trip to the battlefield of Waterloo. Scotland and the Lake District (hence the Wordsworthian epic, among other early writing) came next. Then, in 1833, the Ruskins struck out further afield, heading to the Rhineland, Switzerland, and Italy.

Ruskin spent more than half his life abroad. His accounts of his travels are a strange mixture of occasional homesickness for the comforts of Denmark Hill and Herne Hill and, later, Brantwood, and a yearning to go away again. When he faced crisis, one of his first reactions often seems to have been to take off for the continent, or at least for a hotel or inn, where he was used to staying. He liked to proceed slowly by carriage, generally only in fair weather. Later, though he did go by rail, he declared himself an enemy of railway building and rail travel, which 'transmutes a man from a traveller into a living parcel'.[19]

The Ruskins – and later John himself – toured Europe with quite an entourage and in some style. An 'avant-courier' went ahead to haggle with innkeepers and avoid the 'trouble and

disgrace of trying to speak French or any other foreign language',
as Ruskin put it, while the family and servants followed behind,
at a modest pace of seven miles an hour, or 40 or 50 miles a day,
in a six-person carriage complete with hidden compartments for
luggage, luxurious cushions, and snugly fitted windows.[20] As railways took over from coaches in the second half of the century,
Ruskin maintained an impractical, but romantic nostalgia for the
coaching days. He built a coach-house at Brantwood and kept a
coachman and horses. In 1876, he ordered a tailor-made luxury
'double brougham' – featuring more 'secret' compartments – and
made a special celebratory journey from London to Brantwood,
via Sheffield, on the old coaching routes.

It is a cliché to say of modern tourists that they wish to 'see
the world'. It is true of Ruskin, too, but he has some obvious advice for the frazzled, time-poor 21st-century sightseer. It was the
quality of what he saw, not the quantity that mattered. Recalling
his childhood journeys with fondness, he made much of the fact
that he always had a good view. Perched on a chest containing his
clothes, his 'horizon of sight [was] the widest possible'. 'We did
not travel for adventures, nor for company, but to see with our
eyes, and to measure with our hearts,' he said, echoing his judgement of great artists as those who see and feel.[21]

I have tried to plot the places Ruskin visited in his lifetime
on a Google Map. It is quite a task, given his peripatetic life and
work and the number of places he visited, stayed in and recorded,
in drawings, paintings or daguerreotypes. But if you zoom out, it
quickly becomes obvious that he was a traveller of habit. Most of
the places that he visited regularly, or with which he had an emotional attachment, lie on a diagonal axis running roughly from
Brantwood to Venice. Ruskin called the continental leg of this
route, to Venice, often via Paris, Dijon, Chamonix and Verona, his

'old road'. He went back again and again, looking for new ways of seeing old haunts.

The family's continental tour of 1833 broadly followed this trajectory, though they took a wider loop through Germany than in later years, and doubled back without visiting Venice, the city that he helped shape and that shaped him. The tour was significant nonetheless. Ruskin's father's partner, Henry Telford, had presented the child with an illustrated copy of Samuel Rogers' poem *Italy* on his 13th birthday. The poem was, for Ruskin, almost an irrelevance. Indeed, when the precocious boy met Rogers a few years later, he offended him by praising the illustrations and forgetting to mention the verse.

The book was, however, an eye-opener. Many of the engravings were based on original works by Joseph Mallord William Turner. This was the artist, 35 years Ruskin's senior, whose fame and career were to become entwined with the young prodigy's. Ruskin's mother's suggestion that the family should visit some of the places depicted in the books whose engravings had so intrigued her son was therefore both inspired and inspiring.

So, working their way south-eastwards towards Italy in the spring, the party arrived at Schaffhausen, a small town on the banks of the Rhine that was 'one of the portals of Switzerland', according to a guidebook of the time, 'with little within [it] to deserve notice'.[22]

The family was later arriving than usual. It was already dark and they had to ditch their usual habit of a stroll after dinner but before sunset. The following day, however, they took their constitutional, arriving in early evening at a garden terrace with a view towards the mountains.

Remember that Ruskin was a boy for whom a clear view of Croydon could provoke ecstasies. Six hundred miles from south

London, this was sublimity of a quite different order. At the time, Ruskin was amassing new knowledge of art and architecture, under the influence of his first exposure to Turner's naturalistic combination of feeling and seeing. The experience prompted him to write a sub-Wordsworthian poem ('The Alps! The Alps! – it is no cloud / Wreathes the plain with its paly shroud!'). Looking back, though, Ruskin endowed this glimpse of the serried Alps, where he was to spend years of his life, with a mystical quality.

'There was no thought in any of us for a moment of their being clouds,' he wrote of this vision in *Præterita*, published five decades later. 'They were clear as crystal, sharp on the pure horizon sky, and already tinged with rose by the sinking sun. Infinitely beyond all that we had ever thought or dreamed, – the seen walls of lost Eden could not have been more beautiful to us; not more awful, round heaven, the walls of sacred Death.'[23]

Ruskin's first sight of the mountains that he grew to love was also the spark that helped launch the young genius into a career of dazzling and exhausting variety. He saw the world and would change the way future generations saw it, too, and in order to see it, he almost always needed to draw it.

Chapter IV

Drawing and Painting

Drawing....is mainly to be considered as a means of obtaining and
communicating knowledge. He who can accurately represent the form of
an object, and match its colour, has unquestionably a power of notation
and description greater in most instances than that of words.
(A Joy for Ever)

⊱ *I* ⊰

In 1837, Ruskin went up to Christ Church, Oxford. As did his
mother. Margaret Ruskin and her niece Mary Richardson took
rooms on the High Street, round the corner from her son's college. Ruskin visited them virtually every evening for tea. His
father came up at weekends. (Appropriately enough, the ground
floor of the same address – no. 90 – is now a branch of the
Patisserie Valerie chain of tea-shops.)

This was the kind of odd set-up that would have raised eye-
brows at any point in the university's history. But it was particularly strange in the 1830s.

Oxford at the time was nothing like the centre of scholarship
that it is now. Many students – all men, naturally – were more
interested in drinking, gambling and hunting. Ruskin was not.
At 18, he was already a well-travelled poet, geologist and expert

draughtsman. He had his sights set on the Newdigate Prize for the best verse composition.

What is more, as the son of a Scottish businessman, young John was not a natural fit with the English aristocrats and heirs of the gentry. His father had bought Ruskin the elevated status of 'gentleman-commoner' in college. But gentleman-commoners were the same students who mocked Ruskin when he won the right to read an essay of his in the college hall.

Ruskin did not hold much affection for his undergraduate years, despite meeting some lifelong friends and mentors in Oxford and developing his geological skills under William Buckland, an eccentric Christ Church don known for eating his way through a menagerie of exotic animals he kept in his home.

He was also tortured throughout his time at Oxford by unrequited love for Adèle-Clotilde Domecq, daughter of his father's business partner, Pedro Domecq, wealthy Paris-based member of the Spanish sherry family.

The 1833 Ruskin family trip to the continent had been the occasion for the first meeting between the gauche young John, then 14, and Adèle. When the Ruskins had reciprocated and invited the Domecqs – Adèle and her four sisters – to stay at Denmark Hill two years later, Ruskin had fallen in love.

In pure commercial terms, this would have been a useful match for John James and Pedro, had it progressed, though it is hard to see how staunchly anti-Catholic Mrs Ruskin would have stood for it. But Adèle, 'a graceful oval-faced blonde', though two years Ruskin's junior, was already playing in a far more sophisticated league. Bilingual in Spanish and French, with passable English, she was already groomed and dressed for the Parisian social scene. Indeed, all four sisters were eventually married into French aristocracy.

Ruskin, like many teenage boys, was ill-prepared for flirtation. His chat-up lines were strained, even by adolescents' standards. He tried to impress Adèle by boring on about the Spanish Armada, the Battle of Waterloo, and the doctrine of transubstantiation. He wrote an adventure story *Leoni: A Legend of Italy*, which she subjected to 'rippling ecstasies of derision' and, once the Domecqs had left, Ruskin penned a seven-page letter on the 'desolation and solitudes of Herne Hill', whose French the girls ridiculed. The 'fiery furnace' of the four sisters 'reduced me to a mere heap of white ashes in four days', he recalled nearly fifty years later, as though the wound was still fresh, which quite possibly, given the way his emotional life had evolved, it was.[1]

The encounter would be mainly comic, if not for the fact that it contained some of the seeds of Ruskin's hopeless adoration and pursuit of the young Rose La Touche a quarter of a century later, the emotional disaster that ultimately helped to unhinge him. Ruskin, already super-sensitised to emotion in nature, obviously felt true love deeply. His pining caused him real pain. He brooded about Adèle for four years, writing bad poems for and about her. More ominously, emotional setbacks seemed to weaken him mentally and make him physically ill.

This was the somewhat fragile state in which he went up to Oxford in 1837. He was a slight, eccentric 18-year-old, just under 6ft tall, and already standing out in the greatcoat or frockcoat, high-collar and light-blue stock that would be his increasingly quaint formal dress for much of his life. The stiff, classical education did not suit Ruskin's talents. Still, despite the proximity of his parents, his unconventional upbringing, and his tendency to melancholic poetical musings about his failure to win Adèle, he was at least tolerated, even liked, by his fellow Oxford students.

Disappointingly, there seems to be no evidence to support the tale that when his heartier colleagues tried to drink him under the table, he outlasted them all, having learnt from his wine-merchant father how to hold his alcohol. But the future dean of Christ Church, Henry Liddell – later father of Alice, the heroine of *Alice in Wonderland* – did write that Ruskin had told the 'odd set of hunting and sporting men' he mixed with that 'they like their own way of living and he likes his; and so they go on'. He added 'I am glad to say they do not bully him, as I should have been afraid they would'.[2]

In later life, Ruskin had plenty to say against 'ways of living' that displeased him. He was also to take some criticism for his own odd lifestyle. But it is impressive that in this company and in these potentially hostile surroundings, Ruskin survived, through mutual respect or possibly mutual incomprehension. As one of his biographers puts it, touchingly, Ruskin 'maintained himself socially – as he would do all his life – by being exceptional'.[3]

The young man's draughtsmanship, the first talent noted by Liddell, was one of the gifts that marked him out. Even though he was not taught drawing at Oxford, Ruskin found ways to exercise his skill, building on tuition he had received from a range of artists, encouraged by his father. An 1837 sketch of his splendid Christ Church rooms with their pilasters and embellishment round the window seat and swagged and furbelowed curtains, reveals the precise attention to architectural detail and decoration that was to become one of the hallmarks of his work.

He was to get more practice than he might have anticipated. In spring 1840, after studying to the point of exhaustion and in distress at the news that Adèle Domecq was to be married to another man ('I have lost her,' he wrote in his diary, somewhat exaggerating the extent to which he had had her in the first place), Ruskin coughed up blood. He went immediately to his mother. The main reason for her presence in Oxford was, after all, to be 'on hand in case of accident or sudden illness'. His parents promptly withdrew him from the university.

Ruskin was to return to Oxford, with both triumphant and disastrous consequences for his health and reputation, as professor of art and founder of the school of drawing in his fifties. As a young student, he had benefited from the geological knowledge of the eccentric Buckland. He had (in 1839) finally won the coveted Newdigate Prize. But except for fulfilling just enough of the residency and exam requirements to claim an unorthodox honorary degree, a 'double fourth', in 1842, his undergraduate days were now over.

Suspecting tuberculosis, doctors had advised a trip abroad. The Ruskin family, as we have already seen, never needed much prompting to harness up a coach and four and take off to the continent. They began a 10-month trip through France, Switzerland and Italy that autumn. In preparation, Ruskin stocked up on sketchbooks, ready to record the experience in the way he knew best.

⨶ 2 ⨶

When aged nine or ten, Ruskin recalled later, 'I could literally draw nothing, not a cat, not a mouse, not a boat, not a bush, "out of my head"'.[4]

We could dismiss this as the disingenuous self-deprecation of someone who already knew he had become a master draughtsman. Except it contains an important fact: Ruskin really could not 'invent' a drawing. He was not good at imaginative composition – the ability to lay out a painting to the greatest pictorial effect, even at the expense of strict accuracy to the scene painted. By contrast, Ruskin's great talent was in rendering a view, or the details of an object, with stunning precision. He would call this 'truth'.

Later in his autobiography, he recalled when, in 1842, he had realised the importance of truth in art:

> I noticed a bit of ivy round a thorn stem, which seemed, even to my critical judgment, not ill "composed"; and proceeded to make a light and shade pencil study of it in my grey paper pocket-book, carefully, as if it had been a bit of sculpture, liking it more and more as I drew. When it was done, I saw that I had virtually lost all my time since I was twelve years old, because no one had ever told me to draw what was really there! All my time, I mean, given to drawing as an art; of course I had the records of places, but had never seen the beauty of anything, not even of a stone – how much less of a leaf![5]

Once again, this episode was almost certainly made up by Ruskin later – or confected from several related events. But it was a revelation that illuminated much of his thinking about the vital attributes of great art and artists. One of his most famous aphorisms, still widely quoted, was included in the second volume of his five-volume masterpiece *Modern Painters*. It is aimed at 'young artists', whose 'duty is neither to choose, nor compose, nor imagine, nor experimentalise'. Instead, Ruskin urged them to 'go to Nature … rejecting nothing, selecting nothing, and scorning nothing; believing all things to be right and good, and rejoicing always in the truth'. Only then 'when their memories are stored, and their imaginations fed, and their hands firm, let them take up the scarlet and the gold, give the reins to their fancy, and show us what their heads are made of'.[6]

This characteristically demanding requirement helps explain Ruskin's strangely detached attitude to his own work. He rarely, if ever, considered himself to be an artist, or that his extraordinary paintings and drawings were art, and he almost never sought to exhibit them publicly. Looking back at his output, he wrote to the illustrator Kate Greenaway that his drawings were 'all such mere hints of what I want to do or mere syllables of what I saw that I never think, or at least never thought, they could ever give the least pleasure to anyone but myself'.[7]

Charles Eliot Norton, a pushy American and frequent correspondent with Ruskin, who became his literary executor, assembled his own collection of Ruskin's drawings and arranged a rare exhibition in the United States in 1879. Ruskin's note for the catalogue again underlines his own prosaic reasons for drawing: 'Few of these drawings were undertaken as an end in themselves, but most of them as a means by which to acquire exact knowledge of the facts of nature, or to obtain the data from which to deduce a principle in art, or to preserve a record...' and so on.[8]

That word 'data' leaps out for 21st-century readers living in a world where 'big data', culled from trillions of examples, lies behind myriad businesses and applications for forecasting the weather, directing traffic or improving manufacturers' efficiency. (That big data technology is often based 'in the cloud' would probably have infuriated Ruskin, a dedicated lifelong observer and chronicler of real clouds.)

Ruskin was a master of 'small data'. His 'data-points' ranged from the diagrammatic sketches of the dimensions and structure of doorways, walls and arches in his Venice notebooks, to the detailed pencil, pen, ink and watercolour details of the corners of buildings, or mountain ranges, or trees. That has led some to agree with his own view of himself as a producer of strictly functional drawings. In his autobiography, he recalled how his father 'doubted and deplored my constant habit of making little patches and scratches of the sections and fractions of things in a notebook which used to live in my waistcoat pocket'.[9]

But it is harsh to compare him with some of the 'minor artists' whose company he enjoyed. These days, one can easily make the case for Ruskin as a great artist, and an influential one, even if he himself did not.

The 2014 exhibition *John Ruskin: Artist and Observer*, organised by the National Gallery of Canada and the National Galleries of Scotland, did exactly that, with stunning effect. One critic remarked that 'at times, his images have an uncanny accuracy that prefigures 20th-century hyperrealism', the term applied to sculptures and paintings of exceptional fidelity to reality that emerged in the 1970s.[10]

Ruskin would not have liked that comparison much. Despite his emphasis on truth, he had a contradictory habit of dismissing artists such as James Tissot, the French genre painter known for his scenes of everyday life, for lacking purpose and producing 'mere coloured photographs of vulgar society'. In his twenties, in *Modern Painters*, Ruskin entertainingly dumped on Canaletto's crowded Venetian panoramas as 'nothing but coloured Daguerreotypeism'. Later, he confusingly criticised some of the Pre-Raphaelite painters he had championed for the verisimilitude of their work, for trying a bit too hard and producing highly accurate natural landscapes that lacked emotion.

The sterile term 'data' does not adequately describe the passion and excitement with which Ruskin often drew. He used his waistcoat notebook, but when he set to it, his meticulous style was highly demanding of his energy and time. Later when he became obsessed about specific paintings, he would devote exhausting hours to copying them – in some cases, almost certainly taking more time than the original artist had spent completing the work.

As I mentioned earlier, drawing was a process of mental decluttering for Ruskin and he may have turned to close sketching to anchor his increasingly unstable mind later in his career. But in his prime, he described drawing as a 'sort of instinct like that for eating and drinking' – he was hungry to record everything he saw, and that appetite remained. Writing later as a prematurely elderly 65-year-old, he says of his youthful exploration of Pisa that 'there was too much always to be hunted out… or watched'.[11] Looking back, he conceded, 'I wish I knew less, and had drawn more'.[12]

The 2014 exhibition included the great *Study of Gneiss Rock* (colour plate 5). Besieged by midges and interrupted by bad weather, Ruskin worked on this study over months in 1853 in Glen Finglas, Scotland, sitting alongside John Everett Millais, who was developing his portrait of the critic against a backdrop of rocks and rushing water that includes the same veined surface. A 2013 photograph of the area on which Ruskin focused reveals the perfection of the drawing.[13] It reminds me of the fantastical and absurd 1:1 scale map that Jorge Luis Borges described in a one-paragraph story more than a century later. Back in London, Ruskin himself wrote to a friend that he had 'got maps of all the lichens on the rocks' to help Millais reach the same level of detail in the gnarly background to his portrait.[14] If Ruskin had bothered lifting his head from examining this square metre of gneiss, he might have noticed that the young Pre-Raphaelite painter was falling in love with his beautiful and frustrated wife, Effie. But more of that later.

Any struggling artists will have already spotted one crucial difference with their lot. Ruskin could easily afford not to exhibit, sell, or even finish his work. He was cushioned by the wealth accumulated by his father. This created a dangerous emotional debt to his parents, but at the same time it shielded him from the need to produce drawings or paintings in fashionably popular style. Ruskin himself was never complacent about his comfortable existence. It may even have driven him to produce more as he sought to repay his father's investment in kind.

His comfortable situation also led to some profound, and still relevant, insights into the way in which great art can be undermined by commercial pressures. 'The very primary motive with which we set about the business, makes the business impossible,' he said in an 1858 lecture at the opening of the Cambridge School of Art (later incorporated into what is now Anglia Ruskin University). 'The first and absolute condition of the thing's ever becoming saleable is, that we shall make it without wanting to sell it.'[15]

Even more profoundly, as he wrote in *The Laws of Fesole*, a later attempt to codify drawing techniques for use in schools, if you are trying too hard, you are likely to fail: 'If you desire to draw, that you may represent something you care for, you will advance swiftly and safely. If you desire to draw, that you make a beautiful drawing, you will never make one.'[16]

Ruskin cared for many of the places and, occasionally, people, he drew. It did not mean he necessarily always 'advanced swiftly'. What makes his pictures so precious is that they are often a record not only of buildings, towns and landscapes, but also a graphic insight into how his mind was working. In that way, they are closer to the way many artists' work evolved in the 20th century.

An 1863 watercolour of Baden, Switzerland, for example, sprawls over five different sheets of paper, suggesting that he enlarged his view of the town as he worked, expanding out-wards from an initial close study of the buildings of the town centre, adding sheets of paper in a sort of collage as he worked. Characteristically, he moaned in his diary at the time about how hard it was to complete his drawings.

His extraordinary late-career graphite and watercolour views of the Grand Canal, which he drew in the 1870s, com-bine a fanatical precision with an impressionistic touch – take that, Canaletto! – as the buildings fade into the distance. Again, Ruskin's own record of his work is peppered with evidence of his frustration and fatigue. One was later exhibited in Oxford with the description 'given up in despair'. On another, he writes 'left off tired'. Looking back on his career, Ruskin wrote of his 'ever-more childish delight in beginning a drawing; and usually acute misery in trying to finish one'.[17]

Yet it is the fact that Ruskin left mainly unfinished 'syllables' that attracts modern critics, professionals and amateurs like me back to his drawings and paintings. They seem to open an op-portunity for interpretation and imagination to fill the gaps that he left.

Ruskin never underestimated how hard it was to make an honest recording of what he saw. One problem he identifies is familiar to every artist who ever took up a pencil: that our brains continually get in the way of the truth.

Here he is, writing in the fourth volume of *Modern Painters*, explaining what he called the 'universal law of obscurity'. This is the simple fact that 'WE NEVER SEE ANYTHING CLEARLY' (his capitals – Ruskin could be a no-holds-barred user of upper case and italics for emphasis):

Take the commonest, closest, most familiar thing, and

strive to draw it verily as you see it. Be sure of this last fact, for otherwise you will find yourself continually drawing, not what you see, but what you know.[18]

The directness is typical of Ruskin. One of the excitements of reading him is that you never know when he is going to interrupt his prose to address the reader directly. He goes on to set a simple-sounding drawing exercise: 'Sitting about three yards from a bookcase (not your own, so that you may know none of the titles of the books), ... try to draw the books accurately, with the titles on the backs, and patterns on the bindings, as you see them'.

As he points out, you need to give 'the perfect look of neat lettering... which, nevertheless, must be (as you will find it on most of the books) absolutely illegible'. The same test – and the same challenge – applies if you try to draw the pattern on a piece of patterned cloth, or the blades in a bank of grass, or the leaves in a bush, he writes. 'You will soon begin to understand under what a universal law of obscurity we live, and perceive that all distinct drawing must be bad drawing, and that nothing can be right, till it is unintelligible.'

As a lapsed amateur artist I often feel, reading Ruskin, the sting of his criticism of inept or merely mediocre drawing and painting. But there is something wonderfully right about Ruskin's simple advice to draw what you see, not what you know. It is all too easy to ruin a sketch of a building by trying to draw all the windows you know to be there, rather than just the ones you can see – in other words, by over-thinking the task. An artist, Ruskin says later in the same book, should not be a 'thoughtful man' but 'a perceiving man', stretched out like a 'four-cornered sheet' to catch everything he sees.

↽ *3* ↾

It was not as an artist, or even an art teacher, that the young Ruskin made his reputation. It was as an art critic. Without his ardent advocacy, the reputations of J. M. W. Turner and, later the Pre-Raphaelite partners, might easily have crumbled in the face of hostility. How did Ruskin achieve this pre-eminence? Initially, by sheer precociousness.

Ruskin's 13th-birthday present from his father's business partner – that book of poetry about Italy illustrated by Turner – set fire to the young Ruskin's artistic sensibility.

Turner at the time was an established painter but he had started to paint in a freer, more highly coloured style that critics disliked. After reading one attack on the painter in 1836, the 17-year-old Ruskin wrote an impassioned defence. His father forwarded it first to Turner, who wisely advised against rushing it into print.

In June 1840, convalescing in London after his Oxford illness, Ruskin finally met Turner – '*the* painter and poet of the day'. Ruskin was a sickly 21-year-old student with a Biblical turn of phrase and an extraordinary eye, built on close study of great artworks, and a deep knowledge of the geological foundations of Turner's beloved Alpine peaks. Turner, 65, had a reputation, in Ruskin's words, for being 'coarse, boorish, unintellectual, vulgar', but he was an instinctive artistic genius. They got on, despite their differences. Ruskin described Turner in his diary as 'a somewhat eccentric, keen-mannered, matter-of-fact, English-minded – gentleman: good-natured evidently, bad-tempered evidently, hating humbug of all sorts, shrewd, perhaps a little selfish, highly intellectual…'.[19]

J. M. W. Turner (print after), Peace – Burial at Sea, *exhibited in 1842*

Ruskin was no mere Turner fan-boy. Two years later, on the continent with his parents, he read the vitriolic criticism of Turner's latest works, which included the impressionistic pair, *Peace – Burial at Sea* and *War. The Exile and the Rock Limpet.* These experimental demonstrations of 'cold' and 'hot' colours depicted respectively the burial at sea of Turner's artist friend David Wilkie, and the exiled Napoleon on St Helena, against a red and gold sunset. Contemporary critics suggested the paintings could have been hung upside down with little loss and described the ship in *Peace* as 'a burnt and blackened fish kettle'.[20]

Ruskin conceived the idea of a pamphlet rebutting the attacks, but – as so often – he was unable to rein in his ideas. He later explained how he found 'nothing could be done except on

... enormous scale'.[21] He was not joking: the 'pamphlet' became, over time, the five volumes of *Modern Painters*.

This was the central work of Ruskin's early life. Seventeen years elapsed between publication of the first volume in 1843, when he was only 24, and the last, during which time he changed his mind, contradicted himself, and in general displayed – as he did in his drawings – the evolution of his thinking about art, artists, religion and, increasingly, society. Even in the first volume, though, he wrote with the force and certitude of opinion of a much older man, while at the same time reflecting the staunch Evangelical and therefore anti-Catholic prejudices of his parents.

The young Ruskin came up with a rich and still relevant recipe for great art, combining the vital ingredients of truth and 'greatness'. 'The greatest picture,' he wrote, 'is that which conveys to the mind of the spectator the greatest number of the greatest ideas.' By extension then, 'he is the greatest artist who has embodied, in the sum of his works, the greatest number of the greatest ideas'. He was talking about Turner.

The subtitle to the first volume (partly suggested by his publisher) was itself a brazen assertion of the superiority of contemporary artists 'in the art of landscape painting to all the ancient masters', with Turner singled out. In his introductory chapter, Ruskin writes with blazing certainty: 'It will of course be necessary for me in the commencement of the work to state briefly those principles on which I conceive *all right judgment of art* must be founded' [my italics].'

Instead of putting his own name on the title page, he signed off the volume as 'A Graduate of Oxford' in back-handed recognition of what he had gained from his interrupted and not entirely happy university studies.

Modern Painters went to a second edition within a year, by which time the identity of the Oxford graduate was out. It was obvious from the private declarations of poets and authors, including Tennyson, George Eliot and Wordsworth himself, that he had created waves. Charlotte Brontë wrote later: 'I feel more as if I had been walking blindfold – this book seems to give me eyes.' An anonymous obituarist for US newspapers summed up the revolutionary impact of *Modern Painters* in 1900: 'All this was then a sort of blasphemy, but he made it become authority.'[22]

While Turner may have been less nonplussed now than he had been seven years earlier, his young champion's forthrightness helped underpin his reputation and launched Ruskin's.

The relationship was still a strange one. It mingled adulation, and high-minded art criticism, with something rather close to insider trading in the nascent art market, with Ruskin junior applauding Turner publicly and Ruskin senior stepping into the market to buy his works.

Ruskin would have loved to travel in Europe with Turner in person, though their trips never coincided. Instead, he visited the places that Turner had depicted. He often drew the scene himself and then described how the older artist had imaginatively tampered with reality, in a way Ruskin could never bring himself to do in his own work, to create a better image.

Meanwhile, Ruskin's father was demonstrating he had the commercial acumen, the critical skills, and the money, necessary to buy a fine collection of Turner's work, on his own account.

Ruskin's support for Turner was loud, occasionally off-beam and often over the top. In *Modern Painters* he describes Turner at one point as 'glorious in conception – unfathomable in knowledge – solitary in power – with the elements waiting upon his will, and the night and the morning obedient to his call, sent as a prophet of God to reveal to men the mysteries of His universe, standing, like the great angel of the Apocalypse, clothed with a cloud, and with a rainbow upon his head, and with the sun and stars given into his hand'.[23] No wonder the proud but embarrassed Turner muttered that Ruskin 'sees more in my pictures than I ever painted'.

Still, at a point where his reputation was under attack, Ruskin shored up the artist's earlier success, recreating a market for paintings of the 1830s that Turner had been unable to sell. Ruskin also had a role to play after Turner's death, as we shall later see, cataloguing – and possibly censoring, or at least filtering – the thousands of pictures that the artist bequeathed to the nation when he died in 1851, and that can still be seen (in rotation, there are so many) at Tate Britain.

Ruskin did contribute to a Turner myth. One modern biographer of Turner has even argued that Ruskin helped create an exaggerated legend of the painter as a 'rags-to-riches urchin who had overcome adversity to create a body of work that was largely misunderstood' but that required Ruskin himself to spot and salvage its genius.[24] Even so, it is hard to imagine Turner without Ruskin, or vice versa – they briefly formed the odd couple of mid-19th-century art and art criticism. This is one reason it is hard to forgive film director Mike Leigh for allowing an unfair caricature of Ruskin into his otherwise impressive and moving 2014 film *Mr Turner*. The critic was played for laughs by Joshua McGuire as a pretentious lisping popinjay.[25] But Turner might not have merited a biopic at all, if the author of *Modern Painters* had not stuck his blue-cravatted neck out to explain and defend his later work.

꙾ 4 ꙾

The second great campaign of the first half of Ruskin's career was to champion the young rebels of the Pre-Raphaelite Brotherhood, including Millais, William Holman Hunt and Dante Gabriel Rossetti. The PRB were Young British Artists more than a century before Damien Hirst and his contemporaries burst into view. Like the YBAs, they courted publicity, aimed to shock the art establishment, and, over time, developed in different directions.

Why did Ruskin choose to back them? The paintings seem to occupy the extreme opposite end of the spectrum from Turner's impressionistic work. But they combined, again, two elements that excited the young critic: 'absolute, uncompromising truth in all that [Pre-Raphaelitism] does, obtained by working everything, down to the most minute detail, from nature, and from nature only'.[26] To Ruskin, these were artists living his injunction to reject nothing from nature, select nothing, and scorn nothing.

Like Turner, these painters had also attracted a hostile reception from the mainstream media of the day. Unlike the older painter, the young bucks of the Brotherhood had deliberately sought to excite the critics. The rich colours ('borrowed from the jars in a druggist's shop' as The Times complained) and realistic figures of their early work were bound to stand out against the muddy landscapes and traditional figurative works displayed at the Royal Academy. But the attacks were strong enough to provoke Ruskin into their defence – and he did so in typical hyperbolical style.

In rebuking his fellow critics, Ruskin let loose the bold judgement, in a letter to The Times in May 1851, that the Pre-Raphaelites 'could lay in our England the foundations of a school of art nobler than the world has seen for 300 years'.

That verdict still seems a stretch. Enter any gallery of Pre-Raphaelite work – say, Manchester City Art Gallery, where Ford Madox Brown's brilliant London street tableau *Work* is on display – and the bright colours still shock. Ruskin said it was simply that the public was used to seeing only the light from an artist's 'dim painting-room, not that of sunshine in the fields'. The appeal of the paintings is just a bit too obvious, though. Millais's *Christ in the House of his Parents* – deemed 'revolting' and 'loathsome' by *The Times* in 1850, in part for having depicted the son of God in such mundane surroundings – is powerful. But Hunt's later *The Shadow of Death*, also set in the carpenter's workshop and now in the Manchester gallery, is hard to like, with its portrait of a toothy, bearded Christ stretching in a pose that foreshadows his crucifixion.

In fact, if you go back to Ruskin's first letters to *The Times*, you will find he, too, is tough on the Pre-Raphaelite artists. He slates the 'commonness of feature in many of the principal figures' and singles out Millais' depiction of his figures' hands as 'almost always ill-painted'. Emerging from this detailed critique, the over-charged praise is even more striking. It is one indication of how Ruskin was, by this stage, as adept at using his prose to create a shock as he was appreciative of artists' technical ability to provoke emotion.

Still, the critic's attempt to shoehorn Turner into the brotherhood does read oddly. Ruskin's 1851 pamphlet on the movement, written shortly after the painter's death, is mostly about Turner. In an 1853 lecture, he calls him 'the first and greatest of the Pre-Raphaelites'. Few would now agree.

Throughout his career, Ruskin wrestled publicly with

contradictions in his own opinion. During the long composition of the five volumes of *Modern Painters*, for instance, it troubled Ruskin that he had in effect set up Raphael (1483-1520) as the beginning of the end of any art or architecture worth considering. Yet shortly after he finished the first volume, he was blown away in Venice by the work of Tintoretto – who was born the year before Raphael died. That revelation required some reworking of his views, to say the least. He was forced to re-examine his certainty about the chronology of the decline of Italian civilisation before the final volume of *Modern Painters* came out, and to reassess the gifts of some clearly exceptional but (for the evangelically Protestant younger Ruskin) awkwardly Catholic painters – Fra Angelico, Veronese, as well as Tintoretto.

In a world where opinion and taste are too often fixed, and any divergence from an earlier opinion attacked as inconsistency, there is plenty to learn from Ruskin's constant, honest, quest to update his own views, as his research yielded new revelations about art and architecture. He combines a version of the admission attributed to that 20th-century polymath John Maynard Keynes – 'When the facts change, I change my mind' – with a frank acknowledgement of his own contradictions.

Ruskin did find a way of linking Turner and Millais in the 1850s. In the same pamphlet where he concentrates mainly on the older painter, he imagines an ideal combination of both – the one, Turner, with 'considerable inventive power' and 'exquisite sense of colour' and the other, Millais, with 'the eye of an eagle'. He calls them the 'culminating points of art in both directions'.

As a thumbnail appreciation of the two artists, this is acute. It also suggests, again, the way in which Ruskin looked constantly for what could connect, rather than separate, artists, and ultimately whole fields of study.

In the 1853 lecture, he describes a fantastical vision of how painters might chronicle and record developments in multiple fields, if they were to divide into 'two great armies of historians and naturalists'. The historian-artists would paint 'with absolute faithfulness' historically significant buildings, cities, battlefields. The artist-naturalists would similarly record plants, animals, scenery, clouds, even 'each recess of every mountain chain of Europe'. The output would be stored in national galleries, to be put 'within reach of the common people'. 'Would not that be a more honourable life [for artists], than gaining precarious bread by "bright effects"?' Ruskin concludes.[27]

This sounds like a strong case for what we now call 'interdisciplinary studies' – not to mention national galleries and museums. Ruskin describes the connections between these different ways of seeing and recording the world, not as a cumbersome and dry academic concept, but as an invitation to break down barriers between art, science, history, botany, and zoology.

Here in this description is a sort of analogue prototype for a world wide web, recording and storing all knowledge and making it publicly available for the good of the public. Ruskin, obviously, intended nothing of the sort. But if there was anyone in 1851 capable of combining the multiple disciplines he described, it was the geologist-draughtsman-historian-critic himself.

 5

In his day, Ruskin was valued as a teacher of drawing – which he developed through face-to-face classes at the new Working Men's College in the 1850s. To spread his methodology, he published *The Elements of Drawing* in 1854. It comes with a health warning

– 'If you desire only to possess a graceful accomplishment, to be able to converse in a fluent manner about drawing, or to amuse yourself listlessly in listless hours, I cannot help you'. It also carried a '12' certificate, as not 'calculated' for the use of anyone younger, unless they were willing: 'I do not feel it advisable to engage a child in any but the most voluntary practice of art,' he wrote. A child with a talent for drawing 'should be allowed to scrawl at its own free will, due praise being given for every appearance of care, or truth, in its efforts'.

The manual went to six editions in his lifetime. But its 'elements' are not for the faint-hearted. The ability to record beautiful things that 'cannot be described in words' and to understand 'the minds of great painters' are noble and desirable powers, wrote Ruskin, but they 'cannot be got without work'. Ruskin himself spent hours perfecting the drawing of trees, which he sets as an exercise early in the book. The temptation, he pointed out, 'is always to be slovenly and careless, and the outline is like a bridle, and forces our indolence into attention and precision'.

Despite, or quite possibly because of, its smack of didactic Victorian rigour, *The Elements of Drawing* is still recommended by amateur artists seeking a manual. 'I have attended quite a few drawing classes, worked from the antique, tried different methods and in the end I came down to the conclusion that John Ruskin's method is the best there is,' offers one satisfied reader in a 2012 five-star review on Amazon.com. At the same time, Ruskin's advice is often couched in the same exquisite prose as much of his output. Talking his readers through a laborious exercise in shading, he offered this: 'Work with it as if you were drawing the down on a butterfly's wing.'

As a teacher of drawing Ruskin was generous, both in his group classes, and in his individual advice – often offered by letter

– but he rarely softened his hard line on the need to put in the hours. In the 1880s, he was advising Frank Randal, from whom he commissioned many works for his Guild of St George, to repeat a study of wood carving on choir stalls 'over and over until he [Randal] was happy with the result'. But when Ruskin was satisfied, he had no difficulty praising his pupils. Again, to Randal, on his choir-stall drawings: 'The little sketches show that singular quickness and rightness that you have in catching action and character which no man can teach.'[28]

Professional artists still find inspiration from Ruskin's work. These days, though, it is more likely to spring from a modern reading of his thoughts on architecture or nature or social reform than directly from his old-fashioned strictures on drawing. I contacted finalists for the John Ruskin Prize about their encounters with Ruskin's legacy.

Sumi Perera, who describes herself as an interdisciplinary artist, said she drew on Ruskin's 'moralistic principles as a social reformer and how he fought tirelessly to uphold his fairly radical views and opinions' for her entry for the John Ruskin Prize, *2B or Not 2B (To Be or Not To Be)*, for which she produced graphs of the sound of pencils scratching. Anne Guest, shortlisted in 2015 for *Every Move You Make*, a patchwork of pencil drawings mimicking CCTV images, was 'encouraged by the fact that Ruskin's interests were so vast'. Carol Wyss, who won the inaugural prize in 2012, tapped Ruskin's concern about the environment for her large-scale etchings of plant forms. 'He appreciated nature by looking closely at it, saw that everything is interrelated and that humans are part rather than on a hierarchical top of it – thoughts which are very urgent in our time of environmental crises,' she says.

Robin Sukatorn, who won the 2015 student prize with his

Robin Sukatorn

graphite drawing of a crowded rally in Manchester, at which Labour leader Jeremy Corbyn gave an impassioned speech, told me that he found some of Ruskin's drawings 'a bit too measured and methodical'. Yet he echoed Ruskin when he said drawing was 'a way of seeing more closely'. After winning the prize, Sukatorn went on to produce a book, *Drawing Democracy*, of similar sketches of political events. In his work, he shows an impulse to connect, as Ruskin did, politics, art and society. 'I want my work to have some sort of utility and relevance beyond the art world,' he said.

In 2017, when the Big Draw opened its John Ruskin Prize to artists working in three dimensions, it did not extend the scope to include photography, except as part of a wider work. The prize already accepted digital entries where, in theory, no pencil had ever touched paper, but Kate Mason, the charity's director, said the judges had asked themselves – as Ruskin would have done – 'where was the hand of the artist?' in photography.

'There's a whole raft of other ways that people can express themselves and develop their visual literacy,' she said. Occasionally, in judging the 2017 prize, she said panellists had paused to consider whether Ruskin would have liked an entry. 'Sometimes the answer was: maybe not – but he would have found it interesting' and the piece would be sent through to the next round. Ruskin, she pointed out (with some understatement), was 'a bit quirky' and enjoyed trying out new ideas.

Nobody wants to hold back artistic progress, but it is worrying if artists have lost patience with drawing, relegating it to something that the genteel or the retired, with time on their hands, do in their spare time. I say that as someone who has rarely picked up pencil and sketchbook since I was in my twenties (but has now started to do so again).

Anne Howeson, a tutor at the Royal College of Art, shares that concern. Her drawing-based stop-motion film about regeneration at King's Cross was shortlisted for the 2017 John Ruskin Prize, but she also has strong feelings about the importance of drawing as research and thinking. Echoing Ruskin, and student prizewinner Robin Sukatorn, she pointed out that drawing 'helps you to see'. She has also detected a shift away from drawing among her students. They are following the zeitgeist, she said, which involves thinking conceptually before picking up pencil and paper – if they pick it up at all. She told me: 'Although students say they love [drawing], they're surprised by the amount of focus and attention it needs.'

You can almost hear Ruskin grumbling in the background. In one injunction to his students to put in the necessary hard hours, he wrote that if he 'finds the first steps painfully irksome, I can only desire him to consider whether the acquirement of so great a power as that of pictorial expression of thought be not worth some toil; or whether it is likely... that so great a gift should be attainable by those who will give no price for it'.

Oxford's Ruskin School of Art is the direct descendant of the drawing school Ruskin established when he returned as the university's first Slade Professor of Fine Art in 1870. It started life in the university's Ashmolean Museum but now occupies a Tudor-Gothic-style building on the High Street. (It is not far from where Ruskin's mother stayed when he was an undergraduate, though in those days it was the site of a busy coaching inn, the Angel.) Further from the city centre, a second more modern site provides a workshop for printmaking, wood- and metalwork.

I will touch on Ruskin's original idiosyncratic vision for the school later, but it has been a while since drawing was a central part of what students learn there. Indeed, in 2014, the school decided to change its name from the Ruskin School of Drawing and Fine Art – dropping the 'drawing' and the 'fine art'. I visited between university terms when the Victorian shell was empty and preparations were under way to welcome a new intake of students. Even empty of students, it felt quite unlike anything that Ruskin would have recognised from his stints at Oxford in the 1870s and 1880s, which was one reason for changing its name.

Anthony Gardner, the friendly Australian art historian who has headed the school since 2017, said it was essential to 're-mind people that we're a modern art school'. The message sent to prospective students by the old name, he told me, was 'it's Oxford, it's Ruskin, it's 19th-century heritage'. That had had a subtle but detectable influence on the sort of candidate who used to apply to study there. 'We had a lot of people wanting to do fairly conservative landscapes,' he said. 'We weren't necessarily as engaged with contemporary art as our research and teaching strengths emphasised.'

As for Ruskin's rigid vision of a top-down teaching of the practice of art, 'we've almost gone the exact opposite to that', said Gardner. Students might arrive with drawing skills, but art was now 'about the conceptual and the material meeting each other in ways which are distinctive and creative and can articulate the student's voice in the most rewarding ways'.

It would be untrue to say Ruskin is totally absent, though. Gardner, who came to Oxford as an associate professor in 2012, said that even though there had been strong support for rebranding the school, nobody had thought of dropping the founder's name altogether. And while Gardner does not assign John Ruskin to the syllabus, the thinker's 'ethos does filter through'. In the third year of the Bachelor of Fine Art course, which also covers the history and theory of art, some students engage with Ruskin in their dissertations. Gardner said he saw a link between his own field of research into connections between art and politics. It is the same thread Robin Sukatorn picked up from Ruskin's public championing of art, education, galleries and museums. Like Ruskin, Gardner said, we need to ask how we can 'engage each other more, particularly as students become more politicised and think about their artworks and the wider world'.

Drawing, it turns out, is not being erased. Like a faint soft-pencil mark in the background of an abstract painting, it is still visible. It may even be due a comeback. The growing prevalence of digital and virtual media in art is directing some students back to older, analogue techniques. Drawing, Gardner pointed out, was 'one of the most interesting mediums' for artists because of the many ways it allowed them to express themselves. Ruskin school research students still think about the 'line and where the line takes you'. In Ruskin's case, the line inevitably took him to Venice.

Chapter V

Buildings

When we build, let us think that we build for ever.
(The Seven Lamps of Architecture)

>✒ *I* ✒<

Venice may be the one city in the world whose guidebooks never date. The basic architecture and street plan – in contrast to London, Manhattan, Tokyo – remains the same now as in the city Ruskin explored on multiple visits between 1835 and 1888, his last journey abroad. This is, at least in part, thanks to Ruskin himself.

These days, you must ignore the roar of the engine, and avert your eyes from the refineries and industrial sprawl of Mestre, but if you take the Alilaguna ferry from Marco Polo airport it is just about possible to conjure the same emotions as Ruskin, as what starts as a faint scribble on the horizon gradually gains definition as a great city. He describes how a traveller, pushing off quietly in a gondola into the mysterious lagoon, bound for Venice, watches the 'strange rising of its walls and towers out of the midst, as it seemed, of the deep sea'.[1]

Ruskin's first visit, in 1835, was eclipsed by his more profound reaction to Venice in 1841 – when he called it 'the Paradise of cities' – though his slow convalescence from the attack that had cut short his time at Oxford took the shine off his stay. (At this point in his life, he thought he was going to die young, like the consumptive poet Keats, whose grave the Ruskins had visited in Rome.)

But it was on his third tour in 1845 that the 26-year-old plunged deep into a more mature and lasting appreciation of Italy, and Venice's, art and architecture.

The first volume of *Modern Painters* had been a modest critical success. This trip fuelled the second volume. It ignited his interest in, and concern for, the buildings and streetscape of Italy's historic cities, and the design of buildings in general. This burning excitement also prompted him to write *The Seven Lamps of Architecture*, and the three-volume masterpiece *The Stones of Venice*. Much to the perplexity and occasional distress of his father, who really wanted Ruskin to build on his success as an art critic and finish *Modern Painters*, this was a conflagration that was never doused.

Two of four great 'art attacks' that changed Ruskin's life occurred on this seven-month trip.

One was the first sight of Jacopo della Quercia's marble sarcophagus of Ilaria del Carretto, 'lying on a simple pillow, with a hound at her feet', in Lucca cathedral. Ilaria was the wife a wealthy merchant and ruler of the city, and her statue is virtually all that remains of a more lavish tomb. Collingwood, Ruskin's first biographer, points out that Ruskin 'never dwelt on the story' of the young woman.[2] But he more than dwelt on the sculpture, revisiting the cathedral a number of times in his life and compulsively drawing it. He spent two weeks on one such drawing in 1874, by which point he was starting to associate Ilaria with his doomed love for the young Rose La Touche. In *Modern Painters*,

Ruskin called the sculpture '*truth* itself, but the truth selected with inconceivable refinement of feeling'. His writing drew others to Lucca – one reason why there is an 1899 plaster cast in the Victoria and Albert Museum in London.

Ruskin's other epiphany on this trip was his encounter with Tintoretto's work in Venice, which he experienced in two intense days in September – first at the Accademia galleries and then at the Scuola di San Rocco.

Even today, a visit to the cavernous buildings of the Scuola – one of the great 'confraternities' of Venice – is a semi-mystical experience. You will find fewer tourists here than elsewhere and Tintoretto's great cycle of paintings looms out of the half-darkness of the echoing rooms, building to the drama of his *Crucifixion* upstairs in the Sala dell'Albergo, as it did in Ruskin's day. These are masterpieces of figure painting, humanised by perceptive details, such as the ass eating palm leaves that Ruskin noted in the background of the *Crucifixion*. 'I never was so utterly crushed to the earth before any human intellect as I was today, before Tintoret,' Ruskin wrote to his father after his first sight of the paintings, using, as he always did, the abbreviated version of the painter's name.

So breathtaking did he find the experience that he 'could do nothing at last but lie on a bench & laugh'. That was not my first reaction to the cycle, but I still have a strong memory of the shadowy drama of the Scuola – and the impact of Tintoretto's muscular narrative of the crucifixion – from my first visit to Venice as a 16-year-old in 1981.

When he does tackle the *Crucifixion* in the third volume of *Modern Painters*, Ruskin devotes fewer than 1,000 words to it ('I will not insult this marvellous picture by an effort at a verbal account of it,' he writes), which is close to muteness by Ruskin's verbose standards. In *Stones* he describes the *Crucifixion* as 'beyond all analysis, and above all praise'. In her book *How Do We Look* – a companion to the recent BBC series *Civilisations* – Mary Beard twits Ruskin for not trying hard enough to explain the paintings.

These are signs, though, of just how profoundly the painting affected him. Turn to his letters, and something about Ruskin's youthful first reaction to Tintoretto remains exciting and infectious. Earlier on the trip, Ruskin had started giving 'degrees' to painters (a first for 'pure religious' artists such as Fra Angelico, Raphael and Bellini; seconds for Michelangelo, Giotto, Leonardo and so on). Now he wrote to his father, with schoolboyish hype, to say, 'Just be so good as to take my list of painters, & put [Tintoretto] in the school of Art at the top, top, top of everything, with a great big black line underneath him to stop him off from everybody…'

This trip had spurred another impulse in Ruskin, too: concern for the very survival of the buildings and the art they contained. In the 19th century, Venice had been, and would be again, a war zone. While the young critic no longer feared as much for his own life, in 1845, and in subsequent visits in the late 1840s, he was genuinely terrified that a combination of military conflict, poor restoration and modernisation would destroy what he had only recently discovered.

It precipitated Ruskin into a frenzy of chronicling the art and architecture he saw, before it was too late.

In writing about the glories of the city, Ruskin, burning shoe leather on land and testing the patience of his personal gondolier on water, managed somehow to combine a tight focus on the tiniest details that an average traveller would always miss, and a wide-angle view of the city and its surrounding lagoon and islands.

In *The Stones of Venice*, he described the approach to Saint Mark's Square and the first impact of the cathedral's gilded domes and multicoloured façade: '[A] multitude of pillars and white domes, clustered into a long low pyramid of colored light; a treasure heap, it seems, partly of gold and partly of opal and mother-of-pearl, hollowed beneath into five great vaulted porches, ceiled with fair mosaic, and beset with sculpture of alabaster, clear as amber and delicate as ivory, – sculpture fantastic and involved, of palm leaves and lilies, and grapes and pomegranates, and birds clinging and fluttering among the branches, all twined together into an endless network of buds and plumes' and so on for one long 400-word paragraph.[3] In another wide-angle moment, he later described his favourite spot: in a boat, moored to a post somewhere halfway between the Giudecca and the tiny island of San Giorgio in Alga ('Saint George of the Seaweed'), at sunset, gazing at 'all the Alps and Venice behind you by the rosy sunlight: there is no other spot so beautiful'.

But Ruskin could also narrow the focus, to note the way in which the architect of San Marco had pierced 'minute and star-like openings' into the 'lily capitals' that topped some of the cathedral's pillars, creating a 'system of braided or woven ornament... universally pleasing to the instinct of mankind', reminiscent of the intertwined decoration of the illuminated manuscripts he had long studied.[4] He seems to be telling the tourist, you may gain as much – sometimes more – from close examination of the place you are visiting, as you would from the picture-postcard view. He was also addressing a readership that would never see Venice in person, and rarely even have access to accurate images of the place. His prose was the high-definition film documentary of its day.

><del>n</del> *2* <del>n</del>

The 1845 trip was significant also as his first visit abroad without his over-present parents. Even so, he rarely travelled alone. On this occasion, he went with John Hobbs – a family servant known as 'George' to avoid confusion with John and his father John James – and Joseph Couttet, a trusted guide whom the family had first hired in Switzerland in 1844 and who was to serve their son for 30 years. The trip could have laid the foundation of an independent life, away from parental oppression, but they pulled him back to Denmark Hill with passive-aggressive letters. By the end of 1845 he was home.

Ruskin was not in full physical or mental health. Yet as an emerging art-world celebrity, heir to a merchant fortune, he was eminently marriageable, and, in 1847, he started to court Euphemia Chalmers Gray – known as Phemy to her family, or, as Ruskin and posterity were to call her, Effie.

To understand Ruskin, you need to understand his marriage, so here I digress – as Ruskin himself rarely did – from the immutable stones of Venice's buildings to the difficult human and fleshly concerns of his relationship with Effie.

The union's private details have been pored over by scholars – and pawed over by prurient outsiders – from virtually the moment that it was annulled in 1854, with Ruskin's 'incurable impotency' cited as the reason.

The truth of the dysfunctional relationship will never really be clear, though, because of both wilful and accidental destruction of documents, faulty memoirs and deliberately misleading testimony. Yet it continues to be the subject of books, plays, an opera, a silent movie in 1912, and in 2014 a feature film, *Effie*

Gray, starring Dakota Fanning as Effie and Emma Thompson as her confidante (and Ruskin's nemesis) Lady Eastlake. The movie was the subject of dispute and litigation over its originality and its long gestation caused enormous angst among devoted Ruskinians as they waited to see how badly their hero would emerge. Pretty badly, it turned out.

Robert Brownell has produced an exhaustive analysis of the union, called *Marriage of Inconvenience*. Its conclusions (of which more later) are convincing, and, though the book is harsh on Effie, it contains the best and most sympathetic description of these troubled and over-analysed six years. It was, Brownell writes, 'essentially a story of respectable, decent people who found themselves in an impossibly difficult situation'.

Effie and Ruskin had met before, in 1841, when she was just 12 and stayed at Denmark Hill until the visit was cut short by her sisters' deaths of scarlet fever. Ruskin, then 22, wrote a children's fairy tale, *The King of the Golden River*, at her insistence. (The tale still works: illustrator Quentin Blake – in lots of ways an heir to Ruskin's ideas on observation, drawing and understanding – has produced a new edition for the 2019 bicentenary of Ruskin's birth.) Ruskin embedded in the book many of the economic and social themes to which he would keep returning.

Effie returned, too, visiting Denmark Hill again in 1846. It seems the teenager only recognised quite late that Ruskin had fallen in love with her on that trip. Ruskin's parents, meanwhile meddled in the management of their son's love life as they did in all his affairs. They saw more promise in a match with Charlotte Lockhart, granddaughter of John and John James's favourite novelist Walter Scott.

In a letter, the always blunt John James Ruskin laid out, in language more appropriate to the servicing of thoroughbreds or mating of prize cattle, how worried he was about his son's health. Ruskin was still glum about having 'lost' Adèle Domecq and his father ranked Effie Gray below Charlotte, but grudgingly advised him to 'go on with EG but not precipitately'. John James added that his son should wait six to twelve months and then show his hand, 'if her *health* is good'.

Ruskin did not wait that long. The couple were engaged in late 1847 and the wedding went ahead the following April, in the absence of Ruskin's parents and friends for reasons that will shortly become clear.

Even without the quantity of misinformation and missing information about John and Effie's marriage, it would be hard to guess what went on. If we know anything about marriage, or any long-term relationship, it is this: surface impressions rarely convey the form, scale or, frankly, the weirdness of what can happen behind closed doors. As one obituary of Ruskin put it in 1900, wildly understating the case, their married life was 'strongly tinctured with an unusual form of romance'.[5]

In the annals of poor matches, though, any outsider would have judged the wedding of Euphemia Chalmers Gray and John Ruskin to be singularly ill-omened.

The wedding date – 10 April 1848 – was finally decided only four days beforehand.

The groom, as we know, was a melancholic, intellectual prodigy and reluctant celebrity with a hidden health problem, possibly (in his mind, at least) terminal, an autocratic streak, a fear of sexual intimacy and a knowledge of women drawn mainly from the study of art, the Bible, the novels of Walter Scott and the idealised traditions of courtly love. Before the wedding, Ruskin admitted to Mrs Gray: 'I think, always, that if I had been a woman, I never should have loved the kind of person that I am.'[6]

Effie, the bride to be, was a bright, attractive, flirtatious, extroverted 19-year-old, with an eye for the boys (and they for her), an impatience about book learning, and an incipient desire to enjoy the high life and high society.[7]

The bridegroom's parents were wealthy, overbearing, overprotective worrywarts, over-eager to solve problems by throwing money at them. They were on the record as considering the bride second best and their son too good for almost anyone. Mr and Mrs Ruskin were already friends of Mr and Mrs Gray: the father, George, was a lawyer, on the brink of bankruptcy and disgrace having bet heavily on railway securities, and his wife, Sophia, had already borne eight children.

As for the venue – Bowerswell, Perth, the bride's family house – it was at imminent risk of repossession by the bank in the event of her father's financial ruin. It was also the place where Ruskin's grandfather had lived, had gone mad and had slit his throat – while Ruskin's mother had been caring for him. Hence the older Ruskins' understandable absence from the wedding.

Despite these portents, it seems the wedding itself went well enough. From Perth, the newly weds then drove on to Blair Atholl, an exhausting, hours-long coach ride away. 'John and I had no difficulty in abstaining on the first night,' Effie later wrote in a letter from Venice. As the writer Mary Lutyens pointed out drily 'Nor does he seem to have had any difficulty in abstaining on any other night'.[8]

Here, then, is where I answer the question that many people still blurt out when they hear the name John Ruskin. 'Wasn't he the guy who was afraid of his wife's pubic hair?'

Of all the myths, this one remains the most persistent, because it so precisely sums up a popular image of Ruskin himself, as a hands-off, passionless twerp whose sole experience of the female form came from close observation of (hairless) nude sculpture. So widespread is this assumption that the film *Effie Gray* doesn't even need to allude to it. Ruskin, played as a full-on prig by Emma Thompson's husband Greg Wise, simply takes one look at Effie and walks out of the bedroom.

Even Lutyens, though – who promoted the pubo-phobia explanation for non-consummation – had to withdraw the theory after learning that Ruskin had seen some early Victorian porn while at Oxford. Other ideas include that the churchgoing couple postponed the moment on religious grounds (they married during Lent), that Effie was on her period, or even simply that Ruskin was repelled by her body odour. They remain purely speculative or implausible.

Brownell offers the exhaustively researched and less lurid hypothesis that this was indeed a marriage of convenience, brought about in haste to rescue the Grays from the utter disaster of bankruptcy. Ruskin, as an honourable if confused young man, proposed abstinence, hoping that the couple might fall in love naturally – as was sometimes the case even in arranged marriages.

It was not to be. Ruskin was guilty of adopting a high-handed tone towards Effie from the start. He wrote love letters, but of a rather formulaic kind. He also kept sending bossy instructions about how his teenage bride-to-be should behave. Effie's 'best conduct', Ruskin wrote to her in 1847, would be to return to 'a schoolgirl's life – of early hours – regular exercise – childish recreation – and mental labour of a dull and unexciting character'.

This, as quickly became clear, was not the new Mrs Ruskin's style at all. As even Collingwood, the biographer closest to Ruskin himself, says in his cautious account of the match, Effie was 'a perfect Scotch beauty, with every gift of health and spirits' whereas Ruskin was of 'a retiring and morbid nature'.

The honeymoon, whatever happened on the wedding night itself, hardly allowed them to start bridging this gap.

The 1848 revolutions that had spread across Europe seemed – at least from the comfort of south London – to be threatening civilisation itself. These bloody insurrections prevented the newly married Ruskins from taking off to John's beloved Venice until the following year. Instead, the couple took a short tour of Scotland and the Lakes, and spent the summer studying chilly, damp and draughty English cathedrals and churches – with Ruskin's parents in tow.

The modern fixation on the writer's sexuality is sad. The topic overshadows and distracts from the many ways in which Ruskin's thinking inspired modern progressive movements and organisations. It is also hypocritical. Even in the modern era of openness about sexual habits, few would choose to submit their own bedroom behaviour to the spotlight. As far as I can tell, Ruskin never had full sexual intercourse. Ford Madox Brown, who disliked the critic despite his championing of his fellow pre-Raphaelite painters, invented the cruel term 'Ruskinised' as a synonym for 'castrated'.[9] But Ruskin wasn't 'asexual'. Plenty of evidence, including his own diaries and letters, suggests he had sexual dreams and fantasies. He was tormented before, during and after his marriage by sexual frustration.

Instead of acting on these impulses, Ruskin poured them into his work. Commenting on one landscape painting, one modern critic writes how it and other drawings of geological formations shaped like female genitals indicated Ruskin's desire to be 'invaginated by the physical world'. That is certainly overdoing the Freudian interpretation.

Ruskin was in lots of ways a man of the world, but in this specific area, he was also an innocent. Looking back at the life of Joseph Couttet, Ruskin later wrote how, while out on one of their expeditions, the grizzled, eternally optimistic Swiss guide would listen patiently to the young writer's gloomy musings. Eventually, though, Couttet would slip back and whisper to one of the other servants 'le pauvre enfant, il ne sait pas vivre!' – the poor child, he doesn't know how to live. It was an accurate and poignant observation.[10]

In Venice, with Effie, in 1849 and later, Ruskin certainly preferred to caress the cold stones of the Doge's Palace and the basilica of San Marco rather than his new bride. The city was 'the object of his displaced sex drive', writes one biographer.[11] That is hard to deny – but also, perhaps, not so unusual. The Peggy Guggenheim museum in Venice, just across the Grand Canal from the Gritti hotel in the palazzo where the Ruskin's stayed in 1850, sells a book bag stencilled with nymphomaniac Guggenheim's observation that 'to live in Venice or even to visit it means that you fall in love with the city itself. There is nothing left over in your heart for anyone else'. Strangely, though, the Ruskins were probably at their happiest there, if for quite different reasons.

⤙ 3 ⤚

Ruskin would probably be relieved to visit Venice today, if only to find it was still standing. The city can still look like a mixture of benign neglect – all that apparently crumbling brickwork – and 19th-century restoration. In 1846, he memorably wrote to a friend that 'The rate at which Venice is going is about that of a lump of sugar in hot tea'.[12]

When he and his new wife arrived for a longer stay in 1849, the place was a dangerous mess.

The city bore the scars of the previous year's unsuccessful nationalist uprising and ultimate occupation by Austrian forces. It must have felt like a city on the frontline, with shell and bullet damage on many of the palaces and churches, and cannon drawn up in front of the Doge's Palace. Ruskin worked round them, trying to annotate every column. The city's inhabitants were riven by factions, cowed by the occupiers, and in many cases simply trying to find ways to survive. 'The more I see of the town,' he wrote to his father in December 1849, 'the more my fixed impression is of hopeless ruin.'

Ruskin's notebooks underline just how seriously the critic took his mission of trying to save it. Nowadays, they are housed at Lancaster University in the Ruskin Library. The building was designed in 1998 by Sir Richard MacCormac, who wrote that 'it fulfils Ruskin's expectation that architecture should be metaphorical'. It is situated on an 'island' on the Lancaster campus – 'like Venice' – and separated from the rest of the university by a causeway, as Venice is from the mainland.[13] Inside its curved, lozenge-shaped shell, it holds an extensive and varied collection of paintings, writings, and objects that his most devoted disciple John Howard Whitehouse collected after his death. (Whitehouse was responsible for saving them from dispersal and destruction, following a chaotic house-clearance sale when Ruskin's heirs sold Brantwood in 1931.[14])

The notebooks are mostly ordinary 19 x 12cm lined tablets, of between 160 and 200 pages, divided into categories ('Doors', 'Houses', 'Palaces' and, rather sweetly, 'Bits'), and no different, really, from the modern equivalent you might buy today in any high-street stationer.

Some of Ruskin's sketches are rough – reassuringly so for amateurs like me, in awe of his more worked-through drawings.

They are often just ways of reminding himself of what buildings looked like, or of their dimensions and load-bearing character-istics. They are the annotations of an engineer as much as of an architect or artist. Then occasionally, you will turn a page and encounter something more exquisite: a carefully worked detail of an arch, or a capital, with a light watercolour wash, that reveals Ruskin's great, but lightly worn artistic gift.

As tourists, the overwhelming experience of Venice on a short break is one of rushing past streets, skipping hidden patios, and trying to ignore crumbling palazzi that hint at architectural treas-ures, in haste to get to a better-known landmark. Ruskin had time on his side. He stayed for months on end. And he never rushed. At one point in his 'Doors' book, he notes the existence of a building 'in the bottom of a dark & filthy alley'. Naturally, despite the dark and the filth, Ruskin went down the alley to sketch it – and he went back day after day to sketch more, me-thodically going house to house to detail masonry, arches, style and decoration.

The notebooks remain a great guide to the mind of the man in this prolific, but personally troubled, mid-career period. They still make clear his determination to fill what he saw as a void in Venetians' knowledge of their own culture and history. Ruskin's diligence was awe-inspiring. When later visitors went back and checked his notes against the buildings and found he was as accu-rate as he was painstaking. They mark him out, as one critic puts it, as 'a hero of architecture, feeling it, smelling it, noting it down in its every detail, drawing its minutest part for us'.[15]

The notebooks also help to humanise Ruskin and Effie. At the back of one smaller book, which Ruskin was using ahead of the 1849 visit, he listed things he must not forget for the trip – a table for his *camera lucida*, pencils, tracing paper, a small sketchbook, notebooks (for him and for Effie). Like a stressed 21st-century tourist, worried he would leave behind the one thing he certainly needs, Ruskin also scribbled 'passports'.[16]

The template on each page, into which Ruskin entered the same information about different buildings, is in Effie's handwriting. Perhaps, at this early stage in their marriage, she filled it out willingly, looking for ways to assist and please her edifice-obsessed husband but such 'mental labour of a dull and unexciting character' was certain to wear her down in the end.

Surveying Venice was not always a pleasure for Ruskin, either. In an 1859 letter to his friend Norton he described how the charm of the place wore off because of the 'hard, dry, mechanical toil' of analysing its architecture. He describes Venice not as a paradise but as the 'Queen of Marble and Mud'.[17]

To Samuel Rogers, whose poem *Italy*, with its engravings by Turner and others, had inspired him as a boy, Ruskin wrote in 1852 about how desolate the city could be in the winter. He moaned about his grumpy gondoliers, who understandably disliked being moored to a post in the middle of the Grand Canal all day, while Ruskin sketched. He complained about the deafening toll of bells while he worked in *campanili*, and lambasted the lazy church sacristans who were never around when Ruskin wanted to pester them for the ladders and scaffolding that would give him the vital close-up view of works of art.

Ruskin also explained, in a way that now reads as insufferably superior, his worries about Venetians' failure to see that they were living in a sinking city. If 'the present indolence and ruinous dissipation of the people continue, there will come a time when the modern houses will be abandoned and destroyed, St. Mark's Place will again be, what it was in the early ages, a green field, and the front of the Ducal [Doge's] Palace and the marble shafts of St.

Mark's will be rooted in wild violets and wreathed with vines'.

Ruskin was not a fan of all Venetian architecture. While the passages of *Stones* shedding light on the creativity of the medieval stoneworkers of the Doge's Palace are wonderful, he had a bracingly rude turn of phrase when writing about buildings of the Renaissance and post-Renaissance – the point at which he decided Venice had started its inexorable decline.

He maintained, for example, a hard-to-explain dislike of everything by Palladio, whose cool and calm 16th-century churches are now a tourist trail highlight. Not to Ruskin: he deplored Palladio's smooth, white, undecorated facades. He described the Church of the Redentore on the Giudecca, as 'small and contemptible, on a suburban island', and said of San Giorgio Maggiore, magnificently situated across the channel from San Marco, that it was 'impossible to conceive a design more gross, more barbarous, more childish in conception, more servile in plagiarism, more insipid in result, more contemptible under every point of rational regard'.[18]

The self-aggrandisement of late-Renaissance Venetian worthies also repelled him. It is hard to see how he reconciled this with the depiction of dozens of Doges in paintings by his heroes Tintoretto and Veronese in the ducal palace, albeit in careful allegories that glorified the Venetian empire rather than the individual leaders.

The 1668 Church of San Moisè, which you are almost bound to pass en route from the Accademia bridge to Piazza San Marco, adorned with busts of, and references to, the families that financed and built them, was 'notable as one of the basest examples of the basest school of the Renaissance', according to Ruskin. These days, he would doubtless add Versace, Prada and Michael Kors to his excoriation of modern materialism: their Venice branches sit side by side on the square dominated by the over-decorated church.

꙳ 4 ꙳

'I don't think the Ducal Palace will stand 50 years more,' Ruskin told his father in 1852, before warning him that he was about to freight home yet more plaster casts of some of its sculptures, another consignment in what may count as some of the bulkiest 'wish you were here' postcards in history.

Well, here is the Doge's Palace, still standing more than 150 years later. How far is the building's persistence thanks to the man who described it – for its vibrant display of multiple architectural influences – as 'the central building of the world'?

Certainly, Ruskin's warnings about the threat caused by bad restoration – or, worse, demolition – were heeded in his time. As I mentioned in the last chapter, Ruskin castigated his own tendency never to finish drawings. But in the case of one of his best-known works – his matchless graphite and watercolour drawing of the Ca' d'Oro, from his 1845 visit (colour plate 8) – he had a good excuse. He felt he was working against the clock, as ham-fisted restorers attacked its precious decoration. He told his father that he was 'vainly attempting to draw it while the workmen were hammering it down before my face'.

Astonishingly, it was only in 2018 that Venice devoted the first exhibition to Ruskin alone, held inside the Doge's Palace, mixing watercolours, notebooks, and daguerreotypes.[19] 'We owe a great debt to John Ruskin – not just us [the city] but the whole of Europe,' according to Gabriella Belli, director of the foundation for Venice's civic museums.[20]

But if Ruskin did help save Venice and laid the foundation for 20th- and 21st-century ecological movements to prevent its glories sinking into the lagoon, he also prepared the way for the floods of tourists who followed him. *The Stones of Venice*, which appeared in three volumes from 1851 to 1853, was an unwieldy sort of guide book, but it inspired others to seek out Venice's wonders and lit the path for the crowds that today fill the streets and canals year-round, to whom Ruskin is virtually unknown. Within his lifetime, the city decided to replace with replicas 42 of the most dilapidated carved capitals Ruskin studied on the façade and colonnade of the Doge's Palace. These original stones of Venice are now out of harm's way in its museum.

This was just one consequence of Ruskin's chronicling and campaigning. He found a useful local ally, later in life, in Count Alvise Piero Zorzi. The count helped lead an 1876-7 lobbying effort to prevent a clumsy restoration of San Marco, whose highly patterned exterior Ruskin revered. Sarah Quill's *Ruskin's Venice: The Stones Revisited* brilliantly matches Ruskin's descriptions and sketches with her photographs of the sites he chronicled – a graphic demonstration that his fears for many of the buildings were not realised.

Ruskin also appreciated some of the risks, if not the contradictions, in his own championing of the island-city. He loathed the railway bridge that he saw under construction when he visited in 1845, bringing more visitors to the city, at speeds that gave them no chance of reflecting on the countryside through which they travelled. (This was always Ruskin's principal gripe against travelling by rail – and it is a good one. By luxury carriage, remember, the Ruskin family averaged a leisurely 7 miles an hour.)

Again, writing in 1872, he was already complaining about the whistle and roar of pleasure steamers berthed near his residence 'going through his head like a knife'.[21] It does not take much of a stretch of the imagination to picture him flying a 'No Grandi Navi' flag from his rooms as part of today's campaign against multi-storey cruise ships that clog the port, interrupt the skyline and pollute the waters of the city and beyond.

Just under five years later, in 1876, Ruskin was back, staying at the Grand Hotel. When he decided he needed a cheaper option, he took rooms above an osteria called La Calcina, facing the Giudecca on the opposite side of the Zattere from San Marco. There is a very comfortable hotel of the same name there now. It makes much of the Ruskin connection, even though his stay was relatively brief and the hotel has mostly been rebuilt since. It calls itself 'Ruskin's House', a forgivable exaggeration, and in 2018 it backed a prize in Ruskin's name for writing on architecture, specifically essays on the Ruskinian theme of how to reconcile the need to conserve cities with the demands of future development.[22]

La Calcina's menu, less forgivably, features 'La Ruskin' pizza, topped with mozzarella, honey, goat's cheese, pinenuts, walnuts and rocket. (Among the odder lines of inquiry I pursued for this book was trying to find out whether Ruskin had ever commented on pizza. He and his family did visit Naples on their Italian trip in 1840-41, only ten years after the Antica Pizzera Port'Alba, which claims to be the world's oldest pizzeria, opened its doors. But it seems that if Ruskin did have a view on the merits of thin crust over thick, either he did not express it or it has not been uncovered.)

When I stayed, in 2018, La Calcina was restoring the rooms that would have given the writer his view of the Giudecca – and of the Palladio churches of San Giorgio Maggiore and the Redentore that he hated. It was, however, a less peaceful spot in

Ruskin's day. He describes 'the rattling and screaming, night and day, of the cranes and whistles of steamers which came to unload coals on the quay'. At the time, Ruskin used to break up long sessions of sketching, studying and writing with physical exercise, including rowing and, more eccentrically, log-splitting (also one of his Brantwood pastimes). But he adds, with hindsight: 'The effort made to do thoughtful work in spite of their noise was, I doubt not, in great part the cause of my first illness.'[23] The main threat to the guests' mental health in the 21st century is the constant traffic of fellow tourists, and that is part of Ruskin's legacy.

~ 5 ~

What Ruskin distilled from his extraordinary period of devotion to chronicling Venice's buildings in the 1840s, in all their crazy crumbling detail, was something much more ambitious than a mere guide book.

His sonorous opening to *Stones* made clear that the decline of Venice was a metaphor and a warning to the British empire of what might happen if it made the same fatal mistakes that the Venetians had. It was written, after all, barely 50 years since the last Doge had ended eleven centuries of Venetian independence by caving in to Napoleon – a long downfall that Ruskin dated in part to the Renaissance's rediscovery of cold, classical design over freestyle Gothic architecture. If the British could learn the right lessons, he wrote in his second volume, 'the London of the nineteenth century may yet become as Venice without her despotism, and as Florence without her dispeace'.

The second great insight that Ruskin drew from his study of Gothic architecture, both in Venice and beyond, was the importance of the free agency of the worker. In the second volume, the chapter entitled 'The Nature of Gothic' – actually more of a pæan to 'northern' Gothic style than the Byzantine-Arab-Greek mix visible in Venice – was one of the most directly influential things that Ruskin wrote. It inspired, as we shall see, the founders of the Working Men's College, the designer William Morris, the Arts and Crafts Movement and, indirectly, the British Labour movement.

But even before *Stones*, *The Seven Lamps of Architecture*, published in 1849, established architecture, in the words of one biographer 'as a moral presence in the life of the average Victorian'.[24] Helping to animate that moral presence was the state of mind of the anonymous worker.

The young writer was typically strict and definitive about the difference between architecture and mere 'building'. 'Building does not become architecture merely by the stability of what it erects,' he pointed out in *Seven Lamps*.

What distinguished the architecture from building, Ruskin thought, was decoration. Great decoration required its creators to be moved by something more than the promise of a wage at the end of the day: 'The right question to ask, respecting all ornament, is simply this: Was it done with enjoyment – was the carver happy while he was about it?'[25]

At this early stage in Ruskin's career, the utilitarian factory owners of industrialising Britain may not have picked up this message, but it was surely the first signal of what was to come in the second half of Ruskin's life. In the 21st century, when discussion of how to measure 'gross national happiness' rather than 'gross national product' is alive, and the importance of instilling meaning and purpose at work is becoming more evident, these words have a modern ring and relevance.

Ruskin had also grown to recognise, as the preface to the first edition of *Stones* made clear, that while 'men may live without buying pictures or statues', everyone 'has, at some time of his life, personal interest in architecture'.[26] He appealed not only to those architects or worthies who can 'influence the design of a public building' but also to anyone who 'has to buy, to build, or alter his own house'.

In other words, here – in three volumes covering everything from how to build a wall, to what to carve into the pillars of your palazzo – is a manual that will also help you design your extension or select your cottage or suburban semi-detached. What is more, doing it right will not only make you feel better, it will make your friends, neighbours and passers-by feel better, too.

Amazingly, this advice seemed to stick. Ruskin himself bemoaned the fact he had failed to influence architecture, but you only need to open your eyes and look around the modern city to see that Ruskin's exaltation of the Gothic, in northern cathedrals from Lincoln to Rouen, and in Venice's churches and palazzi, did find its way into British, and international, buildings.

Near my house in St Albans, outside London, is a former infant school from the 1880s in the Gothic style, next to a pair of terraced late 19th-century red-brick homes with Venetian-style arched windows and variegated brick. At the end of my street is the registry office, built in the Gothic style in 1867 – as a prison. Their little-known builders and architects and the people who commissioned them owed a debt to Ruskin.

He was not the only person talking this language. Augustus Pugin – who, unlike Ruskin, did design buildings – had promoted the Gothic Revival in the first half of the 19th century. (Ruskin, still suspicious of Catholics, professed not to have read him in any depth.)

And here is one of those paradoxes that one runs across all the time with Ruskin: he *hated* a lot of what was built broadly to his own prescriptions, in part because he saw the Gothic Revival as fake. He was a conservative conservationist – not anti-restoration, but preferring to employ restorers to preserve the historic bruises and scars of old buildings rather than remake them wrongly. Ruskin panned restoration as 'a Lie, from beginning to end', pointing out that the need to restore a building was often the consequence of wilful neglect.[27] That is a point of view that has, appropriately enough, inspired the Venetian-born 20th-century designer Carlo Scarpa (who, like Ruskin, did not qualify as an architect). He respected the city's ancient architecture while opposing any attempt to mimic it. 'Buildings that imitate look like impostors, and that is just what they are,' Scarpa said, echoing Ruskin.[28]

Yet many of the buildings that Ruskin grumbled about in his lifetime would have been doomed were it not for the conservation movement that his work inspired.

Here is a short list of some buildings, mostly now loved by the public but detested by Ruskin:

The Palace of Westminster. Built to a design by Charles Barry and decorated and fitted out by Pugin, Ruskin called it 'the absurdest piece of filigree, and, as it were, eternal foolscap in freestone'. (He didn't much like the democratic process that went on inside it, either.) He naturally made an exception for the ancient Westminster Hall, which he put in the same sacrosanct bracket as the Doge's Palace.

St Pancras Station – and indeed any station.

George Gilbert Scott's massive towered and turreted masterpiece was later celebrated by everyone from John Betjeman, who helped save it in the 1960s, to the makers of the Harry Potter films, who preferred it to neighbouring King's Cross as the location for 'Platform 9¾', from which the Hogwarts Express departs. Although the station uses multicoloured stone – the polychromy beloved by Ruskin – the writer hated the way in which the style was being applied to railway termini.

Here is one of his best passages, from *Seven Lamps*: 'Better bury gold in the embankments, than put it in ornaments on the stations. Will a single traveller be willing to pay an increased fare on the South Western, because the columns of the terminus are covered with patterns from Nineveh? – he will only care less for the Ninevite ivories in the British Museum: or on the North Western, because there are old English-looking spandrels to the roof of the station at Crewe? – he will only have less pleasure in their prototypes at Crewe House. Railroad architecture has, or would have, a dignity of its own if it were only left to its work. You would not put rings on the fingers of a smith at his anvil.'[29]

Bradford Wool Exchange. An unexpectedly uplifting Venetian palace in the heart of the Yorkshire city, the exchange is still worth a visit. It is home to a branch of Waterstones that may be the grandest bookstore in Britain (though one, as I have mentioned, that did not stock any work by Ruskin at the time of my last visit). This building – or the plan for it – was the cause of one of Ruskin's greatest outbursts, when he was invited to speak to Bradford's burghers about their plans for a new exchange, only to crush them by saying he didn't care for their design, because *they* didn't.[30] By the time his lecture was published in 1867, the design had been chosen, complete with gargoyle likenesses of some of the local worthies on the outside. Ruskin, tapping the same allergy to self-aggrandisement that prompted his vitriol against Venice's San Moisè and its busts of the founding families, detested it.

Every instance of suburban Gothic in the land. In spite of having urged houseowners in 1851 to look to the shape and style of their humble dwellings, Ruskin disliked the sprawl of suburbia. By 1872, he was complaining in a letter to the *Pall Mall Gazette* that he had had 'indirect influence on nearly every cheap villa-builder between [Denmark Hill] and Bromley; and there is scarcely a public-house near the Crystal Palace but sells its gin and bitters under pseudo-Venetian capitals copied from the Church of the Madonna of Health or of Miracles'. One of the main reasons he was leaving London (for Brantwood), he wrote, was because he was 'surrounded everywhere by the accursed Frankenstein monsters of… my own making'. Or, as an estate agent would now put it: period properties of charm and character.

Ruskin lent his growing reputation in his own lifetime to a few projects that, in his eyes, combined the art and craftsmanship of the Gothic style with meaning and purpose. The best example is what is now the Oxford Museum of Natural History, built in the 1850s as what we would now call an interdisciplinary hub where arts and sciences would meet.

Today, visitors show more interest in the exhibits, which include casts and models of the extinct dodo, than in the ornamented shell that contains them. But take a coffee at the gallery level and examine both the overall effect and the close detail. The internal pillars were made from different types of rock, carefully labelled, to help turn the whole building into a geology lesson worthy of the young Ruskin's mineralogical obsession. Outside, there is a rare example of Ruskin's design skills put into practice, in the decorative twin arches to the right of the main entrance, under the well-known 'cat window'.

The creative spirits behind the decoration were two Irish brothers – the red-bearded James and John O'Shea – who carved

exquisite designs. The whole place still reverberates with the originality of its conception. That reflected the direct involvement of
Ruskin. In 1856, he even appeared on site to give what must have
been a rather lengthy, though apparently impromptu, lecture to
the workmen on Christian Socialism, the misguided opinions of
political economists, and the pride the workers should take on
being able to work skilfully with their hands. The happy carvers'
reaction was not recorded.

Even this building, though, to which Ruskin devoted time
and creative effort in the early 1850s, was not a complete success
in the critic's eyes. It used too much structural iron to support its
glass roof, he believed. The detailed stonework was more successful. While the O'Sheas and their fellow sculptors may have been
happy in their work, this did not make them as pliable as Ruskin's
theory of the contented stoneworkers of Venice suggested they
should be.

They certainly lived up to, and exceeded, Ruskin's original
enthusiastic ambition, expressed to his friend Henry Acland, the
Oxford doctor and scientist and joint champion of the project,
that the museum would be 'the first building raised in England
since the close of the fifteenth century, which has fearlessly put to
new trial this old faith in the ... genius of the unassisted workman'.[31] The sculptors ignored the proposals from the keeper of
the museum, and some of the designs suggested by Ruskin himself. They insisted they would only sculpt from nature (a good
Ruskinian precept), not from blueprints and had plants brought
from the botanical gardens every morning on which to base their
ornate carvings.

It turned out, too, that fine ornament was costly. The original plan for a richly decorated entrance had to be dropped, or
at least cut short, leaving some rough unfinished blocks. These

contributed to a persistent urban myth, propagated by Acland and Ruskin at the O'Sheas' expense. The story went that James O'Shea was ordered to stop carving monkeys on one window, on the grounds that the hint of Darwinism would cause a scandal. He changed them to cats instead and was fired. When reinstated, he was told the money had run out. In revenge, O'Shea carved parrots and owls into the portal arch to caricature his intransigent university paymasters, until Acland ordered him to destroy them.[32] As recent research has suggested, apart from the tight budget, nothing fits in this story – the parrots and owls are still there, for one thing, and something of a highlight for today's visitors.[33]

A crotchety Ruskin was, later, unfairly disparaging of James O'Shea. 'I never meant that you could secure a great natural monument of art by letting loose the first lively Irishman you could get hold of to do what he liked in it,' he said in an 1877 lecture in Oxford, although this was almost exactly what he had suggested.[34] The building remains, however, a memorial to the noble early ambitions for its overall design and the sculptors' skill. Less obviously, it is also a reminder that putting the whole of any Ruskinian theory into practice was usually harder, and often dearer, than it first looked. As Ruskin put it, grudgingly, in a letter also written in 1877, the museum was at least 'a first effort in [the] right direction'.[35]

⤛ 6 ⤜

Anyone with a vague knowledge of Gothic style can start spotting it today across London's suburbs, or pick up the scent of Venice in the extraordinary late 19th-century town halls of industrial cities.[36]

It is harder, though, to detect Ruskin's influence among more modern architects' work. The explosion of organic ornament in the work of Gaudí, the Catalan designer of Barcelona's flamboyant Sagrada Familia cathedral, has clear links to Ruskin's ideas. The architect was avowedly interested in the theories of Ruskin and of his French counterpart Viollet-le-Duc, whom Ruskin envied for his fame, even if he objected to his radical restorations.[37]

You can just about see the influence of the gothic in the highly decorated early 20th-century skyscrapers of Louis Sullivan, pioneer of the vertical, though you must put out of your mind Ruskin's coruscating condemnation of the high-rise, which he said could only be achieved by 'pulverising our mountains and strewing the duly pulverized and, by wise medical geology, drugged, materials, over the upper stages'.[38]

But in the low-rise layers of Frank Lloyd Wright's prairie houses, and the unadorned socialist cathedrals of Gropius and the Bauhaus, or the geometric shapes of Le Corbusier – all architects allegedly influenced by Ruskin – there seems at first to be nothing that Ruskin would admire and little that visibly linked him to these 20th-century designers.

For guidance, look back at Ruskin's 'lamp of truth' – one of the seven principles laid out in the 1849 work.

'The idea that a building should express what it is rather than what it would like to appear as – i.e. not disguising poor materials as fine materials but expressing itself through its elements, materials and workmanship – was very much at the heart of modernist ideology,' Edwin Heathcote, the *Financial Times* architecture correspondent, explained to me.

Modernist architects, in other words, looked selectively to Ruskin for that moral notion, rather than for overall stylistic guidance.

Frank Lloyd Wright was a slightly different case. His Welsh Unitarian mother was by all accounts almost as overbearing and religiously motivated as Ruskin's. She used to hang engravings of English Gothic cathedrals in Wright's nursery. She also tried to instil in Wright a deep sense of righteous purpose. He was strongly affected by the Arts and Crafts Movement. Wright took another useful pointer from his unlikely-seeming Victorian inspiration: the idea of that architecture should belong to a place.

Ruskin's strong conviction that architecture represented, and sprang from, the place it was built is reflected in our modern determination to build with local materials, inspired by local vernacular influences. This was the kind of determination with which Wright approached, among other masterworks, Fallingwater, the 1964 Pennsylvania home he designed to be built over a waterfall – exactly the kind of link between architecture and nature that Ruskin considered sacred. You will find this importance of provenance and local sourcing again in Ruskin's commitment to craft and ultimately in his medievalist yearning for a return to types of work and lifestyle linked to the land.

Wright also plainly saw something that he could develop as an American style and movement, building on Ruskin's idea that 'Architecture is possible only to a people who have a Common Pride, and a Common-Wealth, – whose Pride is Civic – and is the Pride of All'.[39] Finally, as a designer and maker of furniture and furnishings for his buildings, Wright developed Ruskin's concepts of craft and brought them into the 20th century.[40]

Ruskin was a great protector and exponent of palatial and ecclesiastical architecture. It may come as a surprise to see how much he wrote about ordinary homes – from Westmoreland cottages to Swiss chalets. Brantwood itself was originally a cluster of cottages, which Ruskin and the Severn family, who lived there as, variously, housekeepers and carers, expanded.

Another surprise is how relevant his attacks on the poor taste and impatience of housebuyers still sound.

As early as 1849, in *The Seven Lamps of Architecture*, Ruskin had harsh words for the throwaway culture of homeowners and builders. 'I cannot but think it an evil sign of a people when their houses are built to last for one generation only,' he wrote in *Seven Lamps* – the kind of maxim that house builders (and buyers) of the 21st century should take to heart.[41]

This is far more serious than a mere critique of interior design. Ruskin went on to blast the poor dwellings being thrown up at the time to house the workers of industrial cities: 'Those comfortless and unhonoured dwellings are the signs of a great and spreading spirit of popular discontent,' he wrote, suggesting that a failure to revere and conserve hearth and home is a sign of having abandoned the Christian 'household God'.

There is no reason why after years of decluttering and minimalism, we should not be overdue a revival of the sort of decoration that Ruskin studied, worshipped and occasionally designed. After all, while we may not wish to clog our rooms with old-fashioned furniture, we still covet homes for their 'original features', as likely as not the sort of curlicues and mouldings that our Victorian antecedents installed, echoes of Pugin or Ruskin.

This revival may also be handmade. The artist Grayson Perry's richly decorated 'A House for Essex' (created with the architect Charles Holland), owes a debt to Ruskin.[42] It is a home, but also a chapel, with a story, and an excess of decoration – mosaic floors, specially commissioned artworks and tapestries by Perry. It advertises itself as 'a testament to the idea that art and architecture can lift our spirits' – a thoroughly Ruskinian sentiment.[43]

But such a revival would also be aided by technology. Ruskin is often caricatured as being anti-machine and he did evolve a pre-industrial philosophy that was feudal and largely unattainable. But Ruskin was not against technology as such; he was against meaningless labour, which seemed to be encouraged, in his day, by the heedless and rapid shift to mechanisation. Computers and computer-aided design, as well as the latest advances in engineering and materials, offer the chance to produce a new type of decorative architecture, on a grand as well as a fine-detailed scale, without having to worry about grinding down the worker.

Wright himself recognised this as early as 1901. In an address to Chicago's Arts and Crafts Society, he urged craftspeople to move on from Ruskin and William Morris's purism and use new mechanical tools 'to emancipate the beauties of nature in wood': 'The machine, by its wonderful cutting, shaping, smoothing, and repetitive capacity, has made it possible so to use it without waste that the poor as well as the rich may enjoy to-day beautiful surface treatments of clean, strong forms that the branch veneers of Sheraton and Chippendale only hinted at, with dire extravagance, and which the middle ages utterly ignored.'[44]

7

John and Effie Ruskin enjoyed another six-month stay in Venice in 1851-52 as he continued to work on *The Stones of Venice*. 'Enjoyed' may not be the right word. The marriage was under strain and Effie's passion for socialising – chiefly with the Austrian military occupiers and the high society around them – was in sharp contrast to Ruskin's reclusiveness.

There were moments of fun together. Effie wrote approvingly

of their outing during the Carnival in February 1852, when the couple wore the traditional masks and disguises and 'John, who was as grave as possible, did the thing capitally'. But Ruskin's parents continued to worry about their 33-year-old son's health, sending food parcels, and making Effie remark in one letter on her fear that the Ruskins 'from leaving John so long really ill when he was younger, can never be persuaded that he has grown out of it'.

In 1852, the couple returned, with varying degrees of reluctance, from Venice to London. This six-month stay had allowed for more leisure for both than the meticulously annotated 1849-50 work trip. But Ruskin himself was despondent, irritable, and, if you believe his own hypochondriacal accounts, unwell.

The previous December he had learnt of the death of Turner. This made Ruskin brood self-indulgently about his own mortality. He had been named an executor of Turner's will, which was an accolade he appreciated, even though he was hurt the painter had left him none of his works (he later resigned the role).

Turner was to remain a powerful force in the critic's life and John and John James's appetite to accumulate as much of Turner's work as possible was unabated. Ruskin's father was in constant communication with Ruskin, who urged him to buy more Turner drawings. Ruskin senior did some sharp work acquiring Turners in the immediate aftermath of his death, when it had yet to become public that the painter had bequeathed most of his unsold work to the nation – a move that was bound to lead to an upward spike in the value of those works still on the market.[45]

Effie, meanwhile, had tried to put the fateful date of departure from Venice out of her mind. She continued to attend parties in the city and beyond (with and without her husband) until just before the couple left. Of her time in Venice, she wrote, 'I cannot

conceive any life so happy so free from care, so perfectly independent and yet not dull'.

Ruskin would not return to Venice until 1876, alone and de-
pressive to the point of psychosis.

What seemed to lie ahead of him and Effie in 1852, though,
as they worked their way back to England on the familiar route
via the Alps, was exactly the semi-suburban domesticity against
which Ruskin was later to rail.

Before they went to Venice, his father had installed the couple
in Mayfair, where they could connect with the fine arts world.
Now, the lease was up on that house on Park Street. John James
took it on himself to acquire and, at some expense, furnish 30
Herne Hill. It was on the Norwood ridge that had once excited
young John's visionary powers, next to what used to be the family
home. The young Ruskins, whatever their differences, were united in their dislike of both the house and its contents. Ruskin said
it was fit for a clerk.[46] You do not have to use much imagination
to see how Effie considered her father-in-law's choice of location, house and furniture a further constraint on her own freedom,
compared with the relative independence of her life in Venice.

The second and third volumes of *The Stones of Venice* appeared
in 1853. Ruskin worked on them at his parents' home in nearby
Denmark Hill, where he always preferred to study, rather than
in the new house. It is tempting to think he had the vulgar décor and unattractive architectural style of 30 Herne Hill in mind
when he suddenly addressed the comfortable mid-19th-century
homeowner, in this passage from 'The Nature of Gothic':

> And now, reader, look round this English room of yours, about
> which you have been proud so often, because the work of it
> was so good and strong, and the ornaments of it so finished.

Examine again all those accurate mouldings, and perfect pol-
ishings, and unerring adjustments of the seasoned wood and
tempered steel. Many a time you have exulted over them, and
thought how great England was, because her slightest work
was done so thoroughly. Alas! if read rightly, these perfect-
nesses are signs of a slavery in our England a thousand times
more bitter and more degrading than that of the scourged
African, or helot Greek.[47]

Effie, meanwhile, threw herself back into London society. She
was probably naïve about the reputational risks of appearing in
public, often alone. She lacked support from Ruskin and his parents, but she was also keen to show herself off. Effie had long
been impressed by young Ruskin's social standing and growing
connections, forged by the success of his early work. The public platform that Ruskin's fame had built, and that he mostly
shunned at this stage in his career, was ideal for her.

Effie's social life was also now increasingly enlivened by her
meetings with the rising stars of the Pre-Raphaelite brotherhood
whom her husband supported. She won the attention of the
dashing John Everett Millais, in particular. Once a child prodigy
with a gift for portraiture, Millais was encouraged – or at least
not discouraged – by Ruskin to invite his wife to model for
the painting that we know as *The Order of Release*. Effie's face is
used for the head of the prisoner's wife, but a different model
sat for the bare feet. The idea that the young Mrs Ruskin might
have modelled barefoot for Millais was a scandal that caused unpleasant gossip.

Ruskin himself was either oblivious to the backchat or possibly starting to look for ways to get out of the unhappy marriage.
It is hard otherwise to explain how his plan to visit the Highlands
with Millais and Effie, thrust together in a small cottage at Brig

John Everett Millais, Detail from The Order of Release

o'Turk near Glen Finglas in the rainy summer of 1853, would ever end well for his relationship with his young wife. This is the scenario – the epitome of Victorian awkwardness about sex – that understandably fascinates screen-writers, playwrights and authors.

Millais, who was trying to complete the sober streamside portrait of his mentor and champion Ruskin, was simultaneously tortured by proximity to Effie. 'I should feel considerably better for a wife in Scotland,' Millais wrote to a friend that September. 'There is such a want of humanity. These chilling mountains make one love little soft, warm, breathing bodies.'[48]

Was this a deliberate attempt by Ruskin somehow to trigger annulment, which might theoretically have provided a painless and private way out for Ruskin and Effie, at a time when divorce was impractical and socially unthinkable?[49]

If it was, then it backfired horribly. On April 25, 1854, Effie left London by train for Scotland, never to return. That evening a 'suit of nullity' was delivered to Ruskin's father, together with Effie's account book, keys and wedding ring. Ruskin seemed to receive the news with cool equanimity. Two weeks later, the Ruskin family trio set off for a planned trip to the continent. The newly liberated Ruskin later recalled his 'immeasurable delight' at taking the ferry, 'with the hope of Calais at breakfast, and the horses' heads set straight for Mont Blanc to-morrow'.[50]

As is now clear, the annulment marked the start of a far more tortuous and unpleasant journey for Ruskin, leading to sexual despair and mental derangement and spilling over onto his reputation for a century and a half.

The failure of the marriage, so loaded with the prejudices, preconceptions and prurience of its era, took on a significance for Ruskin followers and critics that it never deserved. It overshadowed Effie's life, too.[51] But while she certainly suffered during the relationship, Effie did emerge from the catastrophic partnership with Ruskin with an array of connections that helped her forge a new life as wife of Millais, mother of their eight children, and – as Lady Millais – a noted society hostess.

Gladstone once told his daughters: 'Remember there was no fault: there was misfortune, even tragedy. All three were perfectly blameless.'[52] A century and a half later, rather than dwelling on unverifiable detail, or assigning and reassigning blame at the expense of the brighter legacy of Ruskin, Effie and Millais, it is surely healthier to draw a Gladstonian line under the whole thing.

Rumours about Effie's relationship with Ruskin and its breakdown continue to reverberate, however. When a property reporter for *Mail Online* wrote in 2015 about the sale of a flat at Park Street, part of what was once the Mayfair residence of John and Effie, the 'notorious scandal' of their annulled marriage was cited as though it was a selling point and as fresh as the latest gossip from *Celebrity Big Brother*. The flat needed 'extensive renovation', the *Mail* wrote – a bit like Ruskin's reputation.

Chapter VI

Landscape and Nature

*God has lent us the earth for our life; it is a great entail. It belongs as much to
those who come after us, and whose names are already written in the book of
creation, as to us; and we have no right, by anything we do or neglect,
to involve them in unnecessary penalties, or deprive them of benefits
which it was in our power to bequeath.*
(The Seven Lamps of Architecture)

I

In May 1858, John Ruskin took off on a four-month trip through
France to Switzerland and Italy.

It was fifteen years since the first volume of *Modern Painters*
had appeared and what he had thought would be a mere pamphlet was not yet finished. Turner – the great inspiration for the
work – was dead. Indeed, despite having resigned the role of executor, Ruskin had spent much of the previous few months at the
National Gallery, carrying out the exhausting task of examining
and cataloguing Turner's bequest to the nation.

As he toured through Switzerland, he actively sought out
places that Turner had drawn or painted, occasionally sketching
the same scenes himself and reporting varying degrees of frustration as he compared himself unfavourably to the master.

Ruskin, in his late thirties, was still young-looking, slightly built, and, by all accounts, charming company. Charles Norton, later Ruskin's literary executor, met him in 1856 and described a complete absence of 'common English reserve and stiffness'. To Norton's eye, Ruskin did not behave like a celebrity, despite his undoubted public fame, but showed 'an almost feminine sensitiveness and readiness of sympathy'.

He was also a lively and open conversationalist – a bit of a contrast to the stern, sometimes hectoring personality he projected, and still projects, through his prose: 'He had often an almost boyish gaiety of spirit and liveliness of humour, and always a quick interest in whatever might be the subject of the moment. He never quarrelled with a difference of opinion, and was apt to attribute only too much value to a judgment that did not coincide with his own.'

Norton noticed something else. Although Ruskin was 'one of the pleasantest, gentlest, kindest, and most interesting of men', he also seemed 'cheerful rather than happy. The deepest currents of his life ran out of sight.'[1]

This was a retrospective view – written four years after Ruskin's death – and it is impossible to rule out that Norton was colouring his first recollection of meeting Ruskin with the dark events that were about to crowd into the writer's life.

The disintegration of his marriage with Effie was one shadow, but at that point it probably seemed a small one. Unlike, say, Ruskin's failure to win over Adèle Domecq, the annulment did not trigger mental or physical collapse.

More ominously, just before his 1858 continental trip, Ruskin had met for the first time Rose La Touche, then a ten-year-old girl, a meeting that was to evolve over the next 17 years into a desperate, unconsummated passion that would ruin both their lives.

Ruskin was also struggling with his realisation, based on his survey of the thousands of drawings Turner had left to the nation, that some of the artist's legacy was not as great as he had very publicly announced it was in the early volumes of *Modern Painters*. That is an understatement: Ruskin judged only 1,900 of the 19,000 works in the Turner bequest suitable for exhibition; 30 per cent of the rest he categorised as 'entire rubbish'.[2]

Two myths, or semi-myths, have persisted about Ruskin's attitude to the Turner bequest. Myth one is that the chief source of his disgust was the discovery of erotic drawings which he then arranged (myth two) to be burnt. Ian Warrell, a Turner scholar and former curator of 18th- and 19th-century art at the Tate gallery, has established beyond reasonable doubt that there was no such bonfire.[3]

Yet Ruskin would not have regretted consigning much of the bequest to the gallery incinerator. He wrote to his father in June 1858 that Turner had suffered a 'moral decline', leading to work 'encumbered with sensuality, suspicion, pride, vain regrets, hopelessness, labour, and all kinds of darkness and oppression of heart'. Publicly, Ruskin maintained his support for Turner, but his annotated catalogue for the initial selection of 100 watercolours supposed to represent the artist's work (recreated in a 1995 exhibition at the Tate), revealed the high standard to which he held the painter. 'Out and out the worst sketch in the whole series; disgracefully careless and clumsy,' he wrote of one, before reverting to high praise for another: 'There is no laziness, and no failure; but intense haste and concentration of power; every line and blot being of value.'[4]

As he worked his way south through Switzerland towards Italy, Ruskin even started to confess – for the first time in his life – that he was tiring of mountains themselves, preferring to see them as a backdrop to low-level lakeside walks. Writing from Isola Bella on Lago Maggiore, he admitted he was looking forward to the bright lights of Turin, where he was to spend five or six weeks.[5] And later, from Turin, he declared that he didn't 'care so much… as I used [to]' about sunsets. Instead, 'I am gradually getting more interested in men and their misdoings' – a foreshadowing of his swing to social criticism, of which more later.

All the while, Ruskin's spiritual beliefs were evolving from those he had absorbed and practised as the devoted son of his evangelical mother, suspicious of Catholics and Catholic art, to the more open-minded, non-sectarian views of his later years. The evolution was to reach a turning point later in that crucial year of 1858 in Turin – an episode Ruskin referred to as his 'unconversion' and told and retold in differing versions for the rest of his life.

One August Sunday, he attended a service at a church of the Waldensian Protestant sect. The sermon was given by a 'poor little wretch in a tidy black tie… expounding Nothing with a twang'[6] (writing later, Ruskin described this hapless preacher as 'a little squeaking idiot'[7]). From there, he visited the city's royal galleries to continue his study of Paolo Veronese's grand and colourful *Solomon and the Queen of Sheba*. Rubbing in the contrast in another account, in *Præterita*, Ruskin wrote how a military band was playing the background, sounding 'more devotional… than anything I remembered of evangelical hymns'.[8]

Before the grandeur of Veronese's painting, Ruskin suffered his third art attack. He was 'struck by the Gorgeousness of life which the world seems to be constituted to develop, when it is made the best of'. And he posed the question, as much to the younger Ruskin, who had disparaged Catholic art, as to his readers: 'Can it be possible that all this power and beauty is adverse to the honour of the Maker of it?'

Ruskin was never an atheist, but this was the definitive break with the Bible-thumping creed that his mother had drummed into him as a child. As he wrote later in *Præterita*: 'That day, my evangelical beliefs were put away, to be debated of no more.'[9]

Despite the fast and confusing flow of some of these currents, Ruskin was still capable of the clarity of thought that brought the long-delayed final volume of *Modern Painters* to fruition in 1860. It opens with an extraordinary tour de force describing Ruskin's central theory of the interconnectedness of art, nature and society. He called it The Law of Help.

Artistic composition, Ruskin wrote, 'may be best defined as the help of everything in the picture by everything else'. Similarly, 'in a plant, the taking away of any one part does injure the rest. Hurt or remove any portion of the sap, bark, or pith, the rest is injured. If any part enters into a state in which it no more assists the rest, and has thus become "helpless," we call it also "dead."' So finally, 'intensity of life is also intensity of helpfulness – *completeness of depending of each part on all the rest* [my emphasis]. The ceasing of this help is what we call corruption; and in proportion to the perfectness of the help, is the dreadfulness of the loss. The more intense the life has been, the more terrible is its corruption.'[10]

Here was a clue to how Ruskin would spend the rest of his life: promoting a happy, ethical, collaborative society, in which each part depended on all the rest. Yet significantly, this law of help had its roots firmly embedded in nature.

 2

Ruskin's 1858 wobble about the joys of the mountains was unusual. While the writer may sometimes have complained about the time he spent in the bitter Venetian cold researching the history and architecture of its stones, he rarely griped about being outdoors in the mountains whether in France, Italy, Switzerland, Scotland or the Lake District.

Read almost any of his letters or diaries describing his time in the fresh air, and you will find a refreshing contrast to the unjust impression of Ruskin as the stereotypical dry academic, locked in his study, or the pretentious and over-refined critic, warm indoors at the Royal Academy or British Museum. While no athlete (and no great fan of athletic pursuits for their own sake), he loved to row and to walk, until a rupture sustained while dancing in his sixties forced him to be less ambitious.

With Joseph Couttet, their Swiss guide, young Ruskin and friends made some adventurous climbs in the Alps. In May 1849, for example, Richard Fall, one of Ruskin's few boyhood friends, joined him for part of the continental tour he was taking with his parents (he had left his wife Effie, unhappy and unwell, with her own parents in Scotland). In a vivid passage from Ruskin's diary, he described how he and Couttet took Fall up a snow-covered path to a mountain hut on the northern slopes of the Mont Blanc massif, before descending a snowy couloir at speed, using their poles and feet to break the fall.

'We slid down the two thousand feet to the source of the Arveron, in some seven or eight minutes, Richard vouchsafing his entire approval of that manner of progression by the single significant epithet, "Pernicious!"', Ruskin recalled. In an unintentionally hilarious footnote, he made clear that they could have gone faster, but the descent included 'ecstatic or contemplative rests'.[11]

That summer, Couttet guided Ruskin on the 'tour du Mont Blanc'. To give you an idea of what this entailed, the modern version of this tour is 170km long and involves a cumulative 10,000m of climbs and descents through France, Switzerland and Italy. Even with modern equipment, one trekking company advises customers to prepare by walking four to six hours a week in hilly terrain, combined with 'low-to-mid intensity gym work or some jogging, cycling or swimming'.[12] Ruskin took his time, as usual, but the 30-year-old was evidently no weakling.

This visit also allowed him to draw. From April to September, he generated 47 drawings, including the magnificent *Cascade de la Folie, Chamonix* – a dramatic view of a waterfall carving through the foreground with snow-covered peaks on the horizon (colour plate 4) – and filled notebooks with geological, botanical and meteorological observations.

In the light of some of these high-spirited, youthful expeditions there is a whiff of hypocrisy about his later tirades against climbers who, in Ruskin's eyes, desecrated the Alps with their desire to 'conquer' the peaks he liked to admire. This group of pioneers honoured him with membership of the Alpine Club, formed in 1857, rather as the Royal Institute of British Architects tried to garland him with a medal in 1874. (He turned the medal down, accusing builders of 'injurious neglect' and destruction of great architecture.) As Simon Schama puts it in *Landscape and Memory*, 'it is hard to decide which is more amazing: that the Alpine Club ever asked John Ruskin to be a member, or that he consented to join'.

Ruskin's principal objection was consistent with his later criticisms of modern economics and Britain's reckless industrialisation. It was that alpinists had turned even his beloved mountains into a form of competition. Even so, when he accused early mountaineers of treating the Alps as 'soaped poles in a bear-garden' down which they slid with 'shrieks of delight', had he forgotten – or deliberately chose to ignore – the fun he had had with Fall and Couttet fifteen years earlier?[13]

Ruskin's love of geology underpinned his understanding of, and love for, the mountains. It was his first and lifelong enthusiasm. His father once wrote proudly that 'from Boyhood he has been an artist, but he has been a geologist from Infancy, and his geology is perhaps now the best part of his Art'.

Ruskin was no dabbler. In 1864, he remarked in a letter that he had passed 'eleven summers and two winters in research among the Alps', examining what they looked like and how they had been formed. He claimed he often spent ten hours or more a day in the mountains.

'He understood the physical structure of rocks,' Howard Hull, the amiable and encyclopaedically well-informed director of Brantwood told me, as we looked out across the lake below Ruskin's house to the crags of Coniston Old Man that Ruskin loved. 'He understood the process of erosion, how rocks would split' and went on, in some of his later works to describe in microscopic detail, for example, how agates are composed.

If he was a brilliant scientist, Ruskin was also a person who understood nature as a whole – as a spiritual, artistic and emotional experience as well as an occasion for geological and scientific research. He knew 'more about scenery than most geologists, and more about geology than most artists', his biographer Collingwood wrote.

This is where John Muir, the pioneer of US national parks, was mistaken when he accused Ruskin, in a letter to a friend, of trying to force his readers 'to take beauty as we do roast beef or medicine, at stated times, the intervals to be measured by a London watch instead of inhaling it every moment as we do breath'.

In fact, Muir was a Ruskin fan and corresponded with him.

His 1886 edition of *Modern Painters* is peppered with annotations. Muir's cultural legacy was very similar. The Sierra Club initially paralleled Ruskin's Guild of St George – although the Sierra Club is more like another Ruskin legacy, the UK's National Trust, in having become almost a mass movement. Both men 'confronted the dilemmas presented by human presence, influence, and responsibility on the earth'.[14] But Muir misread, perhaps deliberately, how deeply Ruskin inhaled nature and how much he wanted others – particularly artists – to breathe it in. 'The beginning of all my own right art work in life depended not on my love of art, but of mountains and seas,' Ruskin said in an 1872 lecture at Oxford, from the series entitled, significantly, 'The Relation of Wise Art to Wise Science'.[15]

Nature was the thread that connected his work. Ruskin's great knowledge allowed him to form personal relationships with some of the great medical and scientific figures of the time, including Charles Darwin, whom he had first met when a young undergraduate, in the circle of eccentric Oxford geology professor William Buckland.

Ruskin was rude in public about Darwinism, but he and the naturalist shared comparable intellects, keen observational powers, and an interest in botany and science in general. Ruskin, as we have seen, could more than hold his own in scientific discussion, though Darwin – for all his powers, no polymath – struggled to reciprocate when it came to art appreciation. After visiting the Ruskin family house in 1868 in Denmark Hill, where Ruskin showed off his collection of Turners, Darwin admitted that he could not make out what Ruskin saw in the paintings, though he politely kept quiet to avoid offending his host.[16]

Ruskin made no great concession to the sciences in how he wrote about nature, bringing the same thrilling literary inventiveness and breadth of knowledge to his observations on meteorology as he did to his analysis of paintings or buildings. As Sara Atwood has pointed out, for Ruskin, 'there was nothing odd about describing clouds as "spherical hollow molecules and pure vapour" in one breath and as the Graiæ of Greek myth in another'.[17]

Mountains erupt out of his books in unexpected places. When Ruskin lectures about walls early in *The Stones of Venice*, he covers mere bricks and mortar but he also surprises the reader with the Matterhorn as an example of the strength of layered masses of 'imperfect and variable' materials. The passage apparently startled major Victorian architects into varying the colour and size of the stones they used in their buildings.[18]

Mountains are mentioned some 500 times in *Modern Painters* – one of the books that so interested John Muir. The fourth volume, for which those visits in the 1840s and 1850s proved invaluable, is such a pæan to peaks, with separate chapters on aiguilles, crests, precipices, banks and stones, that the president of the Geological Society singled it out in an obituary of Ruskin in 1900 as recommended reading for geologists everywhere.

⤙ 3 ⤚

'The valley is gone... and now every fool in Buxton can be in Bakewell in half an hour and every fool at Bakewell in Buxton,' John Ruskin wrote in 1871, as part of his indictment of the development of the train line between the two Derbyshire towns.[19]

The railway had destroyed the beauty of Monsal Dale in what is now the Peak District, he claimed. Construction of its tunnels and Headstone Viaduct in 1863 had 'heaped thousands of tons of shale into its lovely stream'.

Trains plied this route for just under a century and in 1970, eleven years after the line itself was closed, a preservation order was applied to the viaduct. The story since then is, oddly, something of a tribute to Ruskin's vision.

When I visited in August 2017, I joined hundreds of hikers, day-trippers and cyclists enjoying the traffic-free 'Monsal Trail' laid on the route of the old railway line, between Blackwell Mill and Bakewell.

The viaduct he hated is a highlight of the trail. Plaques record the line's original construction and the engravings they reproduce confirm what Ruskin had observed – the blasting of cuttings through the dale did smash its natural beauty.

But in its current form, with trees allowed to overgrow the old track, the trail, now virtually invisible from the road opposite, is a vibrant fulfilment of another fervent wish of Ruskin's. In 1875, he wrote how he was 'looking always forward hopefully to the day when their embankment will be ploughed down again, like the camps of Rome, into the English field'.

One can go further. It is conceivable that the Peak District national park through which the Monsal Trail runs might not even have existed had Ruskin's influential voice not been heeded in the late 19th century. The Peak District was the first UK national park, approved in 1951, and his beloved Lake District was the second, a few months later. Both were established with the ideal that the parks should 'conserve and enhance the natural beauty, wildlife and cultural heritage' of the areas they cover. The 21st-century development of 'heritage tourism' – a kind of cult of conservation – might not have appealed to him, but the underlying thrust of the great post-Second World War parks movement is pure Ruskin.

You would assume from Ruskin's writing and lecturing that

he opposed all development. He regularly railed against rail. If you take him at his word, he would even have hated the bicyclists on the Monsal Trail. In a letter sent to a magazine in 1888, he wrote that he was 'quite prepared to spend all my best "bad language" in reprobation of the bi-, tri-, and 4-5-6- or 7 cycles, and every other contrivance and invention for superseding human feet on God's ground'.[20]

But he was more pragmatic than these deliberately provocative declarations suggest. He might not have enjoyed seeing, from his drawing room, the steam of the locomotive cutting across the landscape opposite Brantwood to the small station at Coniston (decommissioned a few years after the Lake District became a national park). He remained nostalgic for the slow pace of the coach and horses. Yet he used the railway frequently, often commuting for eight hours from Coniston to Oxford and back when he was Slade professor of art at the university.

On the last leg of his trip to Turin in 1858, he was obliged to take a train from Arona, on the banks of Lago Maggiore, and rather enjoyed the 'luxurious comfort' of his first-class non-smoking compartment, 'lined with cool chintz, and painted with fruit and garlands of flowers on the roof'.[21] He even wrote a rich passage of prose in 1865 about locomotives themselves, describing the 'amazed awe, the crushed humility, with which I sometimes watch a locomotive take its breath at a railway station'.[22]

Ruskin saw more clearly than most how vital was the relationship between man and nature. Its importance went well beyond its cleansing and inspiring impact on the human psyche. He also saw it as a practical relationship. He fought to conserve the Lake District from over-development, but he did not simply want to preserve it unvisited as a perfect æsthetic experience.

For this, among other reasons, Ruskin was one of the three

main cultural pillars of the Lake District's successful 2017 application to UNESCO to be a World Heritage Site – along with Wordsworth and Beatrix Potter, of 'Peter Rabbit' fame.[23] The submission described Ruskin as 'one of the great figures of the conservation movement' in the 19th century and highlighted his promotion of 'the ethical and moral basis of his thinking through works which both derived directly from, and found expression in, the landscape at his feet'.[24]

Sometimes, the landscape really was at his feet. I asked Howard Hull, Brantwood's director, if there was a part of the estate where I should go to feel the presence of Ruskin. I thought he might suggest the turreted bedroom, with its views across the lake and over to the fells beyond, from which a troubled Ruskin had to move late in life after seeing terrifying 'spectres' in the reflections of firelight on his polished wooden bedposts. Or possibly the drawing room where Ruskin worked and was pictured in 1876, with three of his assistants, quietly reading by the light of five tall candles.

Instead, Hull suggested I climb the steps behind the house ('brant' means steep in Cumbrian dialect) up into the elaborate gardens to find 'Ruskin's Seat'. It is signposted, but I still found it hard to find first time, probably because I was looking for a bench facing away from the hillside, through the trees and across the lake towards Coniston village. Instead, the seat – a green-lichened slate throne, whose stone backrest has the point of a Gothic arch – faces away from the lake, so that when you sit there you look at a small beck or brook that runs briskly down past the spot.

Most days, after lunch and letter-writing, Ruskin used to set off, up into the woods, wearing his wide-awake Quaker-style hat and carrying a bill hook, to clear undergrowth or chop wood, one of his favourite pastimes. He is depicted in a silhouette

Howard Hull, Director of Brantwood

self-portrait of 1881, the first to show him with the beard he grew as he recovered from a bout of mental illness. Pied-Piper style, the great thinker is leading a party of guests, assistants and children with picks, poles and baggage to the viewpoints on the moor above[25] (see page 1).

If he stopped at this seat halfway up, though, he must have been alone. Imagine him, deep in thought, applying his intense powers of observation to these few square metres of steep moss, birch- and grass-covered mountainside, pausing for a few moments of reflection, or planning the next phase in the elaborate husbandry of his Lakeland estate.

4

Nearly 200 miles south of Coniston, in the wooded hills around Bewdley in the English Midlands, is another continuing practical experiment that cultivates a direct link with John Ruskin – Ruskin Land.

Here in the Wyre Forest, Ruskin's charitable Guild of St

George still owns two farms at the centre of 6,000 acres of oak forest, orchard, meadow and wildlife habitats. John Iles, who lives in one of the two smallholdings, Uncllys Farm, greeted me there on a damp January day. As he pointed out, it was the 'breathing-in time of the year'. The trees were leafless and the ground sodden.

In the distance, there was the unexpected noise of heavy machinery. A man in a high-technology harvester, guided by computer mapping software, was felling, logging and stripping the wood for eventual sale. Space was being prepared nearby for a sawmill that would increase the return from such sales from £3 to £25 a cubic foot, and should allow the Guild to sell the wood to housebuilders and craftspeople. The vision is that homes and furniture will eventually boast of containing 'Ruskin Oak'.[26]

Iles, a bearded and avuncular enthusiast for the place and its history, used a similar metaphor when asked what the thinking of a 19th-century idealist still brought to this place. 'Depth and purpose' was his reply. He was well aware of the shade of the man frowning down on this mechanisation and commercialisation of the meadows and woods. He 'probably wouldn't like it: he would have had a man with an axe and a bad back', he said cheerfully.

Ruskin visited the area only once and described the land as set 'in midst of a sweet space of English hill and dale and orchard'.[27] The 20-acre gift came from George Baker, a Quaker who was once mayor of Birmingham and an early Companion of the Guild. (The Guild added Uncllys Farm and 100 acres of woodland in 1930, to keep it out of the hands of the Forestry Commission, which would have felled the oaks and replaced them with softwoods.) The original bequest fitted the bucolic vision Ruskin had laid out in an early number of *Fors Clavigera*, his letters to Britain's working men:

We will try to take some small piece of English ground, beautiful, peaceful, and fruitful. We will have no steam-engines upon it, and no railroads: we will have no un-tended or unthought of creatures on it; none wretched but the sick; none idle but the dead.....we will have plenty of flowers and vegetables in our gardens, plenty of corn and grass in our fields....and few bricks.[28]

Ruskin was at first in two minds about what to do with this plot in the Wyre Forest. He variously expressed a wish to keep it as a kind of untouched wilderness, or to build a museum in or on it, 'set there like a temple in the grove of oaks whose roots and stools were older than English history'.[29] Ultimately, he allowed part of it to be cleared and developed to create a smallholding. Like other projects that he or the Guild pursued, the path was not smooth. Ruskin was an absentee overseer and William Buchan Graham, a former lithographic draughtsman who took on the task of clearing and replanting Ruskin Land in the 1880s, complained later about being unsupported, unpaid, and unhoused, despite Ruskin's promises.

Some of the apparent contradictions between conservation and development prevail even today. Part of the forest, which constitutes the largest joined up area of ancient semi-natural woodland in England, is overseen by Natural England, a public agency that advises the British government on protecting Britain's nature and landscape. In many ways that is a Ruskinian project. On its land, Natural England prefers to preserve gnarled trees, helping to create a habitat for rare birds, butterflies and flora. A fence away, Ruskin Land pursues a policy of stripping out the same misshapen growth, whilst retaining as much standing dead wood as possible for bats, owls, birds and invertebrates. Its

John Iles at Uncllys Farm

approach gives preference and space to trees that will emerge tall straight and true, and furnish the raw material for 'Ruskin Oak'.

Over lunch at Uncllys Farm, and a glass of Ruskin Land-labelled cloudy apple juice, Iles explained these policies were not as contradictory as they might at first appear. Different philosophies co-exist in this part of the Severn Valley, he said, but from Ruskin's proposal of an ideal 'beautiful, peaceful and fruitful' place, Ruskin Land was distilling a modern vision of a rural economy, revitalising ancient woodland for the current community.

Neil Sinden lived and worked at St George's Farm, the first Ruskin Land smallholding, from 2015 to 2017, helping with the planting of a new orchard among other projects. He has written that the aim of the Guild and its partners in the forest 'is to provide the raw material, in both a physical and spiritual sense, for a new generation of makers, designers and architects, and to reinterpret Ruskin's ideas about land management, craft and art to the current age'.

Local volunteers look after the herd of cattle, craft items in the wood workshop, help to host events and support the Wyre

Community Land Trust, a social enterprise that manages the woodland for the Guild.

'We're interpreting "fruitful" in an economic way,' said Iles, simply, inviting me to return in the spring, when Ruskin Land 'breathes out'. There is a word for what Sinden and Iles describe – a word that Ruskin himself would never have used: sustainability.

⤞ 5 ⤝

Ruskin's was not exclusively a rural vision. In a lecture on modern manufacture and design given in Bradford in 1859, he compared the homes of industrial workers in nearby Rochdale, with the sunlit existence of their counterparts living among the 'gardens, courts and cloisters' of 14th-century Pisa in Italy.

He described an uninhabited 17th-century cottage:

> the garden, blighted utterly into a field of ashes, not even a weed taking root there; the roof torn into shapeless rents; the shutters hanging about the windows in rags of rotten wood; before its gate, the stream which had gladdened it now soaking slowly by, black as ebony and thick with curdling scum; the bank above it trodden into unctuous, sooty slime: far in front of it, between it and the old hills, the furnaces of the city foaming forth perpetual plague of sulphurous darkness; the volumes of their storm clouds coiling low over a waste of grassless fields, fenced from each other, not by hedges, but by slabs of square stone, like gravestones, riveted together with iron.[30]

Here, again, are the multiple connections Ruskin liked to draw between industrial development, pollution, social deprivation, and art and design. He went on to describe how, far from hoping to build 'a new Pisa' in industrial northern England, he wanted his audience of mill-owners to 'surround your men with happy influences and beautiful things. It is impossible for them to have right ideas about colour, unless they see the lovely colours of nature unspoiled; impossible for them to supply beautiful incident and action in their ornament, unless they see beautiful incident and action in the world about them.... keep them illiterate, uncomfortable, and in the midst of unbeautiful things, and whatever they do will still be spurious, vulgar, and valueless'.

Readers of Ruskin took off in various directions from these urgings. One path led towards improved town planning – and the planting and cultivation of 'garden cities' and 'garden suburbs' in Britain and abroad. Ruskin wanted to preserve the old before he built the new. Hence his backing, with William Morris, of the Society for the Protection of Ancient Buildings. He was also, through organisations such as his Guild of St George, a promoter of a rural ideal of community. But the contradiction between this rosy, sometimes unfeasible vision, and the reality of modern garden cities and communities is not as great as it looks.

Ruskin was as prescient about the need for balance between different activities, and between nature and urban sprawl, as he was about the dangers of overbuilding. In a late lecture on the study of architecture in schools, he contrasted 'cities in which piazzas and gardens opened in bright populousness and peace' with a dystopia familiar to anybody commuting into a modern megalopolis: 'Cities in which the streets are not the avenues for the passing and processing of a happy people, but the drains for the discharge of a tormented mob, in which the only object in reaching any spot is to be transferred to another; in which existence becomes mere transition, and every creature is only one atom in a drift of human dust, and current of interchanging particles, circulating here by tunnels under ground, and there by tubes in the air'.[31]

In other words, Ruskin was not against cities, but he did abhor and fear a particular type of city – the sort that excluded light, nature and interaction between its inhabitants and good art. These were the cities he feared were being built in the second half of the 19th century.

At least in their original concept, the 'garden cities' of the 20th century, mapped out in Britain by Ebenezer Howard and executed by architects Raymond Unwin and Barry Parker, were true to Ruskin's spirit.

Howard used a passage from *Unto This Last* as an epigraph to the first chapter of *To-morrow*, the 1898 book where he laid out his vision of self-sufficient communities. When reprinted four years later as *Garden Cities of Tomorrow*, he replaced it with a passage from *Sesame and Lilies*, in which Ruskin outlined this urban plan: new houses, built 'in groups of limited extent kept in proportion to their streams and wall around so that there be no festering and wretched suburb anywhere, but clean and busy street within and open country without, with a belt of beautiful garden and orchard round the walls so that from any part of the city perfectly fresh air and grass and sight of far horizon might be reachable in a few minutes' walk'.[32]

Unwin was also a believer, having heard Ruskin and William Morris lecture. What Howard, Unwin and Parker built from scratch in Britain was a version of the sorts of places – Abbeville in northern France, Geneva in Switzerland – that Ruskin originally extolled for that balance of piazzas and peace.

Ruskin's town plans were inevitably purist. Pioneering garden city communities have had to some extent to dilute some of their own claims to urban paradise. Letchworth and Welwyn, in Hertfordshire, suffer from the sucking sound of fast-growing cities such as Cambridge and London, which risk turning them into mere extensions of the commuter belt.

Letchworth Garden City Heritage Foundation, which still controls 5,000 acres of land in communal ownership, has the right and authority to insist that residents and builders stick to the original principles. But Graham Fisher, who joined the foundation as chief executive from Toynbee Hall, another institution with Ruskinian roots, admitted it was a 'double-edged sword'. The principles help create a single 'look', he said, 'but many people don't like us saying you can't have a satellite dish on the back of your house'.

What is more, some of the legacy of the early founders and backers has challenging 21st-century consequences. Temperance-promoting industrialists who set up businesses in the garden cities insisted on 'dry' zones. In practice, that meant workers simply hiked out to pubs in neighbouring villages, staggering back to their Arts and Crafts cottages later. These days, you can buy a beer in Letchworth – or even brew one at the Garden City micro-brewery – but Fisher suggested the original constraints had held back its 'night-time economy', as pub and bar culture is euphemistically called.

Artificial perfection was not Ruskin's goal. He would not have loved Poundbury in Dorset – designed by Prince Charles's favourite urban planner Leon Krier[33] – or Seaside in Florida, whose architect the prince consulted about his experimental town. The latter nods to Ruskin by naming some of its streets after the thinker.[34] But there is a clue to the potential sterility of its regulated approach to community in the fact that the town provided the perfect film set for the producers of The Truman Show – about a real person brought up and covertly filmed in an artificial community populated by actors. Seaside has Ruskinian ideals, but as one account puts it, it is 'too real to be Disneyland, too cute to seem real'.[35]

As for the British government's attempts to mask the (necessary) supply of new homes under the banner of 'garden villages' or new 'garden city suburbs', it is hard to know what Ruskin would have made of them.

He might well have been on the frontline defending the green belt that such developments sometimes threaten to swallow. The 'garden' tag looks like spurious greenwashing of a breakneck push for more development, or, as Letchworth's Graham Fisher put it, 'a little bit of cynical branding'. On the other hand, great contradictory contrarian that he sometimes was, Ruskin might also have championed homes for the working man and woman. He might have poured his efforts into advising architects and designers on the planning, building and decoration of these new developments, to avoid their becoming mere 'comfortless and unhonoured dwellings'.

Though he was no great lover of luxury, Ruskin never lived in discomfort – except perhaps when, at one of his lowest points, he took lodgings in the equivalent of a B&B in Folkestone. But that did not mean that he ignored how most people lived. He understood the need, sometimes, to combat what we now call nimbyism in favour of providing a decent, and ideally, a well-designed, roof over people's heads.

The same 1868 lecture that supplied the epigraph for Howard's book also included this realistic assessment: 'Lodging people and providing lodging for them means a great deal of vigorous legislature, and cutting down of vested interests that stand in the way.'[36]

꒰ 6 ꒱

To understand the lasting importance of Ruskin's years of solitary study of the 'law of help', and the vital connection between natural phenomena and the consequences of human activity, we must leap forward to 1884.

In two extraordinary public appearances, the fragile, older Ruskin distilled his hours spent in the mountains, studying lakes, streams and rivers, observing clouds, and 'bottling' sunrises and sunsets 'like his father's sherries'.[37]

The 65-year-old who stood before a packed audience at the London Institution on 4 February that year, to give the first of two lectures on 'The Storm-Cloud of the Nineteenth Century' was not the same lively younger man Charles Norton had met in the 1850s.

Recalling a meeting with Ruskin in 1883, Norton said he retained an 'essential sweetness' but was 'an old man, with looks even older than his years, with bent form, with the beard of a patriarch'.[38]

A drawing by an unidentified member of the audience captures Ruskin in spectacles – a rarity. The amateurish sketch still relays the slightly hunched posture – the result of a spinal weakness that troubled him throughout his life – the lengthening beard and collar-length hair.[39] The packed crowd included many journalists who had recognised from the growing weirdness of lectures the ageing writer was giving in Oxford that he could be guaranteed to cause a sensation of some sort. They were not disappointed.

The lectures were among the last before nervous breakdown curtailed his public speaking career and may be among the best known and (as so often with Ruskin) least read. They have become part of the canon of environmental writing and form part of the basis on which Ruskin's reputation as forerunner and prophet of the modern ecological movement stands. What I had not expected was the degree to which Ruskin paints not only a disturbing picture of the changing weather patterns he had observed — what he had long called 'plague-winds' — but also of his own fragile mental state.

The power of his rhetoric is beyond doubt. But the first lecture is nine-tenths Old Testament prophecy. 'Blanched Sun, — blighted grass, — blinded man' is his famous description of the consequences of industrial pollution. It is frequently quoted as an early warning of the sort of environmental devastation that now haunts newly industrialised countries such as China or Brazil.

Ruskin went on, in a less familiar passage, to describe the causes: 'Remember, for the last twenty years, England, and all foreign nations, either tempting her, or following her, have blasphemed the name of God deliberately and openly; and have done iniquity by proclamation, every man doing as much injustice to his brother as it is in his power to do. Of states in such moral gloom every seer of old predicted the physical gloom, saying, "The light shall be darkened in the heavens thereof, and the stars shall withdraw their shining."'[40]

His presentation was melodramatic, too. Wilson Barrett, the actor-manager who was one of the best-known theatrical figures of the day and a friend of Ruskin's, helped with the visual effects for the first lecture.[41] Using limelight, Ruskin projected coloured enlargements of some of his own drawings of sunsets and cloud formations, including one dramatic midsummer thunder cloud that he had sketched during that pivotal 1858 visit to Switzerland and Italy.

A July thundercloud in the Val d'Aosta, 1858 – one of the illustrations prepared for the lecture and publication after a watercolour by Ruskin

But for all the spectacle, it seems to me that Ruskin fell here into the trap of 'pathetic fallacy', the literary term he had defined – and scorned – decades earlier in *Modern Painters*, attributing feelings to gales and malice to clouds. One modern biographer remarks that his 'belief in the existence of an evil wind was not rational' and points out that references to the devil's work recur in diaries and letters at moments of mental stress.[42]

In his own preface to the printed version of the lectures, Ruskin himself said the newspapers had considered his insights 'imaginary or insane'. Most reports poured scorn on the scant science and abundant Biblical ranting. The London *Evening Standard* printed a long largely sarcastic analysis to the lecture: 'In the clouds and out of the viewless ether, Mr Ruskin, endowed with the poetic vision vouchsafed to him, sees forms and portents denied to the dull eyes of other mortals.... Beautiful in language,

grand in imagery, very forcible in metaphor, and sometimes almost humorous, Mr Ruskin's latest contribution to the theme…
can nevertheless, hardly be regarded as a serious work'.[43]

But he was serious. He was also right. Not about the direct
link to blasphemy, which has its parallels in America's evangelical preachers blaming hurricanes on what they deem to be
moral debauchery, but about the meteorological consequences.
Subsequent scientific analysis showed that sulphur dioxide pollution had worsened and reached a peak in 1880.[44] The diary
entries that Ruskin read out to his audience – as evidence of his
contemporaneous eagle-eyed observations – were vivid ('One
lurid gleam of white cumulus in upper lead-blue sky, seen for half
a minute through the sulphurous chimney-pot vomit of black-
guardly cloud beneath, where its rags were thinnest') *and* accurate.

In other respects, Ruskin was well ahead of his time, too. He
was speaking at the beginning of a long increase in the use of
coal in the UK that peaked in the 1950s. Ten years earlier, in *Fors
Clavigera*, Ruskin had used the metaphor of the 'squirrel cage'
(what we would probably call a hamster-wheel) to describe the
vicious circle of the coal-powered British economy: 'Over the
whole country the sky is blackened and the air made pestilent,
to supply London and other such towns with their iron railings,
vulgar upholstery, jewels, toys, liveries, lace, and other means of
dissipation and dishonour of life', he wrote, going on to advocate
for the less polluting options of wind and water.[45] Only recently
have carbon dioxide emissions dropped to the level prevailing in
the last decade of Ruskin's life.[46]

It is still hard, though, having registered the prescience of
Ruskin's words, to fit them usefully into a modern context. In a
short essay to launch a 2006 debate on Ruskin's relevance in the
21st century, environmentalist Jonathon Porritt acknowledged

that Ruskin was 'a complicated character' for the modern green movement. He touched only briefly on the lectures' 'meteorological whimsy' and spent most of the rest of his essay on the lessons from Ruskin's earlier tirade against laissez-faire economics, *Unto This Last*.[47]

An interesting comparison with 'Storm-Cloud' is Al Gore's hugely successful 2006 documentary on the threat of climate change *An Inconvenient Truth*, based on his lecture tour. It was successful in raising consciousness, if not in reversing global warming. It contains far more science than Ruskin's lectures, but, like Ruskin, the former vice-president used his fame – and the latest communications technology – to spread the message further than a meteorologist might have done. And, like Ruskin's lectures, Gore's presentation also attracted its share of criticism for allegedly skewing the science, or appealing to viewers' emotions over reason.

In any case, Ruskin's late lectures were consistent with his earlier, more scientifically grounded, discussion of mountains and geology in using rich language. To feel the force of the metaphor, you do not have to believe that the 'poisonous smoke' clouding the skies over Matlock in Derbyshire is made of 'dead men's souls', as Ruskin wrote in a *Fors Clavigera* letter pieced together as he recovered from a breakdown in 1871.[48] Ruskin scholar Sara Atwood is right to say 'it is vitally important that we find the words with which to stir these deep emotions and associations, for they are ultimately our best hope for creating transformative change'.

Images still count, too. A recent exhibition in New York entitled *Landscapes after Ruskin* took its energy from the young Ruskin's admonition to painters such as Turner and the Pre-Raphaelites to 'go to nature' and the older Ruskin's horror at the advancing destruction of the natural world.[49] Joel Sternfeld, a photographer specialising in imagery of American industrial and cultural dystopia, curated the show. Its pictures of manmade and natural devastation, including smog, effluent, discarded rubbish, chronicle the creeping storm-clouds of the late 20th and early 21st century.

Ruskin himself would have despised the sterile vocabulary of carbon footprints, sustainability and even global warming, while respecting the ideals of those attempting to protect the environment. As Atwood pointed out in a 2016 lecture, 'the language of science and policy is too often alienating, made up of worn out metaphors and potted phrases drained of meaning through overuse'.[50] Lecturers, campaigners and policymakers can learn something from Ruskin's efforts to make the lexicon of nature fresh and vivid, however overwrought it may sometimes seem today.

7

I met Gabriel Meyer, president of the Ruskin Art Club of Los Angeles on a bright winter's day in 2018 on the small pavement terrace of a café, a 10-minute taxi ride from LAX airport. The air was blissfully free of any 'plague-cloud' of smog or smoke from the forest fires that had raged out of control for weeks north of the city. The incongruity of Ruskin here seemed obvious, but Meyer is an ardent champion of his influence in this quintessentially modern city.

The Club itself was founded in 1888 by Mary Boyce, ostensibly to study the technique and history of engraving and etching. Two years later the club staged what is thought to be the first public art exhibition in LA history, displaying American engravings of works by Dürer, Rembrandt and (perhaps oblivious to Ruskin's antipathy towards the artist) Whistler. Boyce's fellow founder members were all women, many of them wives of faculty members of the University of Southern California. The idea of a women's club was progressive. It embraced the ideals of the Arts and Crafts movement and women's suffrage. The founders 'were at the cutting edge of a social movement that would carry [the US] into the 20th century,' according to the club's history.[51]

Like so many Ruskinians, Meyer, once a freelance war correspondent, told a personal story of how the discovery of Ruskin had helped him free his 'artistic, poetic side' that he had tended to repress because 'it wasn't feeding children'. 'Ruskin put it together for me: I saw it was all related, it was all part of the same reality,' he said.

By the end of the last century, the Club was in the doldrums. It was sustaining a clubhouse – built in 1922 in Mission Revival style – that was draining fees from the dwindling number of members and falling into neglect. Meyer and others saw that harking back to the past was a recipe for disaster in modern LA. Instead, they managed to push the club forward, ultimately selling the house in 2014 (now restored as a private home) and recovering the group's original momentum as a catalyst for civic projects and a forum for intellectual discussion.

'We do "applied Ruskin",' said Meyer with a smile, and the aspects of Ruskin's work that resonate the most are his notions of work and craft – and environmentalism. When we met, plans were under way to award a 'Ruskin Prize' to the poet Lewis MacAdams, prominent campaigner to preserve the Los Angeles River, and for a symposium about Wendell Berry, another poet and environmental activist. When Meyer visited Ruskin Land, he came away with an impression of its 'profoundly Ruskinian' emphasis, 'not on abstractions or abstract solutions, but on the needs and opportunities of a specific place and the challenges of living in community with it'. It is an emphasis that can apply as strongly, and fruitfully, in LA's megalopolitan sprawl as in the Wyre Forest.

From Southern California to Cumbria, Ruskin is regularly invoked, not only as a cultural icon, as in the Lake District's pitch for World Heritage Site status, but as a tribune of environmental preservation.

His name was first attached to such a campaign in the 1870s, when local Lakeland landowners and activists, including Ruskin, rallied against a plan to dam the Thirlmere valley and create a reservoir to slake the thirst of the fast-expanding industrial metropolis of Manchester. That fight failed ultimately. But just as Monsal Dale and its railway diverged from Ruskin's principles only to reconverge on a more balanced modern version, Thirlmere's beauty today owes a lot to the existence of the body of water that Ruskin and his supporters opposed.

Activists recalled that original Ruskin-backed campaign recently in their successful fight against the plan to install a zipwire on the hills above the lake. 'We're calling this the second battle of Thirlmere,' one activist told *The Guardian*.[52]

When the Lake District worthies formed the 'Thirlmere Defence Association' in 1871 for the first battle, they awoke a generation to the importance of conservation. Hardwicke Rawnsley, the Lakeland clergyman who was an early disciple of Ruskin, was a supporter. So were London-based philanthropists Robert Hunter and Octavia Hill, whose efforts to promote better housing for working people had been funded by Ruskin. The trio went on to form the National Trust.

1. Self-portrait, 1873. Outwardly, Ruskin was at the height of his powers at this time. Inwardly, though, he was racked by hopeless love for Rose La Touche and plagued by mental instability. The self-portrait seems to hint at the tension between the two sides of his life and personality. It is inscribed 'Di Pa by himself' by Joan Severn, using her babytalk name for Ruskin.

2. *View of Susa, 1858. This is the first glimpse of Italy for the traveller crossing the Alps from France. Ruskin drew this scene during his four-month journey through France and Switzerland to Italy in 1858. This was the year he underwent his 'unconversion', in Turin, from the staunch evangelical Protestantism instilled by his mother to more open, non-sectarian beliefs.*

3. *Dawn at Neuchâtel, 1866. Ruskin frequently drew cloudscapes and the light at dawn. Here the view is reminiscent of his first view of the Alps: 'Infinitely beyond all that we had ever thought or dreamed, – the seen walls of lost Eden could not have been more beautiful to us; not more awful, round heaven, the walls of sacred Death.'*

4. Cascade de la Folie, Chamonix, 1849. Ruskin underpinned his stunning studies of the Alps with his love and knowledge of geology, often spending more than ten hours a day in the mountains, observing, drawing and painting clouds and rock formations. He described this scene in a letter of 10 July 1849: 'The glacier was seen against the sky through the most fantastic pines, and the grand rocks falling to the source, nodding forwards (like a wave about to break) and the great cascade bounding from its narrow way.'

6. (above) Rocks in unrest, c. 1857. This is copied from a section of one of Ruskin's favourite Turner watercolours, The Pass of St Gotthard, which he studied repeatedly. He also visited the pass, notably in 1845, to understand how Turner interpreted nature. But this swift and thrilling drawing conveys also the excitement and awe Ruskin felt in the Alps, and his fascination with geology – in the case of these rocks, 'gneiss coloured by iron ochre proceeding from decomposing garnets'. The similarity of water in motion and the forms of rocks remained a source of fascination.

5. (opposite) Study of gneiss rock, Glen Finglas, 1853. Ruskin carried out this detailed study – accurate down to the last wrinkle, as modern photographs prove – near the spot in Glen Finglas where Millais was painting his famous portrait of the critic and falling in love with Ruskin's wife Effie.

7. Trees in a lane (possibly Ambleside), 1847. Inscribed by Ruskin 'Best way of studying Trees, with / a view to knowledge of their leafage. / Young Shoots of the Oak and Ash, in Spring. / J.R. 1847. (Unfinished)' Ruskin would spend hours perfecting the depiction of trees, and set the task as an exercise in his manual The Elements of Drawing.

8. (opposite) St Sauveur, Caen, 1848. Drawn on Ruskin's first visit to France with his new wife Effie Gray, this study of niches is intended to demonstrate the natural, living energy of Gothic architecture.

13. Vineyard Walk, Lucca, 1874. Ruskin spent much time in the city's cathedral studying the tomb of Ilaria del Carretto by Jacopo della Quercia, but this painting of a nearby village provides spectacular evidence of his wider appreciation for the beauty of the region and a rare exception to the rule that Ruskin often struggled to finish his work.

Seed of common Rush
J.R. Spoiled.
Brantwood. 72.

At Brantwood, Ruskin was able to apply both his wide-angle lens on the world – as in the painting of Coniston Water (opposite, top) – and his tight focus on nature in the study of a rush (above) and the detailed cloud study (opposite, bottom).

14. Study of common rush ('spoiled'), 1872 .

15. Dawn over Coniston Old Man (the view from Brantwood), 1873.

16. Cloud effect over Coniston Old Man, 1880s.

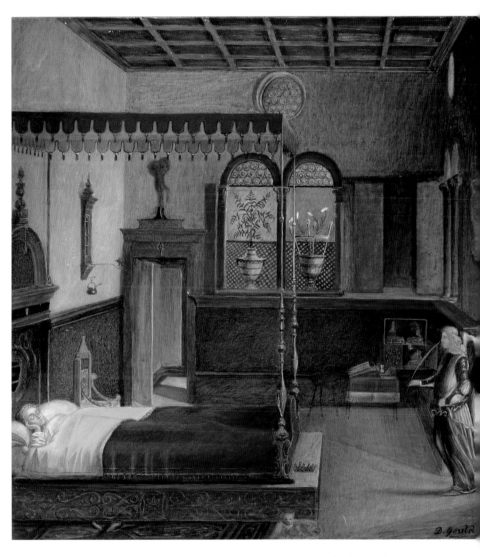

Carpaccio's work provided the fourth and last great 'art attack' that struck Ruskin. He turned the painter's St George into the symbolic slayer of the dragon of capitalism, symbol of his new Guild, while he increasingly associated the painter's Ursula with the late Rose La Touche, obsessively copying the painting of her dream from Carpaccio's cycle of the saint's life.

17. *The Dream of St Ursula after Carpaccio, 1872 (opposite). Ruskin's copy was photographed and retouched by David Gould, who acted as a photo-colourist and made teaching aids for Ruskin.*

18. *St George and the Dragon after Carpaccio, 1872 (top).*

19. *Upper part of the figure of St George in St George and the Dragon, after Carpaccio, 1872 (bottom).*

20. *Northwest porch and corner of St Mark's, Venice, 1877. The Basilica of San Marco remained the touchstone of all architecture for Ruskin, and this beautiful watercolour records the last unrestored section of the façade. It was made to help campaign for its preservation.*

Some Ruskin enthusiasts tend to disparage the Trust in its modern form as a promoter of 'heritage' tourism for the middle classes.

That is true of the genteel end of the movement that Rawnsley, Hill and Hunter launched, with its mugs, memorabilia and flapjacks taken with tea in the converted outhouses of stately homes. But in some of the more recent innovations aimed at broadening the appeal of the Trust there is a strong strain of Ruskin's thinking. The purchase and conversion of 'ordinary' properties – the childhood homes of the Beatles in Liverpool, for example – has an echo of the Guild's early purchase of houses in Hertfordshire (where it still owns cottages in the village of Westmill), and in Liverpool itself. The conversion of homes into 'interactive' spaces, where visitors seek to understand the past, and not just pass reverentially through it, is absolutely in the spirit of the museums for workers that Ruskin inspired in Sheffield.

As for nature, the National Trust has preserved some of the areas where you can still enjoy, more or less, the same views Ruskin enjoyed and extolled.

You can stroll for ten minutes from the car park beside Derwent Water to Friar's Crag, the promontory that opens onto what Ruskin judged to be one of 'the three most beautiful scenes in Europe', and one of the first pieces of land bought by the Trust, in 1901, following a public appeal for funds.

Ruskin did not, to my knowledge, identify the other two, though he might have included 'Ruskin's View' over the Lune Valley from near the churchyard in Kirkby Lonsdale, which he described elsewhere, with typical hyperbole, as 'one of the loveliest scenes in England, therefore in the world'.

At Derwent Water, the tall slate monument has the form of a natural Gothic arch. A large embedded medallion depicts a stern-faced Ruskin. An inscription reminds visitors that his first memory was being taken by his nurse to the brow of the crag.

The Trust and other organisations that aim to conserve the careful balance between humans and landscape are the advocates for the Law of Help that Ruskin laid out in *Modern Painters*, more than 150 years ago.

Writing about Ruskin's epiphany in the Swiss valleys, Fiona Reynolds, former director-general of National Trust, says that 'in describing beauty he recognised the obligations of humans to do more than satisfy our own demands and to fix our spirit instead on what will sustain us for eternity'.[53]

Even at 30, when he wrote *The Seven Lamps of Architecture*, from which this chapter's epigraph is taken, Ruskin foresaw this necessity. Inevitably, his idea of the earth as a 'great entail' now has an ugly piece of eco-jargon attached to it: 'bequest value' or 'intergenerational equity' – 'the unmeasurable value that things today will have when inherited tomorrow by a future generation'.[54] Ruskin put it better, in terms that practitioners of 'applied Ruskin' can use. One of our duties, he wrote, is 'planting forests that our descendants may live under their shade, or of raising cities for future nations to inhabit'.

Chapter VII

Work and Education

*Ignorance, which is contented and clumsy, will produce what is imperfect, but
not offensive. But ignorance discontented and dexterous, learning what it cannot
understand, and imitating what it cannot enjoy, produces the most loathsome forms
of manufacture that can disgrace or mislead humanity.*
(The Eagle's Nest)

⋙ *I* ⋘

In an old Victorian pub on Brick Lane, the vibrant, multi-cultural
thoroughfare in London's East End, is a furniture workshop, filled
with light, all white walls and blond wood. Large windows look
out onto the street – and passers-by can look back in. The working areas with their sanding and cutting machines are separated
by high glazed panels. You could eat your lunch off most of the
work surfaces. Upstairs, in a cramped but tidy office, looking out
through arched windows onto a small park opposite, designers
and production planners work side by side on computers.

It reminds me on a tiny scale of the vast 'lean' production lines
of the world's biggest carmakers, where clutter is a vice, autonomy of front-line workers a virtue, and machines work alongside
human staff.

Brick Lane has its roots in artisanal manufacture, dating back to the 15th century, when it was the centre for the building materials from which it got its name. But despite the history and the Victorian connection, this place feels a long way from Gothic cathedrals, Turner paintings, or handmade Arts and Crafts furnishings.

Where is John Ruskin in all this tidiness and efficiency? He is there, in a large modern screen-printed image – the full heavy-bearded 'Datur hora quieti' pose of his final years – gazing sternly down on a showroom full of simple plywood chairs, tables and chests of drawers. He is also present in the philosophy of the furniture-maker's founder, Olivier Geoffroy, a thoughtful, intense Frenchman with a monk-like halo of curly hair around a bald patch. He is planning a new manufacturing revolution on a manifesto explicitly based on John Ruskin's ideas, but with a technological twist.

And Ruskin is there in the title of the factory itself: Unto This Last, named after one of Ruskin's best-known works which, in 1860, convinced many of the art critic's fans and a whole new readership of outraged industrialists that he was mad and dangerous.

Modern Painters was finally complete. The fifth volume had been published in 1860. John Ruskin had the loftiest platform imaginable for his work. He could have turned in any direction. Doubtless, his growing fan base expected his next steps to take him further into the criticism of art and architecture with which he had made his name.

They had not been paying attention, though. Rooted in Ruskin's earlier writings were ideas on the nature of work, the inequality and oppression of the industrial worker, and the perils of free trade and free markets. Ruskin was moved now to express them more plainly.

Olivier Geoffroy in
the Unto this Last
workshop

He chose as his vehicle the *Cornhill Magazine,* edited by the novelist William Makepeace Thackeray. There, he published four articles attacking laissez-faire economics.

The first essay begins with a head-on attack:

Among the delusions which at different periods have possessed themselves of the minds of large masses of the human race, perhaps the most curious – certainly the least creditable – is the modern *soi-disant* science of political economy, based on the idea that an advantageous code of social action may be determined irrespectively of the influence of social affection.[1]

Ruskin laid out an alternative, coupling competition with

'anarchy' as twin 'laws of death', advocating 'laws of life', such as co-operation and collaboration, and proposing equal wages for workers doing different jobs. (That was the essence of the parable from which he drew the title of the series when the essays were republished in book form in 1862.)

To have an idea of how controversial this was with the newly enriched industrial boss-class, you need to understand that the doctrine of free-market economics – as laid out by Adam Smith, David Ricardo, J. S. Mill and others – underpinned their wealth and, by extension, 19th-century Britain's global industrial dominance.[2]

Ruskin's art criticism had turned him into a provocative but essentially establishment figure. He was what we would now call 'a thought leader' but with aristocratic and court connections. His work seemed, on a cursory read, to bear exclusively on the refined world of art and artists.

This was controversial enough. Ruskin's defence of the Pre-Raphaelite Brotherhood a decade earlier had prompted a press backlash, and his *Academy Notes*, featuring his pointed criticism of Royal Academy exhibits of the late 1850s, had given him a reputation as an 'art-dictator'. They provoked such jealous in-fighting among artists that the series had to be stopped in 1859. Beyond this circle, though, few at the high table of British politics or in the cadre of newly enriched British entrepreneurs and industrialists had taken notice. If they did know about Ruskin, they had boxed him, as neatly as their mass-manufactured products, and labelled him as a maverick from the world of fine art whose ideas had no effect on their interests.

The publication of the *Cornhill* essays, as a result, provoked a fierce response from the mainstream media of the time. The *Saturday Review* condemned the articles as 'intolerable twaddle' and said the world would not be 'preached to death by a mad governess'. The *Westminster Review* accused him of 'patch[ing] his motley with apocalyptic spangles'. Provincial papers were more forgiving – and some of Ruskin's notices outside London were even favourable – but still the counterblast prompted Thackeray to cut short what should have been a six-article series. In the preface to the 1862 book, Ruskin wrote that the essays had been 'reprobated in a violent manner... by most of the readers they met with'.

Yet the fire that Ruskin stoked with *Unto This Last* continued to smoulder, in his own thinking and beyond, despite the criticism. The book sold slowly in the 1860s, but when reissued in the 1870s, it took off and its popularity persisted for the rest of Ruskin's lifetime. The first Labour MPs elected in 1906, responding to a questionnaire, indicated that it was the book that had most influenced them. One of those MPs, Thomas Burt, called it a 'landmark in the history of the labour movement'.[3] It was also the book that inspired Gandhi. He translated and paraphrased it in Gujarati, changed his lawyer's lifestyle, and ultimately India's destiny.

Unto This Last is not an easy read. Like much of Ruskin's work, it has its Biblical thickets. But it is at least widely published. It is short (thanks to Thackeray who implemented a drastic cure for Ruskin's logorrhoea). And it is modern.

I bought a copy in the bookshop at Ruskin's home Brantwood in 2009, when I was largely unaware of Ruskin as a social critic. It opened my eyes to a different side of Ruskin's thinking. In the book, I found plenty of parallels with the critiques, then and since, of the 'socially useless' work of bankers and financiers, the forecasting failings of orthodox economists, and even the scandal earlier that year over MPs' expenses claims.[4] The shock and

disgust of commentators, policymakers, regulators and the public in the wake of 2008's financial crisis echoed Ruskin's angry
denunciation of ill-gotten gains and his fierce antipathy towards
free-market economics.

I will pick up some of the threads of that polemic in the
next chapter, on Ruskin's attitude to wealth and its dark alternate,
which he called 'illth', but much of what he wrote about work
and education in this prolific period of the 1860s has a strikingly
modern tone. *Unto This Last* could even now provide a moral
code to go alongside the legal codes laid down by financial regulators.[5] The essays look, in retrospect, like the hinge on which
Ruskin's career swung from forthright art critic to aggravator of
the British industrial establishment.

〜 2 〜

Ruskin felt temperamentally ill-suited to the rough and tumble
of criticism and counter-criticism that his essays provoked. At the
height of attacks on *Unto This Last* in 1861, he wrote a letter to
his mentor and promoter Thomas Carlyle, a practised polemicist.
'The least mortification or anxiety – makes me so ill so quickly
that I shall have... to live the life of a monster,' he told his older
friend.[6] He also continued to wonder how he should reconcile
this impulse to 'teach peace and justice' with a pull 'towards quiet
investigation of beautiful things'.[7] As it happens, he managed to
do both. But from this point on, as his extraordinary output shift-
ed from artistic to social and economic concerns, his fame as a
thorn in the side of smug Victorian Britain only increased.

In fact, by the time the first essay of *Unto This Last* – 'The
Roots of Honour' – came out in 1860, Ruskin, still only in his

early forties, had been developing these ideas on what constituted worthwhile work and how to educate people to achieve it for more than a decade. In his art criticism, as we know, Ruskin liked to see evidence of the artist's diligence. That was part of the reason he championed the Pre-Raphaelites and defended the 'labour bestowed on those works'.

For those tuned in to the right Ruskin wavelength, a new and different melody was audible amid the orchestral sweep of his writing and lecturing on art and architecture almost as early as the 1840s.

Ruskin had first learnt about work in the real world from his father, the sherry merchant. From his mother, he acquired a sense of guilt about his own work rate that led to workaholism. When travelling, he would often rise at six, take a stroll, then breakfast, before settling down to dedicate two to three hours to drawing, with a further two hours in the afternoon. During his stay in Venice in 1876-77, his routine was even more intense:

'He was up with the dawn to watch the sunrise from his balcony. By seven he was at his writing-table, translating Plato, "to build the day on". At half-past seven the gondola was waiting to take him to the bridge before SS. Giovanni e Paolo, where he painted the Scuola di San Marco, with vista of the canal to Murano... At nine Ruskin returned to breakfast, and did some writing. Then at half-past ten to the Academy, where he made his studies of Carpaccio till two o'clock. Then home to read and write letters till three, at which hour he dined. At half-past four gondola again – to Murano, or the Armenian Convent, or St. Elena, or San Giorgio – Ruskin sketching, and on the way home taking an oar himself. Tea at seven, and, afterwards, evenings spent with his friends or with his studies in Venetian history for *St. Mark's Rest*.'[8]

Like all writers, he could agonise over his own efforts, but his writer's block often took a prolific turn. When one project became bogged down, it was sometimes Ruskin's habit to start, or resume, another. As one biographer has written, many of his books 'were digressions or acts of truancy'.[9] Astonishing though it seems, for example, writing *The Seven Lamps of Architecture* (1849) was a sort of holiday from what would become five volumes of *Modern Painters*. *Seven Lamps* already contained hints of his attitude to the nature of 'good' work with its concept of the 'happy carver'.

Ruskin managed to accommodate the composition of three volumes of *The Stones of Venice*, published between 1851 and 1853, between stretches working on *Modern Painters* and *Seven Lamps*. It was here that Ruskin made his most important and influential statement on the necessity of creating meaningful work for ordinary people.

In 'The Nature of Gothic', Ruskin underlined the importance of 'forming' the spirit of the worker. The sentiment was triggered in part by the European worker risings and revolutions of 1848, the effects of which he had witnessed in Venice and Paris. He sustained it in his later writing and his own career until his final breakdown in his sixties.

'The great cry that rises from all our manufacturing cities, louder than their furnace blast, is all in very deed for this,' he writes in *The Stones of Venice*: 'that we manufacture everything there except men; we blanch cotton, and strengthen steel, and refine sugar, and shape pottery; but to brighten, to strengthen, to refine, or to form a single living spirit, never enters into our estimate of advantages.'

The 'evil' of modern manufacturing, he continued, could be combated only 'by a right understanding, on the part of all classes, of what kinds of labour are good for men, raising them and making them happy'.

As the great boom that propelled Britain into the age of steel and heavy engineering gathered pace, Ruskin was one of a few voices raised against the din of the machine age, including novelists such as Elizabeth Gaskell and Charles Dickens, and the irascible Carlyle. Few others had thought and written seriously about the need to manufacture 'souls of a good quality', as Ruskin put it in *Unto This Last*. Few had expressed concern for the dignity, education and well-being of the workers who went into Britain's expanding factories, as opposed to the quantity of products that came out. Triggered by revolutions, these were revolutionary ideas.

It was around this midpoint in his variegated career that Ruskin – the unconverted evangelist who had once been primed for the Anglican clergy – also started to preach what he practised and practise what he preached.

In 1854, the same year his sexless marriage to Effie was annulled, he had accepted an invitation from Frederick Denison Maurice, an Anglican cleric, to teach drawing classes at the Working Men's College that Maurice had founded in London. Maurice was also a founder of the Christian Socialist movement, which was developing an anti-greed philosophy, and Ruskin was part of a star-studded teaching line-up that included Dante Gabriel Rossetti, the Pre-Raphaelite painter, and novelist Charles Kingsley, who was to go on to write *The Water Babies*.

'The Nature of Gothic' was reprinted as a pamphlet for distribution at Maurice's inaugural lecture to the College and would separately inspire the designer William Morris, and, through him, feed important ideas into the early Labour movement.

As I have already described, Ruskin was a gifted and demanding teacher of drawing technique. But he saw his fortnightly classes almost as much as a way of inspiring and enlivening his students' working existence.

'My efforts are directed not to making a carpenter an artist, but to making him happier as a carpenter,' he told a Royal Commission in 1857. It was a radically different approach even by the college's own progressive standards. His distinctive methods included leading his students on outdoor drawing trips and making them examine in detail plants and fossils. One outraged Pre-Raphaelite, William Bell Scott, described Ruskin's teaching style as 'intellectual murder'. More used to the rigid techniques taught in the Government Schools of Design, which Ruskin abhorred, Scott ranted that the 'pretence of education' in Ruskin's classes was 'in a high degree criminal'.[10]

Here as in Ruskin's other explicitly educational ventures, he aimed to stimulate his students rather than to lay down rigid rules. His drawing classes were deliberately arranged in opposition to the government schools, which were organised by Sir Henry Cole, founder of the Victoria and Albert Museum. Ruskin was an early devotee of the visual aid, which reached a peak later in his lectures of the 1880s, such as 'Storm-Cloud'. He often prepared his own elaborate, detailed, highly coloured illustrations for lectures – a kind of Ruskinian PowerPoint.

At this stage in his career, there is something odd about the image of the slight intellectual, more used to holding forth at the Royal Academy, trying to transmit his artistic insights to hard-handed labourers. In reality, his students were generally part of an artisan elite. But Ruskin was well aware of the gulf between the work of the intellectual, and that of the working men whose welfare he tried to improve. In 1859, in a lecture series collected as *The Two Paths*, he pointed out that before advising workers on morals, 'it would be well if we sometimes tried it practically ourselves, and spent a year or so at some hard manual labour'.

Much later, he recounted a trip to Furness Abbey with a bunch of architecture and art-lovers, and self-deprecatingly contrasted his group, who 'like to have done our eight hours work of admiring abbeys before we dine', with the labourers they met en route, 'employed in work so disgraceful as throwing up clods of earth onto an embankment'.[11]

His Working Men's College talks mingled the inspirational with the practical. This was a proving ground for his public speaking, where he combined high rhetorical flourishes with the engaging, intimate style that made him a lecture-circuit star later in his career.

Ruskin tailored his approach to individual students. He brought in pebbles, lichen, even – according to one student's account – 'a case of West Indian birds unstuffed' to demonstrate a point about colour in nature. Another former student described his talks as 'a wonderful bubbling up of all manner of glowing thoughts'.[12]

You can get a small flavour of what a Ruskin lesson was like from *The Elements of Drawing*, which he developed in part from the talks he gave at the Working Men's College. Picture him upbraiding a student who had complained that he already knew how to 'do a stone': 'A stone,' Ruskin retorts,

> may be round or angular, polished or rough, cracked all over like an ill-glazed teacup, or as united and broad as the breast of Hercules. It may be as flaky as a wafer, as powdery as a field puff-ball; it may be knotted like a ship's hawser, or kneaded like hammered iron, or knit like a Damascus sabre, or fused like a glass bottle, or crystallised like hoar-frost, or veined like

a forest leaf: look at it, and don't try to remember how any-body told you to "do a stone".[13]

As academic Dinah Birch has commented, by rooting his writing and teaching in tangible *things*, Ruskin made a connection with ordinary people and particularly people who were largely self-taught, like him. 'There's a Ruskin for everyone,' she has said.[14]

〜 3 〜

For Ruskin, the celebrity he enjoyed in the late 1850s was a mixed blessing. While he seemed to court publicity and would grow more comfortable with the idea of his public success as he developed his lectures, he was still 'miserable in general society'. This was a phrase he used in an 1848 letter to Effie before their marriage. Even at that earlier date, Ruskin's fame was attracting fans, groupies and stalkers. They would find a way to contact him 'out of mere idleness and curiosity desire to know me – and to talk nonsense about art – or pass their heavy time over my pic-tures – or sketches'. As he wrote to Effie, 'against their inroads nothing but the most rude firmness protects me'.[15]

Rude firmness was still his rule when Maria La Touche, the sensitive, cultured, art-loving wife of an Irish banker and land-owner, got in touch with Ruskin in 1858 to ask his advice about teaching her daughters art. Ruskin at first fobbed her off with a visit from one of his Working Men's Club protégés.

Then, as now, though, contacts and persistence can bear fruit. Mrs La Touche had both, and a face-to face meeting was ar-ranged. Charming, good-looking and only 33, she was to fall a little in love with the 39-year-old Ruskin. But it was her younger daughter Rose, 10 at the time, who charmed the critic.

Ruskin recalled his first sight of Rose much later, after the slow tragedy triggered by this meeting had largely played out:

> Neither tall nor short for her age: a little stiff in her way of standing. The eyes rather deep blue at that time, and fuller and softer than afterwards. Lips perfectly lovely in profile; – a little too wide, and hard in edge, seen in front; the rest of the features what a fair, well-bred Irish girl's usually are; the hair, perhaps, more graceful in short curl round the forehead, and softer than one sees often, in the close-bound tresses above the neck.[16]

There is no denying that Ruskin enjoyed the company of young girls. This description, though, was written in 1888 when Rose had been dead 13 years, and Ruskin's late-life obsession with her was in full flow. At the start, Ruskin and Maria La Touche ('extremely pretty, still, herself' in Ruskin's same retrospective description) formed a warm relationship.

What developed between the young Rose and the writer, entering early middle age, was initially an odd, but not for the time unusual friendship, kept alive by tuition sessions for Rose and her sister Emily at Denmark Hill and at the La Touche's central London house. In return for these occasional art lessons when the La Touches visited London, Rose recounted her experiences of art and architecture while on family travels, dubbing Ruskin 'St Crumpet' to distinguish him from 'St Bun', her governess, a Miss Bunnett, or Archigosaurus, a nod to her sometime tutor's geological-paleontological interests.

Ruskin fell properly in love with the teenaged Rose in the early 1860s, as his reputation as a social critic was growing.[17] When she was not around, Ruskin's love-sickness bled into his letters to friends. Ruskin knew he had to wait until Rose had grown

*Rose La Touche by Ruskin, c. 1872-4.
Inscribed* Flos Florum Rosa, *'Rose,
the flower of flowers'*

up before he could make any serious proposal. The La Touches were staunch members of the Anglican Church of Ireland, and Rose's father John was a convert to a fundamentalist form of Christianity with which he indoctrinated his younger daughter. If anything, it was this – contrasted with Ruskin's 'unconverted' scepticism – that would doom the relationship, more than her youth or the gulf in their ages.

Rose was also fragile. She suffered nervous disorders that started in her early teens and may have developed into what we would now describe as anorexia. As the relationship between Ruskin and Rose developed, the La Touches quite naturally act-ed to protect her. In February 1862, when their daughter was 14, Ruskin wrote to a friend that 'Rosie's got too old to be made a pet of any more' and it was only a few months later that her parents decided to distance Rose.[18] Throughout their relationship there were long stretches when Ruskin and Rose did not meet face to face, but her absence enabled Ruskin to build an idealistic fantasy round the troubled girl.

When they did meet again, it was the winter of 1865-66, as

Rose was turning eighteen. She was not a mature eighteen, unlike, say, Effie Gray at the same age. But her health had improved and she was happy to contribute to the slightly pious atmosphere of the Ruskin parents' Denmark Hill home, where – Ruskin recalled 20 years later – they took 'paradisiacal walks' together in the garden, enjoying the spring-like weather.

The 47-year-old writer behaved like a besotted teenager – shades of the boy who had once fallen for Adèle Domecq. He wrote poems. He monopolised Rose's conversation at dinner. He contacted friends to tell them how happy he was. And then he messed everything up by proposing marriage, to the understandable shock of Rose and her parents.

Rose asked him to allow her to put off her decision for three more agonising years.

 4

I can find no evidence that Ruskin overstepped the boundaries of the time. He sustained his friendship with many of the girls he met well into their more mature years. He directed most of his interest in young women into highly productive – and, for its time, progressive – work on their education.

Around the same time that he met Maria La Touche, for example, another persistent and charming woman – Margaret Bell, the principal of Winnington Hall, a girls' school in Cheshire – contacted Ruskin, initiating links between the critic, Bell, and her students, that were to last for years. *The Ethics of Dust*, a dramatic dialogue with his students about crystallography that is one of his odder books, was inspired by his work with the Winnington girls. A number stayed in touch with him as they grew up.

In the middle of this early period of infatuation with Rose, Ruskin gave his lecture 'Of Queens' Gardens'. One of many paradoxes surrounding Ruskin and his legacy is that this talk helped solidify the thinker's reputation and fame in the second half of the 19th century – and destroy it in the second half of the 20th.

'Of Queens' Gardens', addressed to an audience of middle class men and women gathered at Manchester town hall in December 1864, made a case for women to expand the range of their interests – but within limits set by what Ruskin said were the specific competences of men. He envisaged women dutifully confined to more passive domestic roles.

'Each has what the other has not; each completes the other. They are nothing alike, and the happiness and perfection of both depends on each asking and receiving from the other what the other only can give,' Ruskin said.[19]

Just over a century later, feminist writer Kate Millett attacked Ruskin in her 1970 book *Sexual Politics*. She described the lecture as a 'compulsive masculine fantasy [that] one might call the official Victorian attitude'. As Millett pointed out with controlled anger, Ruskin's superficially benign-sounding division of the world into two spheres, one for men, one for women, in reality reserved the 'entire scope of human endeavour for the one, and a little hothouse for the other'.[20]

Ruskin said: 'The man's power is active, progressive, defensive. He is eminently the doer, the creator, the discoverer, the defender. His intellect is for speculation and invention; his energy for adventure, for war, and for conquest…. [The] woman's power is for rule, not for battle, – and her intellect is not for invention or creation, but for sweet ordering, arrangement, and decision.'

In a hard-fought race to find the part of Ruskin's work that has aged worst, this patronising passage is a strong front-runner.

Understandably, Millett and others used it as a rallying point for modern critics of Ruskin and his unenlightened contemporaries. But there is a snag in this critique. To cast Ruskin only as the stereotypical Victorian patriarch is to ignore how his vocal support for women's education gave the age's early feminists confidence as they fought for the right to work and, ultimately, to vote.

In the same lecture, Ruskin urged his Mancunian listeners to widen the curriculum for girls to include maths, history, science and physical exercise. 'You bring up your girls as if they were meant for sideboard ornaments, and then complain of their frivolity,' he said. 'Give them the same advantages that you give their brothers.' He described as 'the most foolish of errors', the idea that 'woman is only the shadow and attendant image of her lord, owing him a thoughtless and servile obedience, and supported altogether in her weakness by the pre-eminence of his fortitude'. Read now, Ruskin's ideas sound old-fashioned and condescending. Read or listened to in the 1860s, they were radical, popular – and transformational.

'Of Queens' Gardens' was included in the collection of writings and lectures called *Sesame and Lilies* that was one of the most popular of Ruskin's books. It had sold 160,000 copies by the time his editors prepared the collected works in the early 1900s. If you have an old copy of any of Ruskin's work on your bookshelf, it is probably this or *Unto This Last. Sesame and Lilies* was a popular prize at school prize-givings. Special editions were published aimed at this very market, as well as a 'Coronation Edition' presented to the new King and Queen in 1902. The book was an obvious gift for young women – though Ruskin intended it for one in particular: Rose La Touche. Her copy, a gift from the writer, contains the dedication 'Rosie, with St C's love'.

'Of Queens' Gardens' also influenced and inspired educators

of the 19th century. Queenswood School in Hertfordshire was named after the essay, for instance, and put into practice Ruskin's then-revolutionary idea that girls should read widely and study science and art, as journalist and broadcaster Samira Ahmed discovered when she visited the school for a recent radio documentary. She gave Ruskin conditional respect for introducing progressive ideas (though she could not resist introducing him, in an accompanying blogpost, via the old pubic hair myth). 'How did girls' education come so rapidly to include the same ambitions of sporting and scientific prowess as boys? Did Ruskin, even before the female suffrage movement, help set that off?' Ahmed asks in her blog.[21] The short answer is yes, though he obviously was not the only one encouraging these aspirations.

In the 1870s, Ruskin was persuaded to sponsor Whitelands College, based in a run-down corner of what is now smart Chelsea and then one of the few teacher training institutions for women.

His contribution to Whitelands (like his earlier Working Men's College teaching) was eclectic, even eccentric. Ruskin supplied a cabinet of drawings and paintings – conventional enough – but also a set of Edward III gold coins, a copy of the Koran and the inevitable stones and minerals. He also inspired a May Day festival, in which students elect the 'likeablest and loveablest' of their number, which persists to this day, though the college itself is now part of the University of Roehampton.

'In all probability, [Ruskin] wanted to make a contribution to their aesthetic sensibility,' David Peacock, a former principal at Whitelands, told me, but 'his influence on the curriculum was only incidental'.

>⌒ 5 ⌒<

We know what a Ruskin school curriculum would look like, because in 1884, he summarised his vision for a 'scheme of schooling' to take place under his charity the Guild of St George:

> Every parish school to have garden, playground, and culti-
> vable land round it, or belonging to it, spacious enough to
> employ the scholars in fine weather mostly out of doors.
>
> Attached to the building, a children's library, in which
> the scholars who care to read may learn that art as deftly as
> they like, by themselves, helping each other without trou-
> bling the master; – a sufficient laboratory always, in which
> shall be specimens of all common elements of natural sub-
> stances, and where simple chemical, optical, and pneumatic
> experiments may be shown; and according to the size and
> importance of the school, attached workshops, many or
> few, – but always a carpenter's, and first of those added in
> the better schools, a potter's.
>
> In the school itself, the things taught will be music,
> geometry, astronomy, botany, zoology, to all; drawing, and
> history, to children who have gift for either. And finally,
> to all children of whatever gift, grade, or age, the laws of
> Honour, the habit of Truth, the Virtue of Humility, and the
> Happiness of Love.[22]

Ruskin, as this shows, despised the exclusive emphasis of the
time on the 'three Rs' – reading, writing and arithmetic. He
would surely have been appalled by the way Britain's modern
education system concentrates on 'Stem', at the expense of art,
music, languages and the other humanities. Singling out a late

19th-century obsession with sterile mathematical prowess, for instance, he wrote in *Fors Clavigera* that it seemed based on 'the notion that every boy is to become first a banker's clerk and then a banker, – and that every woman's principal business is in checking the cook's accounts'.[23]

But neither in his concern for the working man, nor in his passion for the education of young women, was Ruskin much of a fan of social mobility. In some respects, he was an advocate of 'vocational education'. That is one way of reading his backing for education adapted 'to the material of which the man is made' or his vision for a network of naval schools in British ports and agricultural colleges inland. He saw no point in teaching working men to read Latin or write English, for example. That was to confuse useful education with mere erudition, he wrote.

Instead, he advocated for education by aptitude. In 'Modern Education', an 1852 appendix to *The Stones of Venice*, Ruskin made a strong case for 'education to purpose' – teaching each man to know 'just what will fit them to do their work and be happy in it'. Later, in *Time and Tide* (1867), Ruskin was even more precise, writing that education 'should be clearly understood to be no means of getting on in the world, but a means of staying pleasantly in your place there'.

While Ruskin deserves credit for spreading ideas and education beyond privileged, upper class men, he mainly wanted working men (and women of all classes) to know their place and learn how to be happy in it. 'You do not learn that you may live – you live that you may learn,' he said in an 1869 lecture on 'The Future of England'.[24]

In his 1865 lecture 'Work', Ruskin fleshed out the idea of different types of labour, clearly segregated. 'There *must* be work done by the arms, or none of us could live. There must be work done by the brains, or the life we get would not be worth having,' he said.

One obvious irony is that many late Victorian autodidacts used Ruskin's writings as a basis for their education or found inspiration there to rise beyond their 'place'.

They included Thomas Dixon, who was the 'working man of Sunderland' to whom Ruskin addressed the series of letters that formed *Time and Tide*. A self-educated cork-cutter, Dixon went on to become a cultural patron and philanthropist. Leonard Bast, the tragic, Ruskin-reading young clerk in E. M. Forster's 1910 novel *Howards End*, is a fictional example of the same model of self-improver.

Ruskin imagined and used his influence to campaign for a future in which workers would be better paid, and, incidentally, would also benefit from good books and 'comfortable firesides' like their wealthier counterparts.

But his ideal society would maintain the social strata and be topped by the sort of wise leaders he had extolled in *Unto This Last*. In future, he told the working men of Camberwell, work would be done 'in an orderly, soldierly, well-guided, wholesome way, under good captains and lieutenants of labour'.

⚓ 6 ⚓

Few schools achieved Ruskin's ideals, although some tried. The most notable was probably Bembridge School on the Isle of Wight. It was founded in Ruskin's centenary year of 1919 by Ruskin's most devoted disciple, John Howard Whitehouse, the man responsible for saving most of the writer's archive, now at Lancaster University. The school survived until the 1990s, based on underlying principles of 'success through skill and hard work, the dignity of labour, and the equal importance of craftsmanship and academic studies'.[25]

Whitehouse claimed in 1945 that 'every major educational problem in the new Education Act [which provided free secondary education for all in the UK] had been dealt with' by Ruskin. The scattering of schools that have Ruskin's name in their title is one nod to his influence on early 19th-century educational reform and the spread of schools that were compulsory, universal and free. The first – a board school in Walworth – was named after him in 1899 when he was still alive.[26] There is, understandably, a John Ruskin School in Coniston, near Brantwood, and also a John Ruskin College in Croydon, not far from where Ruskin's mother was born.

The Croydon college is a descendant of a boy's school that was established in Ruskin's name in 1920 with an 'extended curriculum' that included the three Rs, but also woodwork, metalwork and singing.[27] It morphed via a boys' grammar school (whose most famous ex-student is Roy Hodgson, the former England football manager[28]) into today's vocational college, teaching 16- to 19-year-olds qualifications in practical areas including childcare, applied science and digital media.

An 1885 photographic portrait of Ruskin in pensive-prophet mode hangs in the central stairway of the college. Mohammed Ramzan, its principal since 2015, told me the message was 'you can leave a lasting legacy, as John Ruskin did', though he conceded that Ruskin did not have the same aspirational appeal to the school's 1,000 students as their modern idols do. Yet he said the college's ethos, notably its inclusive approach and its philosophy of 'learning by doing', owed something to its namesake's ideas.

Another ambitious route to Ruskin's vision of integrated

education is being followed by Aonghus Gordon, an innovative educator. Gordon learnt about Ruskin in Venice, where he was raised during the 1960s in the bohemian surroundings of his parents' Ruskin Centre for Art Appreciation – ultimately closed by the Venetian authorities, Gordon implies, for being rather *too* bohemian.

His Ruskin Mill Trust takes elements of Ruskin's thinking, combined with ideas drawn also from William Morris and the Austrian philosopher and radical educationalist Rudolf Steiner. Steiner schools, which 'take account of the whole child' owe a debt to Ruskin's insight that hands, head and heart should be engaged together.

Gordon, a Steiner school alumnus, has applied these ideas particularly to young people unable to get access to mainstream education, notably those on the autism spectrum. 'I was always told I would never teach in a regular school,' Gordon told me, 'so I set up my own'.

The Trust has bought up disused or dilapidated Victorian industrial sites – a glassmaking factory in Stourbridge, a silversmith's workshop in Birmingham – and refurbished them for occupational training and therapy, often drawing on the knowledge of retired workers to help guide the students. The curriculum combines craftsmanship, practical work and land husbandry, a template for rounded education a little like the one Ruskin first laid out for his ideal 'schools of St George' in *Fors Clavigera*.

Gordon admitted he had picked the school's principles selectively from Ruskin's many works, absorbing the spirit rather than the letter of what he wrote. ('It's unreadable for most people' is his harsh judgment.) But, a little like Mohammed Ramzan at Croydon's Ruskin College, he recognises that Ruskin the educator was a champion of the excluded. Ruskin wrote about how to bring the destitute and outcast back into society through exposure to a broad range of activities and teaching, including crafts such as pottery, metalwork, glass and stonework.

'The word I use for Ruskin is that he is a "morphologist", who saw how one plant, or piece of rock can iterate bigger principles,' Gordon told me.

By applying Ruskin's interconnected view of the world, combining handiwork with glass and metal and involvement in landscape and nature, his trust develops students' self-awareness and social skills. 'Basically, when they perform a task which combines service and civility and people pass by and say "That's wonderful, did you make it?", they are afforded positive affirmation.'

Ruskin's vision of a broad-based education system was at first ridiculed by proponents of a narrower 'three Rs' approach. Similarly, the work of the Ruskin Mill Trust is an object mainly of curiosity to mainstream schools obliged to fit into the current system of targets and rankings – a system that is spookily close to the 'payment by results' approach to schooling that Ruskin despised. Gordon described this as the 'British dilemma': 'Children who don't enhance the performance of a school get chucked out. [Ruskin Mill Trust] picks up only a tiny part of that.'

 7

The progressive pedagogical spirit that Ruskin brought to the Working Men's College survives there today.

For most purposes, the College now sells itself to the world as the gender-neutral 'WMC'. It relocated to draughty red-brick premises in Camden, north London, a short walk from St Pancras Station's neo-Gothic spires, five years after Ruskin's death.

Ruskin's name still graces the honours board in the building's main hall and students with time to dawdle on their way to classes in creative writing, digital design or modern languages could, until recently, read a short biography posted in the corridor near the main entrance. Now, a Ruskin quotation – 'A little thought and a little kindness are often worth more than a great deal of money' – greets learners and tutors.[29] There is a Ruskin Gallery for art displays by the students. His books can be found in the library, though they are infrequently borrowed and these days the high-ceilinged room's book-shelved alcoves double as ad hoc meeting spaces. On the February night that I visited, classes on offer included rock guitar, jewellery making and beginner's Arabic.

There is drawing, too. In a life drawing class, Paul Peden, a WMC tutor, was picking up the thread of Ruskin's original mission, to launch a group of adult 'learners' – mixed by ability, gender and ethnicity – into a series of quick warm-up sketches of John, their model.

Ruskin was not a great figure painter, though he took pains to copy many figures from the works of Tintoretto and others in his time. He did not think 'figures, as chief subject, can be drawn to any good purpose by an amateur'.

He always preferred to present his students with objects from the natural world. His students were taught drawing 'primarily in order to direct their attention accurately to the beauty of God's work in the material universe'.

Ruskin was not the first or the last artist to put a premium on seeing and drawing, as I have already made clear. But it was hard to ignore the connection in the life class at the vaulted room at the WMC, in the concentration of the life-drawers, in their obvious relish in the process, and in the philosophy of their tutor

– gently nudging his students towards self-improvement. During a break, Paul explained that his aim was simply to encourage his students to 'understand what you see and translate it into the drawn mark'. When he did offer advice on technique, he said it was always to guide them in the task in hand rather than to dictate how to draw.

Helen Hammond, the college's principal, told me the college's long history gave it a firmer foundation than some other adult education centres, as they fight for dwindling central government funding, but added: 'It's true to say that we are not always citing Ruskin.'

That is not just because of the ups and downs of Ruskin's reputation. Work and education have changed since 1900. There are fewer men in the Working Men's College, for a start. The college did teach some women even at the outset. Octavia Hill, later beneficiary of Ruskin's philanthropy and co-founder of the National Trust, was secretary of the women's classes. Now three quarters of students at the WMC are women. Many are seeking work rather than doing work. Either that, or they have precarious roles of the sort that Ruskin would doubtless have attacked as the 21st-century service-economy equivalent of the soulless factory labour of the mid-Victorian era: zero-hours contractors, coffee-shop washer-uppers, part-time carers and cleaners.

The WMC offers the chance of qualifications that will get its students a better job, or any job at all. While about half the college's offering is art classes, the people studying for the fun of it – to make themselves 'happier as a carpenter', if you like – tend to be older and wealthier than the average student.

The other half of the curriculum is more elementary and utilitarian: English for speakers of other languages (ESOL) or basic maths. These lessons in 'skills for work' as the WMC bills the

Helen Hammond

classes are for people, often immigrants, who hope to learn enough to understand their own children's homework, or who simply need the formal qualifications to advance to the first rung of the labour market and take the first step towards the state Ruskin described in his 1851 pamphlet on Pre-Raphaelitism. 'In order that people may be happy at work,' he wrote, 'these three things are needed: They must be fit for it; They must not do too much of it: and they must have a sense of success in it.' A century and a half later, in his book *Drive*, management writer Dan Pink revived interest in similar keys to self-motivation at work. He called them autonomy, mastery and purpose.

These WMC students are people like the ones I met in a maths class that February evening: Susan, who works in a special needs school, and started coming to maths classes to get the basic level required to go further ('I didn't want to do it, but now I love it'), or 52-year-old Steve, who left school at 15, worked in engineering, then facilities management, and now needs to 'reignite' his maths skills to become an electrician.

Where there is demand for courses such as digital media, the Ruskins, Rossettis and Kingsleys to teach them are in short supply. Tutors are paid by the hour and, said Hammond, 'if you want a good digital media person, they can make more money elsewhere'.

Even so, the capacity for education to launch students down new paths, one of John Ruskin's most important gifts as a teacher, remains embedded in the WMC's ethos. An annual 'How WMC Changed My Life' prize is awarded to the student with the most vivid story of transformation.

One woman who moved to London from Chennai, India, in 2016, wrote that without the WMC's English language courses, she 'would not have dared to register' for a yoga teacher training programme. Another student fought through periods of homelessness, disease and trauma, before a WMC creative writing course 'unlocked my mind'. A third, a grandmother and full-time night support worker in a care home, aims to use her English and maths tuition at the college to run her own nursery school and write children's stories: her tutors, she wrote, 'saw potential in me even when I was getting discouraged'.

As a tutor in the 1850s, Ruskin saw potential in many of his students. A number went on to work with or for him.

Henry Swan, an eccentric vegetarian engraver (one of his later obsessions was boomerang-throwing) attended evening classes at the College. He stayed in touch with Ruskin and went on to become first curator of his quirky new museum in Walkley, on the outskirts of industrial Sheffield, which had a mission to educate and uplift local workers.

Another of Ruskin's students was George Allen, a carpenter. He could also have told quite a tale. In later years, Ruskin enlisted Allen as his personal publisher. Without Allen's entrepreneurial flair, Ruskin might well have run out of money just at the point that his health was deterioriating. His books were wildly over-priced for the working men and women at which they were ostensibly aimed partly because of Ruskin's obsession with the craftsmanship of printing, pages and bindings. It was Allen who devised the strategy of producing cheaper editions – including those special gift editions of *Sesame and Lilies* for school prize-givings – to give sales a lift. His name lives on as one half of the imprint Allen & Unwin, whose Australian subsidiary is still publishing.

Arthur Burgess was a wood engraver, whom Ruskin employed as a copyist – praising his fine architectural drawings for their demonstration of his 'gifts of mechanical ingenuity and mathematical intelligence'. John Bunney, a clerk, was inspired to move into art teaching himself, and eventually went to live in Venice. As part of his campaign against the planned 'restoration' of San Marco, Ruskin commissioned from Bunney the vast and detailed picture of the west front of the basilica that now hangs in Sheffield's Ruskin gallery.

🐦 *8* 🐦

This diaspora of people who had met and learnt from Ruskin, was increasingly supplemented in the second half of the 19th century, by the people who, at one remove, were inspired by his work. Gradually, they started to implement his ideas in the workplace.

One was Wisconsin-based Kohler, the bathroom fittings

company that has since diversified into leisure and hotels, including ownership of the Old Course Hotel overlooking St Andrews' famous links golf course. Walter Kohler, self-taught son of the founder, built a company town around the factory his father had set up, and enshrined Ruskin's aphorism 'Life without labour is guilt – labour without art is brutality' at the centre of the company's way of working. [30]

A century on, Ruskin's ideas on work and education are starting to crop up again in unlikely places, though followers inevitably pick and choose from his ideas.

At Solomeo, a hamlet in Umbria, Brunello Cucinelli, the Italian fashion designer, has built a business and a community founded, in part, on Ruskin's insights into the importance of beauty, craft and a fair wage. The village, painstakingly restored, is a symbol of 'humanistic capitalism', and includes a craft school for training young practitioners of old artisan skills. [31] Cucinelli believes the ideal growth rate for his company is 10 per cent, despite the potential demands of the listed company's investors. According to *The Economist*'s magazine *1843*, he 'pays his staff more than the average wage for their jobs, insists they work no longer than eight-and-a-half hours a day', and spends around 20 per cent of his profits on charitable donations. As the designer said in 2014, echoing *Unto This Last*: 'I think there's a return to the idea of the value of work and the value of remuneration. It's about returning dignity to the idea of healthy profits.' [32]

Which takes us back to Brick Lane. When I visited Unto This Last, Olivier Geoffroy, the workshop's founder, pointed out Elodie Le Roy, who runs the small production line. She has one goal that marks her role out from those managers who share a similar title at less idiosyncratic manufacturers, Geoffroy told me: 'To make everybody's job interesting'.

Geoffroy, as the workshop's stress on openness suggested, invites scrutiny and inquiry by his customers. The 'workshop is the brand' is one of his maxims. On the autumn Friday afternoon when he showed me round, Le Roy was diligently tidying up the main workshop while workers planed and polished in the background. It looked pristine to me, but still Geoffroy sounded mildly vexed that a vacuum tube designed to suck away dust and waste from one of the worktables was inelegantly attached to the ceiling.

The differences between how people think of Ruskin the 19th-century sage and how Unto This Last operates in the 21st century is partly intentional, according to Geoffroy.

'The point isn't nostalgia,' he told me. Instead, he is on a quest to find new ways to use all the assets available to his team – including the machine technology Ruskin generally loathed – to become more efficient and to live up to Unto This Last's main motto 'local is logical'. The workshop draws directly from Ruskin's conviction that, in Geoffroy's words, 'you do not have to believe the dominant economic ideology of your time if it contradicts your experience.'

In addition, Geoffroy explained, it is simply not enough to be a great – or even a happy – carpenter: 'The first thing we say is that they can't just be interested in polishing wood with a sander or applying oil to wood, because they would get bored after six months.'

Instead, every day Geoffroy asks his team to find a problem to solve and reinforces the challenge at weekly meetings: 'Can we do this product making less noise? Can we do it faster? Can we do it with less dust and less oil on the workbench? Can we start with less bulky materials?'

Geoffroy takes issue with Ruskin's narrow idea that all

craftspeople should try to be creative and that work is invalidated by a lack of creativity. He prefers to ensure that workers use their imagination. It is a subtle and interesting distinction. 'The absolute requirement today is to have a creative job and everyone would expect that,' said Geoffroy. 'We aren't completely at ease with this. We don't ask people to find a new shape for a chair every day'.

When I asked the founder of Unto This Last, the workshop, what he would want to discuss with the author of *Unto This Last*, the 1860 polemic, were Ruskin to appear on the threshold, Geoffroy surprised me with his answer: productivity, the holy grail of modern economies and economists, and so often a synonym for the deadening, job-cutting, management style of the faceless multinational.

In fact, the lean management techniques of Toyota, when they were first introduced, had a clear human objective – to hand independence to the frontline workers and delegate to them the task of solving problems. US imitators stripped this human side away and made lean production a tool for restructurings and layoffs. This is why Ruskin would probably not object to the robots that Unto This Last is introducing into its workshop, even if he would baulk at the machined perfectionism of the furniture the factory produces.

Geoffroy has bold ambitions to extend the principles of the Unto This Last workshop in other places, creating a network of local workshops. Though it is inspired in part by Toyota's manufacturing lines, this will not be mass production. He described it as a 'system of local production', in which the use of machine technology, bought second-hand from the market for 'unemployed robots', is crucial, not to scale up, but to scale down.

'One of the logics of this process is to reduce this workshop to something smaller,' he explained to me. 'We want to reduce the size of the material that we handle to open the approach to more women – because physical force will no longer be vital.

'It's very human and a logical part of Ruskin's work to do things with less,' Geoffroy added. 'I would argue that productivity and paring things down and thinking how you can do things with less is very much a legitimate legacy.'

In 2012, I sought to reconstruct for the Financial Times Ford Madox Brown's Pre-Raphaelite masterpiece *Work* – depicting roadworks near Hampstead Heath (see overleaf) – using equivalents to the workers that he assembled for his tableau.[33] His exemplars the 'brainworkers' Thomas Carlyle and F. D. Maurice, a penniless flowerseller, beer-drinking navvies, and jobless down-and-outs. Mine included a clergyman, BT workers, a banker, a multimillionaire philanthropist, an unemployed philosophy graduate and a vendor of the Big Issue magazine.

I asked them each what work meant to them. What was interesting was how many of the white-collar workers who made up the majority of the 2012 cast still expressed their work in physical terms and yearned for the honest toil of physical work. 'If you are a brainworker,' said the clergyman, 'you don't quite have the same nobility of labour... Sometimes I'm very envious of straightforward work.'

Ruskin is an unlikely champion for the physical work and Brown was no fan of the writer, despite having considered including Ruskin as one of his brainworkers.

Their mutual dislike represented a great missed opportunity for a meeting of minds, because they thought similarly about the value of work. In 1865, a few months before Brown put his painting – the 'work of my life' as the painter described it – on display, Ruskin gave the lecture entitled 'Work' at the Working Men's

Ford Madox Brown, Work, *1865*

Institute in Camberwell, down the road from his Herne Hill home. In the talk, he cleverly inverted 'work' and 'play'. The former was dignified and honourable, he suggested, the latter mainly the frivolous, useless pastime of self-interested money-grubbers. With some rephrasing, this passage from the lecture could easily be mistaken for a newspaper column aimed at the bonus-hungry bankers of the 21st century:[34]

> The first of all English games is making money. That is an all-absorbing game; and we knock each other down oftener in playing at that, than at football, or any other roughest sport: and it is absolutely without purpose; no one who engages heartily in that game ever knows why. Ask a great money-maker what he wants to do with his money, – he never knows. He doesn't make it do anything with it. He gets it only that he *may* get it. "What will you make of what you

Hunt Emerson, Work, *2018*

have got?" you ask. "Well, I'll get more," he says. Just as, at cricket, you get more runs.[35]

Ruskin was not just an ivory-tower thinker on labour. His genius was to frame the discussion of work in a new way, according to Howard Hull, Brantwood's director. Unlike contemporary 19th-century industrialists, who were starting down the path towards the treatment of people as mere inputs into a process – as 'human resources' and 'human capital' – Ruskin considered what people 'gain from work, not just what they give to work', says Hull. In 2018, he helped organise a new version of Brown's painting in cartoon form by Hunt Emerson, featuring Ruskin himself in the position occupied by Carlyle. Ruskin observes a modern street-scene featuring BT workers as navvies, Somali immigrant passers-by, illthy Mercedes-drivers and jobless people eating junk food.[36]

According to Ruskin's philosophy, to be useful to the world, values and wages had to go hand in hand. And if you happened to benefit from this noble combination, your duty was clear. 'There is no wealth but life', from near the end of the final essay in *Unto This Last*, may be Ruskin's most frequently cited maxim. But Ruskin also knew that wealth had it uses, as I shall go on to describe. That is why he went on to point out that 'that man is richest who, *having perfected the functions of his own life to the utmost* [my emphasis], has also the widest helpful influence, both personal, and by means of his possessions, over the lives of others'.

Chapter VIII

Craft

Fine art is that in which the hand, the head, and the <u>heart</u> of man go together.
(The Two Paths)

>〜 *I* 〜

In 2016, if you did your Christmas shopping at John Lewis, the chain of department stores that epitomises aspirational middle-class British values, you could have bought a 7ft artificial 'Ruskin Pine', with 'rugged upswept branches and pine cones for a realistic look'. For 'a touch of quirkiness', the shop recommended enhancing your tree with 'frosted chestnut baubles and mushroom pegs', most of which could be bought from the range it called Ruskin House. At selected stores, you could even have signed up for a 'treetorial' in how to deck your halls.

The Ruskin House 'look' was inspired by John Ruskin and William Morris, John Lewis explained. It included gold-and-green trimmed glassware, Spode earthenware crockery and a set of maroon jacquard-check tablecloths and napkins, in 'a nod to the Arts and Crafts Movement'.

I doubt Ruskin and Morris were nodding back. The pair are bracketed together so frequently that it is easy to assume that they were an inseparable duo – the Simon and Garfunkel of craft, churning out design blockbusters through the second half of the 19th century.

It is not quite as simple as that. Morris, fifteen years younger than Ruskin (though he died before him) was bound to the older man by ideas, but their artistic and political collaboration was limited. It started with that brilliant chapter from *The Stones of Venice*, 'The Nature of Gothic'.

Morris and Edward Jones – later better known as the Pre-Raphaelite painter Edward Burne-Jones – were undergraduates at Exeter College, Oxford, when *The Stones of Venice* was published in 1853.

Morris liked to chant chunks of Ruskin's work to his fellow students and 'The Nature of Gothic' was particularly resonant. It contained not only the exhortations to enjoyable work that I discussed in the last chapter, but also a three-point code for craft that influenced both men.

How would we recognise the products of 'healthy and ennobling labour'? Ruskin asked. By checking them against these rules:

1 Never encourage the manufacture of any article not absolutely necessary, in the production of which *Invention* has no share.
2 Never demand an exact finish for its own sake, but only for some practical or noble end.
3 Never encourage imitation or copying of any kind, except for the sake of preserving records of great works.[1]

Ruskin and Morris had quite a lot in common. Like Ruskin, Morris was the son of affluent Christian parents. He enjoyed a blissful childhood in what was then countryside just outside central London – Walthamstow, to the north, rather than Herne Hill, to the south – reading Walter Scott and wandering in Epping Forest, indulging Walter-Scottian chivalrous fantasies and developing a love of nature. Like Ruskin, he could have joined the church, but the radical ideas of Carlyle, Ruskin and later Karl Marx set him on a different path.

Morris was also what we might now call an early adopter. Apart from his early appreciation of 'The Nature of Gothic', he was, later, one of the first readers of Marx's *Das Kapital*, which he obtained in a French translation. Combined, these texts formed the pillars for a revolutionary socialist ideal that took Ruskin's ideas further than Ruskin himself would have done.

Morris was plainly an admirer and follower of Ruskin and wrote warmly later about his influence on his thinking. But while relations with Morris were always cordial and occasionally affectionate, Ruskin was closer to 'Ned', as close friends called Burne-Jones, who continued to seek, and occasionally receive, the patronage and attention of Ruskin throughout his career as a Pre-Raphaelite artist.

'Think of knowing Ruskin like an equal and being called his dear boys,' Burne-Jones wrote in 1856, after Ruskin dropped in on him en route to the Working Men's College, 'Oh! he is so good and kind – better than his books, which are the best books in the world.'[2]

It was mainly through Burne-Jones that Morris stayed in touch with Ruskin. Morris offered to be a witness for the writer when his reputation was under fire in the Whistler trial in 1878. Five years later, Ruskin reciprocated when Morris's political views were attacked at a lecture at Oxford, describing him as his 'old and dear friend'. He had kind words for Morris again in 1887, when he likened him to 'beaten gold' or a 'great rock with a little moss on it' to a visitor.[3]

Morris remained indebted to the ideas in *The Stones of Venice* and the later, more overtly political works of Ruskin. Even second-hand reports of the thinker's praise encouraged him. In 1892, a visitor to Brantwood spotted the ornate edition of 'The Nature of Gothic' produced that year by Morris's Kelmscott Press and noted that Ruskin had called Morris 'the ablest man of his time'. Learning of the compliment, Morris ordered up a bottle of fine Hungarian Tokay from his wine-cellar to celebrate.[4]

Ruskin's flattery was in its turn a response to Morris's comment, in the preface to that 1892 edition, that it was not the artistic side of Ruskin's work but the 'ethical and political considerations' that 'had the most enduring and beneficent effect on his contemporaries, and will have through them on succeeding generations'.

The objects Morris created with Ruskin's ideas – beautifully crafted books, furniture and décor – were closer to Ruskin's prescription than Morris's politics. Morris's quest to furnish ordinary people's homes with beautiful and useful things, ran up against the contradictions and inequalities of late 19th-century society like Ruskin's idealistic vision of self-sufficient, harmonious rural communities. But rather than fantasise about an ideal world, Morris persisted in his support for a socialist movement that would change the real one. As Morris told a friend in a letter in 1884, Ruskin was 'not a socialist, that is not a *practical* one… he mingles with certain sound ideas which he seems to have acquired instinctively, a great deal of mere whims'.[5] That is a pretty accurate summary of some of the reasons why many of Ruskin's ideas faded from view soon after his death.

Ruskin was more animated by Morris's interest in craft and architecture. The younger man's maxim, 'Have nothing in your houses that you do not know to be useful or believe to be beautiful' now enshrined in thousands of souvenir embroidery samplers and cheaply framed prints, sounds like a version of those three rules of craft from *The Stones of Venice*. Morris was also a leading light of the occasionally militant Society for the Protection of Ancient Buildings, which hewed to Ruskin's ideas on preservation, rather than heedless restoration, of monuments.

The Arts and Crafts connection came later. Morris only joined the Arts and Crafts Exhibition Society, one of the movement's founding pillars, four years after it was established. The movement itself was only widely identified under that name in the early 20th century, after Ruskin and Morris had died.

It would certainly have surprised and appalled both men – Morris, the early Marxist and militant socialist, and Ruskin, the violent Tory – to find themselves invoked alongside each other in 'treetorials' at John Lewis, consumer cathedral to the modern British bourgeoisie.

So be it. 'Arts and Crafts' is the route that leads from a 21st-century retailer's range of Christmas baubles, via Morris, all the way back to Ruskin. What is more, craft and crafting are the liveliest ways in which Ruskin's ideas continue to animate modern work and design. As the unexpected appearance of Ruskin House suggests, with other examples I am about to describe, this is also one of the few places in Ruskinland where John Ruskin's name is getting a fresh lease on life, from the interiors of four-wheel drive vehicles, to designer bags and wallpaper.

In 1864, John James Ruskin died, aged 78. The 'entirely honest merchant', as John described him on his tombstone, had passed on to his son not only his wealth, but also important notions about how riches could be well-spent, and about the value – moral and economic – of art, literature and music.

He had also handed down a strain of 'violent Toryism' that separated Ruskin's politics from Morris's, and informed unpalatable aspects of Ruskin's beliefs, thinking and work.

Ruskin's 'humanitarian impulses and his prejudices belonged alike to the 1830s,' his biographer Tim Hilton has written. Hilton was commenting on William Gladstone's recollection that Ruskin once said 'I don't think that prisons ought to be reformed, I don't think slavery ought to have been abolished, and I don't think war ought to be denounced'.[6]

Ruskin inherited such illiberal, ultra-Tory views from his father and his father's circle. In early evidence of what we would now call unconscious bias, any psychologist would cite his magnificent 'word-picture' describing Turner's painting *Slavers throwing overboard the dead and dying – Typhoon coming on*, in the first volume of *Modern Painters*. While justly famous as prose, the description only nods to the horrific theme of the painting in a footnote. (Ruskin's father bought the painting for his son and hung it in the entrance hall at the Denmark Hill house, where Ruskin would have passed it every day. The horror of the subject did eventually get to him: he later disposed of the painting because it made him uncomfortable.)

Ruskin was a polemicist. Like today's Twitterati and online opinionistas, he often adopted an extreme stance for effect. Unfortunately, unlike those opinion-leaders, he rarely had to answer to an editor, who could have reined in, or at least questioned, his worst impulses.

Ruskin was also too ready to take up a position because someone he admired requested his support, as he did, two years after his father's death, for Thomas Carlyle. Carlyle's wife, Jane, had died suddenly in 1866. It had not been a happy marriage – also assailed, as it happened, by rumours that it had never been consummated – but Jane's death left her husband bereft. At the same time, Carlyle was spearheading a campaign to defend the governor of Jamaica, Edward Eyre. Laid low by grief, he passed much of the burden to Ruskin, for whom political lobbying was not a forte.

Eyre had in 1865 violently suppressed a supposed rebellion of black islanders, killing hundreds and flogging others with wire whips. More than 150 years later, the wounds from that outbreak of officially sanctioned sadism have not healed. 'That pain will never go away: I mourn the loss of my ancestors', one Jamaican told David Olusoga when the historian visited Morant Bay, where the atrocities took place, for a 2016 BBC documentary series.[7]

Ruskin was not alone in joining an 'Eyre Defence and Aid Fund', chaired by Carlyle. Prominent literati, including Alfred Tennyson, Charles Dickens and Charles Kingsley backed Eyre, too. Against them were ranged members of the 'Jamaica Committee', including John Stuart Mill, Charles Darwin and other progressives.

Ruskin's involvement did not consist of simply adding his name to a petition. Driven in part by his admiration for Carlyle, the writer stood up for Eyre in print, spoke about the case in public, and added his considerable weight to the case against prosecuting the governor. Eyre was in the end allowed to slip into early retirement instead of being tried.

The Eyre affair is not the only shadow on Ruskin's legacy as a social progressive. His earlier dismissal of Indian art is another blot on his reputation as an art critic.

India was one part of the world where Ruskin's ideal of

interconnectedness between craft, culture and the livelihood and fulfilment of the worker was strongest. Here, inspired in part by *Unto This Last*, Gandhi pursued, after Ruskin's death, the ideal of self-sufficiency on a local scale, complete with a central role for the spinning wheel, and homespun textiles that paralleled Ruskin's later influence on Lakeland textile manufacture.

Long before that, India was also a centre for craft skills, and this was evident during Ruskin's lifetime. Such skills were on display in 1851 at the Great Exhibition, which devoted 30,000 square feet to the jewel in the imperial crown and its products – 'superb couches, royal bedsteads with richly-embroidered curtains; marble slabs and carved furniture, in wood and ivory;...fruit and flowers in wax; carved boxes and ornaments in sandalwood from Mangalore; embossed paper and illuminated writings,... together with a large assortment of manufactured articles illustrative of the wonderfully exact and patient industry of Hindoo workmanship'.[8]

Ruskin hated the Great Exhibition, though Effie, his wife, adored the show, going to the opening alone, with a ticket obtained by Ruskin's father. He later dismissed the Crystal Palace in Hyde Park as 'a conservatory'. Much more worryingly to the modern reader, he also openly deplored Indian decorative art and handicrafts.

This work was acknowledged at the time of the Great Exhibition to be superior in almost every respect to the British equivalent. Indian art also showed exactly the kind of expressive craftsmanship that Ruskin liked to praise in, for example, the work of the O'Sheas, the hard-to-control stone-carving Irish brothers who had worked on the Oxford museum.

Owen Jones, a Welsh designer, pointed out in an 1853 lecture about the Great Exhibition that in the use of colour in design

– one of the areas in which Ruskin's famous eye was particularly discerning – 'we [British] were not only behind some of our European neighbours, but in common with these, were far outstripped by the nations of the East'.[9] For later artists working in the Arts and Crafts tradition, the region's anonymous artisans were an inspiration. At the Ashmolean Museum's collection of Pre-Raphaelite art, Millais's portrait of Ruskin in front of the rushing stream at Glen Finglas stares disapprovingly across the room at cabinets filled with ceramics and decorative objects by British craftspeople that drew openly on Indian and other south Asian traditions.[10]

In 1858, Ruskin gave a lecture at the South Kensington Museum, the future Victoria & Albert Museum and already a centre for decorative art from all cultures. It took place at the time of the 'Indian Mutiny', an uprising that started with Indian troops in imperial service and was bloodily put down by British forces. The occasion was a presentation of prizes to decorative sculptors, including his favourite, James O'Shea. It only serves to underline the contrast between Ruskin's over-the-top praise for British craftspeople and his disdain for their Indian counterparts.

In his speech, Ruskin stereotyped Indians and Scottish Highlanders as 'the races of the jungle and of the moor'. The former rejoiced in art and are 'eminently and universally endowed with the gift of it', he said, while the Scots were 'careless of art, and apparently incapable of it', beyond 'the variation of the positions of the bars of colour in square chequers' – that is, tartan.

Ruskin praised Indian artists' 'delicate application of divided hue, and fine arrangements of fantastic line' and acknowledged that Indian art was 'delicate and refined', though he attacked its fantastical decorative themes ('*it never represents a natural fact*'). But these days you need a strong stomach to get through the entire lecture, because he also channelled conservative Britain's revulsion at the (sometimes exaggerated) accounts of the 'mutiny'. The Scots had moral character, he implied, in contrast to the Indians' failings: 'Out of the peat cottage come faith, courage, self-sacrifice, purity, and piety, and whatever else is fruitful in the work of Heaven; out of the ivory palace come treachery, cruelty, cowardice, idolatry, bestiality, – whatever else is fruitful in the work of Hell.'[11]

This speech needs to be seen in part as a sharp jab at the V&A founder Cole, whose design schools, museum strategy, and love of decoration for its own sake Ruskin despised. It was also made at a time of highly charged British indignation at the 'mutiny' and in the context of broad British consensus about the superiority of 'civilised' societies, such as that of the British Empire, and the barbarity of other races and nationalities. In *On Liberty*, even the great progressive – and opponent of governor Eyre – John Stuart Mill stated that 'despotism [was] a legitimate mode of government in dealing with barbarians, provided the end be their improvement, and the means justified by actually effecting that end'.[12]

The same context applied to Ruskin's inaugural lecture as Oxford's Slade Professor of Art in 1870 in which he careered off the topic to extol England's imperial duty. The high-flown rhetoric, or at least reports of it, apparently inspired the young Cecil Rhodes before he set off on his bloody colonial adventures in Africa. It is unlikely Rhodes was present at the inaugural lecture because he did not attend Oxford as an undergraduate until 1873. He could easily have read about the lecture, though, as it was widely reported.[13] In the speech, Ruskin reached for his most grandiose oratorical style. 'There is a destiny now possible to us – the highest ever set before a nation to be accepted or refused. We are still undegenerate in race; a race mingled of the best northern blood,' he said, urging England to 'found colonies as fast and as far as she is able, formed of her most energetic and worthiest men'.[14]

It is important to guard against 'presentism' – applying modern values to historical utterances and acts. It is also impossible to know how Ruskin would have been shaped by 21st-century values in all sorts of areas, from the bedroom to the boardroom, and which of these unpleasant views he would have suppressed – or never developed.

Anthony Gardner, head of the Ruskin School of Art, an Australian who identifies himself 'more as anti-colonial', said the taint of Ruskin's imperialism had been 'a huge consideration' when he considered taking his current role. But after speaking about it to colleagues, he recognised that 'Oxford was not only the heartland of colonial thinking, it was also the heartland of anti-colonial thinking'. He believes the key to interpreting the contradictions of Ruskin is 'recognising the strengths of ideas past and challenging those that have long been proven wrong'.

Still, there are good reasons why plenty of modern Ruskinians prefer not to address these episodes at all. Ruskin was a contradictory and contrarian man. But even within the context of the age, some of his outbursts were ill-judged, prejudiced and extreme. There was precious little that was 'unconscious' about some of his biases.

⤙ 3 ⤚

As Ruskin's critical decade of the 1860s advanced, his professional fame became tangled with his personal distress.

After his ill-judged proposal to Rose La Touche in 1866, her parents had again cut Ruskin off from face-to-face contact with their daughter. Infatuated, Ruskin had continued to construe from tiny hints – her despatch of rose petals in a letter of 1867, for instance – that there was still hope.

But the La Touches had set out to extinguish that hope, by consulting lawyers and, more damagingly, Effie Millais, about the circumstances of Ruskin's failed marriage.

In 1854, it might have seemed to Ruskin that it was convenient not to challenge 'incurable impotency' as a justification for the annulment. But what seemed inconsequential then was disastrously significant now that he was courting a new bride.

The lawyers advised that if Ruskin and Rose married and she bore his children, the annulment would be void and they would be guilty of bigamy. If they could not bear children, then the charge of impotency would stand, disgracing Rose and her family. It is doubtful whether this would have stood up in court. If it had, it would surely have resulted in mutually assured destruction. Presumably, Effie and Millais's marriage would also have been deemed illegal and Ruskin and Effie would have been thrown back into a loveless union. The claim would never be tested. Yet it hung over Ruskin like one of his polluted clouds.

No wonder that in February 1869, on the third anniversary of Ruskin's proposal, Rose, now 21, offered nothing to satisfy the increasingly hysterical writer, who was about to turn 50.

As usual, Ruskin took his distress abroad, and tried to dilute it with hard work of an obsessive kind. In Florence, he spent hours copying the roses on the dress of 'Spring', in Botticelli's *Primavera* in the Uffizi. In Venice, which he was visiting for the first time since his last trip with Effie in 1852, he discovered the work of Carpaccio, including *The Dream of St Ursula* from the wider cycle of the legend of the saint in the Accademia – his fourth great art attack. 'This Carpaccio is a new world to me,' he wrote to Burne-Jones. Neither man was to know that Ruskin's obsession with Carpaccio's world would later overwhelm his fragile mental health.

Back in London in January 1870, he met Rose by chance in the galleries of the Royal Academy. Ruskin tried to return her love letters. He kept them always on his person, between sheets of gold, in a dark blue silk wallet embroidered with a gold 'J' and 'R'. When she refused them, he fled. The rejection rendered him, for once, speechless: he marked a single cross in his diary.

This emotional setback coincided, though, with an important professional advance. Just a month later, on his 51st birthday, Ruskin made a triumphant return to Oxford as the first holder of the Slade Professorship of Art.

Here was an opportunity to implement his ideas about art education on a grand stage and through his own School of Drawing, which over time evolved into the Ruskin School of Art.

It is one of the few institutions in Ruskinland that carries his name and can trace a direct line back to John Ruskin himself. The Ashmolean Museum – in the west wing of which Ruskin first established his drawing school – has tried to recreate his original vision online. In fact, his whole approach has the feeling of an analogue website. He encouraged students at Oxford, as he had at the Working Men's College, to build links between the different items and accumulate knowledge not only of art, but also of, say, ornithology.

Ruskin populated a series of cabinets with artworks, by him, by Turner and by others – prints, engravings, watercolours, even a sculpture or two – arranged into four series: Standard, Reference, Educational and Rudimentary. The Rudimentary series ranged from heraldry, Greek, Medieval and Gothic design to the familiar 'exercises in tree-drawing'. Ruskin's accompanying instructions were characteristically severe, offering students no shortcuts: 'You will have to practise for months before you can even approximately outline' any of the specimens, he pointed out.[15]

Ruskin himself was a bigger draw, though, than the school itself. His opening lecture as Slade professor – the one that included his imperialist call to arms – had to be switched to the Sheldonian theatre to accommodate the crowds. His drawing classes, on the other hand, were only sporadically attended.

Ruskin was a highly public figure at this point. He was widely caricatured. One cartoon from 1872 shows him as an 'Angel of Light' floating under the star of 'High Art' and sprinkling his greatest works like roses onto smog-bound London. Many of the most famous early photographs of him date from the late 1860s and early 1870s: a stern, heavily sideburned figure, staring out at the camera, his hair worn to his collar, with a side parting. In these images, there is little sign of the 'sparkle and vigour' noted by one member of the audience at his inaugural lecture,[16] let alone the quiet humour that friends appreciated. Except in one frame from an 1869 series by society photographers Joseph Elliott and Clarence Fry: in the photograph Ruskin has dropped his chin, furrowed his brow, and frowns directly out at the camera, with a hint of a self-deprecating smile.[17] It is a picture begging for a caption: 'Don't mess with the future Slade professor', perhaps.

Like many prolific public intellectuals today, Ruskin sought multiple outlets for his views. The lectures were one. They were set-pieces, delivered to overflowing theatres and increasingly reported by journalists. Today, Ruskin would surely have been in demand as the polarising host of television series or as a contributor to Question Time. He would also have made a formidable blogger.

In 1870s Britain, this blog took the form of open letters. Ruskin was already a prolific writer of letters to newspapers and magazines. This was the medium he had used to defend the Pre-Raphaelites, among others. Letters were also the format for *Time and Tide*, the 1867 book addressed to the 'working man of Sunderland', the cork-cutter Thomas Dixon, in which Ruskin had laid out some of his views on education.

In 1871, Ruskin took this a step further and started to publish his baggy, apparently endless project *Fors Clavigera*, 'Letters to the Workmen and Labourers of Great Britain'. Despite the subtitle, Ruskin clarified that it was intended for 'masters, pastors and princes' as well as workmen and labourers. The last two groups may not even have read it. Each letter cost the same as half a week's supply of candles. Workers could save up to buy *Fors* or they could save up to buy the means to read it after a long day at work, but they were unlikely to be able to afford both.[18]

The eccentric title alone tells you something about the intricate workings of Ruskin's mind. It means, roughly speaking, 'Fortune with the Nail', based on the idea that fate fixes our destiny unalterably. But – this is Ruskin, after all – there is more to it than that. 'Fors' also stands for the force people need to do good work, and the fortitude or patience they need to carry it through. 'Clavigera' can be fortune's nail, but also the key and club borne, respectively, by fortitude and force.

At any rate, the title of the series gave no obvious clue as to *Fors Clavigera's* content. Its 96 issues, published over 13 years, ranged wildly across different subjects. It must have perplexed readers – assuming they were even able to follow its thread. Freed from the need to lay down a consistent argument, or the requirement to make money from the venture, Ruskin riffed on almost anything that occurred to him. In the counterpart to today's moderated 'below the line' reader comments on online columns, he also included some of the correspondence he had received, responding to criticism and enlarging on themes raised in previous issues.

Even fans concede *Fors* is a recondite, difficult work of mind-boggling breadth. Edward Tyas Cook and Alexander Wedderburn, the tirelessly positive editors of the 39-volume edition of the works (of which *Fors* occupies three), call it 'wildly discursive', ranging 'at will from Monmouth to Macedon, from China to Peru, from Giotto to goose-pie'. They offer little relief for any modern reader who fancies merely dipping into the letters: 'If a work, so heterogeneous and often so obscure, is to be read so as to reach the author's real meaning, it must be read as a whole,' they advise, over-optimistically, in their introduction.

Another lover of the work – modern biographer Tim Hilton – describes the topics Ruskin touched on over a two-month period around Christmas 1872:

'*Fors* began to mock at contemporary Christmas festivities, all Dickens and happiness;… Dante, crimes in Mile End, Chaucer, "Why not shoot babies instead of rabbits?", a recipe for Yorkshire goose pie, the iconography of the penny, "Free fighting in these days: newspaper extract", the *Pall Mall Gazette* on female education, the dragon as a symbol of spiritual enmity, Goethe, drunkenness, Walter Scott, the Poor Laws, "The Otomao Indians who live on clay and crocodile", republicanism, masters and servants, Dickens, Scott again, agricultural labourers, Theseus and Ariadne once again, "Saints, ancient and modern"; and much more.'[19]

On the other hand, as this partial list suggests, *Fors* can amply repay the open-minded browser. It can be a mad and frustrating read, but it is also shot through with moments of insight, humour and self-awareness. In that sense, it is like Ruskin himself at this stage in his troubled life. If you have some inside knowledge of Ruskin's fraught personal situation, *Fors* provides an invaluable running commentary on his fragile emotional state up to 1884, when the series petered out.

Early in its run, *Fors* was almost stopped permanently by a near-fatal illness that Ruskin contracted on an 1871 visit to Matlock, the spa town in Derbyshire where the young mineral-obsessed writer had once holidayed with his parents.

Ruskin's nonagenarian mother was ill (she was to die that December). His beloved childhood nurse, Anne, had recently died. And his cousin Joan, first sent to look after Mrs Ruskin after John James's death, had married Arthur Severn and headed off on honeymoon.

Perhaps this reminded Ruskin of the trauma of his own annulled union with Effie. At any rate, Joan's absence, even for this short holiday, distressed the needy professor. He was in Derbyshire that chilly, wet July to meet them. This first hint to Arthur that they would always have to tolerate a crotchety bewhiskered third individual in their marriage, was combined with an awful prefiguring of the behaviour Joan would have to put up with when Ruskin and the Severns later lived together at Brantwood.

Ruskin caught cold, which developed into 'a severe attack of internal inflammation', including violent vomiting and fever, that nearly proved fatal. Ruskin also seems to have suffered a first mental breakdown, complete with delirium, bad dreams and hallucinations. He was, and would remain, a difficult patient. The local doctor recalled how the professor would ask what would be worst for him – pepper and mustard, washed down with brandy and water, for instance – and take that.

Recuperating from his illness, Ruskin took what looks like an unusually rapid and unconsidered decision to buy the collection of ramshackle Lakeland cottages on Coniston Water where he was to spend much of the rest of his life. The deal to purchase Brantwood was struck by letter with its owner, a radical republican, poet and wood-engraver W. J. Linton, publisher at one time of a *Fors*-like periodical called *The English Republic*.

The acquisition, for a relatively modest £1,500, was not as reckless as it sounds. Ruskin had visited, sketched, and written early poems about this part of the Lake District, and despite his minute study of architecture and pernickety views on it, he was strangely unbothered about the architectural quality of the houses where he lived or stayed. When he visited the property that September, he described it cheerily as 'dilapidated and rather dismal' and later, in *Fors*, as 'a mere shed of rotten timber and loose stone'.[20] Collingwood, his secretary and biographer, reckoned it ultimately cost him at least £4,000 – the equivalent of nearly £500,000 in 2018 – to refurbish and furnish the place.

What the house provided for Ruskin was roots in a community – importantly, for the son of two Scots, a northern community – as well as an opportunity to practise and promote the craft skills that he wanted to sponsor.

When Ruskin mounted his brief defence of William Morris in the 1880s, he described him, according to a press report, as 'the great conceiver and doer... at once a poet, an artist and a workman'.[21]

These are important clues as to what Ruskin came to value as he grew older. He saw craft and artisanship as hands-on pastimes. He recalled sitting next to an 'iron-masked stone-breaker' in Oxford to understand how best to pursue a road-building project and learning from an 'Irish street crossings-sweeper' how to 'finish into depths of gutter' as part of another practical scheme he launched to clean a street near the British Museum in London.

'I have to say that half my power of ascertaining facts of any kind connected with the arts, is in my stern habit of doing the thing with my own hands till I know its difficulty,' Ruskin wrote.[22] It is a rare instance of Ruskin asking us to use our hands, rather than our eyes.[23]

As I have mentioned, it is a bit too easy to picture Ruskin as an indoors figure. He was, however, an active land-owner, pursuing a series of experiments at Brantwood that amounted to a practical expression of the importance of landscape for the people who lived in it and used it. A rapid sketch from 1876 by one of his secretaries shows him on his way to the wood in frock coat, boots, wearing his wide-awake hat and carrying a bill hook.

Though he set himself up as an absent-minded professor, his Brantwood projects were realised according to highly pragmatic plans. With the assistance of his gardener David Downs – 'Downsie' – who always referred to him as 'the young master', Ruskin had an ice-house carved into the rocks behind the house. He planted a moorland garden, now abandoned, that was an experiment in upland agriculture. He had a complex system of underground plumbing and irrigation built, to channel the water running off the moor, and helped construct a harbour on the lake that still survives.

'You can't just have a vague idea, go to your contractor and leave them to it,' Howard Hull, Brantwood's director, told me, drawing a highly practical modern lesson from Ruskin's approach as a landowner. 'You get a good result when you actually are able to give them a detailed brief – and he did that and worked with them a lot of the time.'

꘎ *4* ꘎

From the busy hub at Brantwood, a whole network of local craft started to expand, with Ruskin's endorsement and help.

Lakeland crafts were a stream that shared some of the same ideals as the Arts and Crafts movement but essentially ran in parallel. Crucially, they also fed the reservoir from which flows much modern interest in Ruskin as an enduring symbol of craftsmanship.

Among the organisations that sprang from Ruskin's thinking – and his fledgling charity the Guild of St George – was a woollen mill at Laxey on the Isle of Man, which a Lancastrian silk weaver called Egbert Rydings ran on Ruskinian principles (it was powered by a water mill, rather than steam, for example) to produce a highly durable textile. At one point, Ruskin suggested a square of Laxey cloth should be adopted as one standard for the Guild's currency. Whether it would have held its value is another matter. The clothes that Ruskin and his close associates had made from Laxey cloth never wore out but the Laxey mill did.[24] It failed in its original form in 1900, shortly after Ruskin's death, although family-owned Laxey Woollen Mills still exists.

More successful, and more enduring, was Langdale Linen, set up by another Ruskin disciple, the *Fors*-inspired solicitor Albert Fleming. Disgruntled with his lot, he moved to Coniston in the 1880s and, with the help of his housekeeper Marian Twelves, encouraged local women to revive the Westmorland use of spinning wheels. 'It seems that there is a real demand for genuine homespun goods,' recounted one local press report in 1886.[25] Ruskin Lace, based on a specific technique and developed by the enterprising Twelves, using some designs lent to her by Ruskin himself, explicitly built on the writer's idea of individual creativity. No two pieces of lacework were the same. Machine manufacture would have destroyed the principal attraction of the work, as Ruskin himself had said it would, in 'The Nature of Gothic'.[26]

These were successful, viable, craft-based enterprises that lasted, in some cases, into the 1920s. It is not too much of a stretch to suggest a link from Twelves and her network of local women to Olivier Geoffroy of the Unto This Last workshop on Brick Lane in London, and his plan to make local craft production of furniture operate on a wider scale.

Meanwhile, Hardwicke Rawnsley was exploring another strand of Lakeland crafts. We have come across Rawnsley as one of the founders of the National Trust. But when he accepted a post as vicar of Wray, on Lake Windermere, in the late 1870s, he was already a devoted conservationist and Ruskinian. He and his wife Edith were inspired by a conversation in which Ruskin suggested every parish should have a workshop where 'the blacksmith and village carpenter shall of a winter evening teach all the children who will be diligent and will learn, the nature of iron and wood, and the use of their eyes and hands'.[27] When the Rawnsleys moved north to Keswick they helped found the Keswick School of Industrial Art, expanding on the needlework, woodwork and metalwork classes they had launched at Wray. The Keswick School of Industrial Art survived until the 1980s, when it succumbed – like Laxey at the beginning of that century – to competition from cheaper imports.

Do not confuse this Lakeland arts revival, which the Rawnsleys, Fleming, Twelves and others took forward with impetus and input from Ruskin, with the Arts and Crafts movement. They were only lumped together later. Lakeland arts developed on strong, local foundations, using local materials, local craftspeople (many of them poor women to whom these small-scale business ventures offered 'dignified [paid] labour combined with creative freedom'[28]) and local distribution, through exhibitions and commissions.

It is no coincidence that the principal figures of the Lakeland Arts movement were also those involved in campaigns to protect the region from the advance of the railways. Sara Haslam, who has chronicled the separate evolution of Lakeland Arts, points out that 'like the revival of the [spinning] wheels, the revival of domestic crafts... and the protection of Lakeland were all part of a concentrated effort to protect not only the landscape but also the people who lived and worked in it, and the traditional regional culture which had developed from a particular way of life'.[29] Ruskin himself was, as so often, the person who wove together these disparate strands.

As it turned out, though, many of the people who could afford the work of Morris and many of his Arts and Crafts disciples in Britain were not ordinary working men and women but wealthy business people.

One of the patrons of the Lakeland arts movement was my great-great-grandfather William Long. A Unitarian tanner and hide merchant from Warrington in Cheshire, Long built a large home for his long holidays in the Lakes, where he stayed for the first time a few months after Ruskin's death in 1900. He incorporated the work of craftspeople such as Arthur Simpson, a woodcarver and furniture maker from Kendal who was an ardent Quaker and follower of Ruskin, decorated his 'morning room' with William Morris-designed wallpaper, and, on a small scale compared with Ruskin, collected and catalogued shells.

Long was a friend of Sir Edward Holt, the brewer who had built Blackwell, the quintessential Arts and Crafts house nearby, designed by M. H. Baillie Scott. I have tried and failed to find a direct connection with, or interest in, Ruskin, on the part of my wealthy ancestor, bar the existence on the bookshelves of the Lake District house of one 1909 red-bound Allen & Co pocket edition of Ruskin: *The Crown of Wild Olive*. That is the volume that contains 'Traffic', the showy lecture Ruskin gave to the rich citizens of Bradford, excoriating them for their pursuit of the 'Goddess of Getting-On'.[30]

Those ideas probably would have antagonised an entrepreneurial merchant and free-trader like my great-great grandfather, even as he enjoyed his golfing and walking breaks in the Lake District in the early 1900s. But his edition of *The Crown of Wild Olive* shows no sign that he read Ruskin's work, let alone was moved by anything in it.

He and Holt, though, represent one way in which craft developed in Britain in the late 19th and early 20th century – against the political direction set for it by both Ruskin and Morris.

If the Arts and Crafts movement narrowed and foundered in Britain, it prospered and took on a far wider significance in the US. One proponent was Gustav Stickley, the American designer best known for his now highly collectable craft-influenced furniture.

Stickley's plans for houses, versions of which you still find across the US, allowed Americans to live in Arts and Crafts style homes, often simple bungalows. His 'Craftsman' magazine, published from 1901 to 1916, published more than 200 plans for log cabins, cottages and larger two-storey dwellings. Stickley even sought to follow Ruskin and Morris's prescriptions on free and happy workers, modelling his United Crafts movement, at least initially, on medieval fraternities.

Similarly, Elbert Hubbard, a shrewd and charismatic

businessman, inspired by Morris, was able to turn Arts and Crafts furniture, books and homewares into a wider success, through the Roycroft community in upstate New York, near the Canadian border. His venture was, for a short period, a triumph of mass marketing, built on a base of utopian, agrarian ideals and handicraft techniques. It is questionable whether all the Roycroft production was handmade – though these are the items that collectors now treasure – but discussion of just how much machine-work is acceptable prefigures debates that still rage among craftspeople today.

⤙ 5 ⤚

Today Ruskin's name has come to be associated with a rootedness of products in local materials and communities.

Alli Abdelal, who grew up in a tiny hamlet called Hutton Roof, a few miles north-east of Keswick in the northern Lake District, is tapping that spirit with RUSKIN, a maker of 'affordable-luxury' bags that she and two others founded in 2015. It followed a year-long search for a mill that could transform into usable textile the hardwearing wool from Herdwick sheep, the traditional Lakeland breed with the alabaster face and the elegant grey coat. The search took her out of the Lake District, to Yorkshire, where the material is worsted and woven, and ultimately to Italy, where the bags are made.

Abdelal, who designs the bags, sounds almost apologetic about not having found an all-Cumbrian solution, or at least all-British, solution. Also, she told me, the bags, which retail for up to £550, are not going to sell themselves. That was never a problem for the wealth-cushioned John Ruskin (as his uncommercial line of

Alli Abdelal

books suggests). There is a nice truth about how to produce innovative and beautiful products in Ruskin's comments, cited earlier, at the opening of the Cambridge School of Art: 'The first and absolute condition of the thing's ever becoming saleable is that we shall make it without wanting to sell it'. But it has its limits in a competitive market. Abdelal said, 'I intended [RUSKIN] to be this quieter, more considered approach to design.' But, she added, 'we can't be so quiet that nobody knows about us'.

Her dilemma is similar to that faced and overcome by Olivier Geoffroy at Unto This Last, introducing computer design into his workshop, or John Iles at Ruskin Land, seeking the best way to help the Guild of St George's investment bear fruit. Likewise, her solution: to choose selectively from Ruskin's legacy. And, why not manufacture 'Ruskin' bags in Italy? After all, it was where Ruskin himself spent some of the happiest days of his life and for that reason as much part of Ruskinland today as it was in the 19th century.

John Ruskin himself knew about the value of his name as a brand, even if he did not always approve its use. He agreed to attach his signature to souvenir cups and saucers, a few of which are now on display at Brantwood. His cousin Joan Severn, by then the unofficial vice-president of marketing of the Ruskin myth, probably arranged that merchandise deal.

But as his fame grew, and his public appearances diminished, he was also prone to the entrepreneurial instincts of rip-off merchants, brand-ambushers, and bootleggers, who produced a stream of Ruskin-tagged objects, without any formal permission. Ruskin's own idiosyncratic approach to commerce helped encourage the piracy of his ideas and name. For instance, the mismatch between the cost of his books and the market among working men and women opened an obvious opportunity for publishers of pirate editions, especially abroad, to exploit.

At a distance of more than a century, though, 'Ruskin', the name, has enjoyed an unexpected, though not inexplicable, resurgence as a talismanic reminder of... well, of what exactly?

What could link RUSKIN with Ruskin, a clothing store in Whitstable, on the Kent coast, and Ruskin Design, a Leicestershire workshop for the design, trimming, stitching and fitting of interiors for Land Rover Defenders? And what links that 'Ruskin' with the one who lends his name to a £700 Ruskin ceiling lantern, or a non-electric Ruskin pendant light, at less than a tenth of the price, with an 'intricate cut-out design', all available online, or a craft beer, brewed less than half a mile away from 'Ruskin's View' in Kirkby Lonsdale?

A few of these references are explicit, even if the links are tenuous. The Whitstable shop's owners cite the aphorism 'quality is never an accident, it is always the result of intelligent effort' which they say 'resonated' with them. 'Ruskin is ever evolving,' the founders claim – words that could apply as much to the man's legacy in craft as to the shop itself.

Ruskin Design uses the same quotation in its brochure, though the company's founder, consultant and former Royal Navy petty officer Steve Castledine told me his first inspiration was the so-called Common Law of Business Balance, based on the quotation 'It's unwise to pay too much but it's worse to pay too little'. It is a nice line for customers who may be invited to pay over £15,000 for the full customised package, from 'cubby box' to 'gear gaiter', and even more for the 'vegan interior' that Castledine's 10-person team was working on when I spoke to him.

The truth, unfortunately, is that Ruskin does not seem to have been the author of either sentiment, however Ruskinian they sound. Castledine acknowledged to me that The Common Law of Business Balance may not be Ruskin's. An equally Ruskinian alternative is: 'There is hardly anything in the world that someone cannot make a little worse and sell a little cheaper, and the people who consider price alone are that person's lawful prey', which used to be displayed in Baskin-Robbins ice cream parlours, attributed to Ruskin. The Ruskin Library has 'been asked many times about this quote, or similar versions of it, and have never been able to identify it as being by Ruskin'.[31] As for the 'quality' quotation, the self-contradictory writer appears to say the opposite in his 1851 pamphlet *Pre-Raphaelitism*, viz 'if a great thing can be done at all, it can be done easily'.[32]

A more promising and interesting explanation for the new blooming of the Ruskin brand is that brand managers, marketers and copywriters are picking up and recycling for a new audience the faint scent of many different things that he represented.

Ruskin's Bitter, brewed by the independent Kirkby Lonsdale Brewery has a 'fruity and spicy characteristic, with a lasting dry finish'. You can buy it in the restaurant at Brantwood, among other places. The brewery describes the beer as its 'quintessential British bitter'.

Ruskin might not have appreciated the temptation it offered, though he would have lauded the brewery's small scale and local roots. When he launched *Fors* he asked readers to 'pay me the price of two pots of beer, twelve times a year' for his advice (it worked out more expensive than that, as we have seen). While he did not begrudge working people their beer, he sternly warned them not to spend on alcohol what they might save for better causes, and at one point urged them to turn acres devoted to hops over to parks and free-range livestock. ('Do you know how much corn land in the United Kingdom is occupied in supplying you with the means of getting drunk?'[33]) There is an echo there in the environmental movement's concern about the indirect cost of devoting natural resources, including water, land and forest, to the grazing of cattle for meat-eating fast-food junkies.

But Ruskin's Bitter does sum up nicely what Ruskin, the name, contains: a whiff of his interest in creative work, a drop or two of what he wrote and knew about nature, a strong strain of rural nostalgia, and, above all, those deep notes, via William Morris, of craft and craftsmanship.

According to Rachel Dickinson of Manchester Metropolitan University – like me, an enthusiastic collector of odd recurrences of the Ruskin name in modern commerce – Ruskin is a figure who 'lends weight and authority to ideas'. She pointed me towards the founders of a Glasgow-based textile design company with the wonderful Robbie Burns-inspired name Timorous Beasties. Ruskin's name appears on a few of their lines of wallpaper. For them, the writer relates 'a universal connection between nature, art and society'. Timorous Beasties is exploring how those

Rachel Dickinson

interconnections affect our 'daily experience of furnished spaces, from one-bedroom flats to country villas, to the halls of civic and government buildings, departure lounge backdrops, boutique enclaves, restaurants, and hotels'.

If Ruskin would disapprove of 'departure lounge backdrops' or 'boutique enclaves', he would be even harsher about Land Rovers, whose least considerate owners indulge their off-road capabilities at the expense of the peace of the countryside. Steve Castledine of Ruskin Design admits the links between his company and Ruskin's ideas on craft were 'incidental' in its naming. Yet the patterns for the interiors are still drawn and cut by hand. Castledine may move the workshop to digital design, as much for security against the paper plans being destroyed as anything else. But for Ruskin Design's interiors, as for the manufacture of Ruskin lace in the late 19th century, a move to machine production, though speedier, would be counterproductive.

Castledine has also taken John Iles's idea of placing 'Ruskin Oak' inside homes and furniture as a mark of quality and provenance, one step further. Ruskin Design has trademarked the phrase 'Ruskin Inside', complete with Union flag label. It is a nod to the successful 'Intel Inside' campaign by the US chipmaker, which placed stickers on personal computers and laptops to promote its hidden product. Here, as at other companies that have rediscovered the Ruskin name, a small and selective part of the work and reputation of John Ruskin is still powering the brand.

⤝ 6 ⤞

'The parallel couldn't be more obvious,' writes novelist Jeff VanderMeer of 'The Nature of Gothic', introducing a parallel that seems, at least at first glance to be far from obvious: 'Steampunks seek to reject the conformity of the modern, soulless, featureless design of technology – and all that implies – while embracing the inventiveness and tech origins of Victorian machines. They also seek to repair the damage caused by industrialisation… [It] is a progressive impulse to reclaim the dead past in a positive and affirmative way.'[34]

VanderMeer's *Steampunk Bible* puts John Ruskin at the centre of the modern movement of neo-Victorians, with their steam-powered eccentricity, anachronistic greatcoats and goggles, and fantastical science-fictional homage to Ruskin's era. It is no coincidence that Philip Pullman, whose trilogy *His Dark Materials* conjures a steampunk world centred on Oxford, is a reader of Ruskin. The epigraph to one of the chapters of the third book, *The Amber Spyglass*, is taken from Ruskin's *Time and Tide* ('Labour without joy is base. Labour without sorrow is base. Sorrow without labour is base. Joy without labour is base'[35]). In 2008, Pullman was asked to draw up a reading list of 40 favourite books: there, between Rilke's *Duino Elegies* and Art Spiegelman's *The Complete Maus*, are Ruskin's *Selected Writings*.[36]

Steampunks may highlight one of the most direct 21st-century links to Ruskin's patronage of craft and craftsmanship and to one of his most difficult ideas, that imperfection can be a sign of quality.

In 'The Nature of Gothic', Ruskin wrote that 'neither architecture nor any other noble work of man can be good unless it be imperfect'. It is a hard precept to live down to, above all in a world that has come to expect perfection in finished, machine-produced objects.

Olivier Geoffroy of the Unto This Last workshop aims for a uniformity of finish in the furniture his team produces. The drawback with a more bespoke, craft approach is that 'it creates a personal bond with the workshop', he said. Customers then 'expect a personalized service and, if the edge is rough, they take it personally'.

Yet the reaction against perfection and mass production has a direct link back to Ruskin's ideas. Geoffroy acknowledged to me that 'people would accept some imperfection today – even a rough edge – because they buy the story'.

He added: 'The public today wants a relationship with an economy they can like, relate to, and check. This is the simple idea that keeps the business going. Ruskin was prescient: we can state every day that the public prefers buying from a local workshop because of "social affections"' – the idea Ruskin mentioned in the first essay of *Unto This Last* that he said political economists rejected. Unto This Last 'organises the business accordingly'.

Steampunk Sean Orlando has pointed out that 'modern design can be very cold and rectangular, so hidden as to be æsthetically unreachable, smooth, a zipless totalitarianism.'[37]

A resurgence in handmade and small-production items – of the sort sold through sites such as Etsy and, in the UK, Not On The High Street – is part of the response to zipless totalitarianism. To call this Ruskinian is to stretch a point. How many 'inspirational quote necklaces' can the world accommodate ('When love and skill work together, expect a masterpiece' – another misattribution – yours for $59[38])? But at least some of the impetus for the craft movement comes from the initial impulse given by Ruskin, and the ethos of the back-room artisan often seems a direct echo.

'In a very real way, Ruskin can be read not just as reveries about, say, the delights of Venetian architecture, but as a handbook for any creative person,' according to VanderMeer, who added: 'I love Ruskin's defense of ambition and audacity in art, which I read as an admiration for these qualities in creative work generally. Ruskin loves a risk-taker, understands in his gut that perfection can be a signal of a lack of imagination.'[39]

Etsy, the American e-commerce site, was set up with the intention of meeting many of the same ideals as ventures with 'Ruskin inside'. When the company came to list its shares, Chad Dickerson, its then chief executive, wrote how it had a goal of creating a sustainable 'Etsy economy' that 'transcends price and convenience, [that] emphasises relationships over transactions and optimises for authorship and provenance'.[40] In the same way, Ruskin wrote in the Oxford lecture collected in 1872 as *The Eagle's Nest*, that we should 'cherish, above all things, local associations, and hereditary skill'.

Etsy, and its equivalents elsewhere, have also taken energy from the growing resurgence of respect for analogue, handicraft skills, such as those celebrated in Matthew Crawford's 2009 book *The Case for Working with Your Hands*. In the book, Crawford – a self-described 'philosopher and mechanic' – lays out the dangers of separating thinking from doing. Crawford is rightly rather disparaging of early 20th-century attempts to 'get back to "real life"'. Specifically, he disliked the 'romantic fantasy about the premodern craftsman' which he says led, via the Arts and Crafts movement, to an evangelisation of good taste. It is no surprise that, alongside environmentalism, 'notions of work and craft' are the strand of Ruskin's thought that most resonates at the Ruskin Art Club in Los Angeles, according to its director Gabriel Meyer.

Ruskin does not merit a mention in Crawford's book. But Crawford's ideas about the fulfilment of manual work sound as though they come straight from late Ruskin. 'My work situates me in a particular community,' writes Crawford of his motorcycle repair job and the circle of skilled motorcyclists he serves. 'The narrow mechanical things I concern myself with are inscribed within a larger circle of meaning; they are in the service of an activity that *we* recognise as part of a life well lived. This common recognition, which needn't be spoken, is the basis for a friendship that orients by concrete images of excellence.'[41]

When ideals meet commercial competition, it is often ideals that must flex – or break. Just as Laxey's woollen mill wrestled with how to reconcile craft, provenance and equitable working with the demands of commerce, or Alli Abdelal will fail if she does not sell RUSKIN products, Etsy initially struggled as a listed company to live up to that 'Letter from Chad'. Dickerson himself had to step down in 2017 while users and employees feuded about the way Etsy was 'selling out' its original vision, in an internet-scale version of some of the disputes that broke out later at Ruskin's utopian ventures. Say what you like about Ruskin, he was never a sell-out – in part because he was usually wealthy enough never to need to sell at all.

Completing the circle, there is a strong case for embedding Ruskin's ideals of work, beauty and craft *inside* objects and machines. In *The Seven Lamps of Architecture* Ruskin made what seemed an eccentric plea to architects and builders to use 'wealthy' materials and to continue ornamenting even parts of buildings that were designed to be invisible. '[The] sculpture of the backs of the statues of a temple pediment [is] never, perhaps, to be seen, but yet not lawfully to be left unfinished,' he wrote. [42]

Ruskin took this even further in *The Stones of Venice*, when he mounted a ladder to examine a much-admired tomb of Andrea Vendramin, one of the city's Renaissance doges. He was shocked to discover that the artist, aware that the tomb would be viewed only from below, had not bothered completing the unseen part of the sculpture, leaving one hand and half the face uncarved. The sculptor was guilty of dishonesty, Ruskin wrote, and 'utter coldness of feeling, as could only consist with an extreme of intellectual and moral degradation'. [43]

A century or more later, Steve Jobs instilled a similar attitude in the builders of objects that made his and Apple's reputation. Jobs did not only spend time driving his designers, engineers and sales team to distraction with the external design of Apple machines, he also obsessed about the invisible parts, a habit he once said he picked up from his father, a mechanical and metal worker. [44] So he made his team sand rough plastic seamings on the inside of the casings of Apple II computers, and even complained that the 'lines were not straight enough' on the machines' original logic boards.

From here, it is just a short step towards coding in a way that incorporates both the fulfilment of the anonymous software engineer and the beauty of the computer code itself. Sure enough, here is a passage from *The Pragmatic Programmer*, an influential

programming manual published in 1999, with a strong flavour of
'The Nature of Gothic':

> The construction of software should be an engineering dis-
> cipline. However, this doesn't preclude individual craftsman-
> ship. Think about the large cathedrals built in Europe during
> the Middle Ages. Each took thousands of person-years of ef-
> fort, spread over many decades. Lessons learned were passed
> down to the next set of builders, who advanced the state
> of structural engineering with their accomplishments. But
> the carpenters, stonecutters, carvers, and glass workers were
> all craftspeople, interpreting the engineering requirements
> to produce a whole that transcended the purely mechanical
> side of the construction. It was their belief in their individual
> contributions that sustained the projects: We who cut mere
> stones must always be envisioning cathedrals.[45]

>〜 7 〜<

Charles Dickens was the great chronicler of the drama of industrial deprivation and social injustice. But Ruskin deserves to
be considered in this company. Take this powerful, cinematically
dramatic passage from his 1854 pamphlet 'On the Opening of the
Crystal Palace', written in the wake of a cholera epidemic that
had swept through London's East End that summer:

> If, suddenly, in the midst of the enjoyments of the palate
> and lightnesses of heart of a London dinner-party, the walls
> of the chamber were parted, and through their gap, the
> nearest human beings who were famishing, and in misery,
> were borne into the midst of the company – feasting and

fancy-free – if, pale with sickness, horrible in destitution, broken by despair, body by body, they were laid upon the soft carpet, one beside the chair of every guest, would only the crumbs of the dainties be passed to them – would only a passing glance, a passing thought, be vouchsafed to them?[46]

Ruskin's inspiration was probably what he had learnt while serving on a committee of important men organising relief for the victims of the epidemic and their families. Around the same time, Ruskin's friend Henry Acland, a medical doctor, also published a study of cholera outbreaks in Oxford. Two decades later, again in Oxford, Ruskin found a way to combine that early activism with his determination to bridge the gulf between brain and muscle and unite 'the hand, the head and the heart'.

In 1874, he persuaded some of the university's students to abandon rowing and cricket – the game he had earlier used in his critique of City money-making as mere 'play' – in favour of a little light road-building. (Ruskin was not averse to watching a bit of cricket. His day spent at The Oval in summer 1882 means he was probably 'the only great Victorian writer to witness the English defeat commemorated in the Ashes'.)[47]

Ruskin invited the eager students to join a mission to repair a road in the cholera-ridden village of Ferry Hinksey outside the university city.

The temptation to caricature the venture was irresistible. Contemporary accounts and pictures of the road building exercise show a mocking audience of locals observing the unprepared and ill-equipped undergraduates at work in boaters and shirt-sleeves. In other words, many outsiders viewed it as a folly, in the same way that Morris ten years later was to view some of

Ruskin's legacy as a 'mere whim' rather than a contribution to practical socialism.

But this was not a case of Ruskin wanting to keep his feet dry as he walked into Oxford from the Crown and Thistle Inn at Abingdon, south of the city, where he sometimes stayed while fulfilling his professorial duties. It was also a public health project, an experiment in construction methods, and a useful distraction from the students' more frivolous pastimes. Ruskin challenged them to pour the effort they devoted to games into useful work, draining and bridging the unsanitary marsh around the village and improving the health of the villagers. He wrote to one of the participants Alexander Wedderburn – later one of the editors of the vast collected edition of his works – that 'even digging, *rightly done*, is at least as much an art as the mere muscular act of rowing'.[48]

In truth, the project was a long way from becoming a construction case study. If the idea progressed at all, it was probably because of the assistance of Ruskin's long-suffering gardener, David Downs, rather than any management skills on the part of the middle-aged sage. For want of appropriate materials, the road disintegrated shortly after completion and eventually had to be replaced.

The road was not, however, the principal legacy of the project – and perhaps was never intended to be. The 80 or so builders included a roll-call people who went on to do much more, with Ruskin and without him. They included Wedderburn, Collingwood, future secretary and Ruskin biographer, Hardwicke Rawnsley, later leading light of the National Trust and the Lakeland arts movement, and a charismatic young economic historian called Arnold Toynbee. Others went on to become prominent politicians and civil servants, pioneers in education, novelists, barristers and historians.

Later, they were joined by the most improbable navvy of the lot, Oscar Wilde. The image of the young Wilde pushing Ruskin's wheelbarrow, as he claimed he had done, remains a comic one. The playwright and æsthete joined the Hinksey team only for the later, lighter task of paving the road. But Wilde, who had made a beeline for Ruskin when he arrived at Oxford, maintained a deep affection and respect for the writer – even if his pleasure-based æsthetic diverged from the older man's religiously centred perception of art and work. Wilde recalled later how Ruskin had said to the happy-go lucky undergraduates 'that we should be working at something that would do good to other people, at something by which we might show that in all labour there was something noble'.

This intellectual chain gang, much derided at the time for their incapacity for hard labour, formed powerful bonds. Inspired by Ruskin's teachings and his practical call to action, they helped push through economic and social reforms. Their vehicle was the 'university settlement' movement that aimed to bring shelter, food, and education to people suffering in inner cities in Britain and the US and to narrow the gap between an educated elite and the poor and uneducated. These settlements, including Toynbee Hall (named after Arnold, who died at 30) in east London, helped lay the foundations of the British welfare state and the expansion of publicly funded social work and education.

Many of these unlikely navvies were to admit later that they had joined the road-building in part for the opportunity to breakfast with Ruskin, drawn by his fame and exuberant public lectures. In short, for many, it was less about roadworks than networks. But what a network.

Chapter IX

Wealth and Welfare

THERE IS NO WEALTH BUT LIFE. *Life, including all its powers of love, of joy, and
of admiration. That country is the richest which nourishes the greatest numbers of
noble and happy human beings; that man is richest, who, having perfected the
functions of his own life to the utmost, has also the widest helpful influence,
both personal, and by means of his possessions, over the lives of others.*
(Unto This Last)

I

When I started to write about John Ruskin in the Financial
Times in 2009, I got a mixed response. One chief executive of a
large British company contacted me to ask what were the 'lessons
for the modern merchant' from *Unto This Last*, obliging me to
outline them in more detail.[1]

But I also received a few reactions that Ruskin himself would
have found wearily familiar as he channelled his moral outrage
at the state of Britain into political writings in the second half of
his career. 'It strains credulity to suggest the swivel-eyed theories
of Ruskin may seriously have something to offer today,' wrote
one reader from the US. 'I didn't know you were a leftie,' joked
a City financier.

Ruskin did not know he was a leftie either. He was a man

brought up and kept in comfort largely through subsidies from his hard-working father while his parents were alive, and a generous inheritance afterwards – £120,000, the equivalent of some £10m today, plus houses and other properties and paintings worth £10,000.[2]

He could hardly attack wealth without being accused of hypocrisy. Indeed, my fifth lesson from Ruskin for 21st-century CEOs was still 'create wealth'. But there was, and is, that important proviso touched on earlier – that the rich man should use his wealth to influence positively the lives of others.

John James Ruskin had never been entirely comfortable with his son's political and economic pronouncements. Apart from worrying for years that his son was too distracted to finish *Modern Painters*, he knew that John did not really understand business. Ruskin's commentary was fuelled by moral outrage. In the real world, Ruskin was openly self-deprecating about his lack of management and financial acumen, often referring to it later in the chatty updates he sent out via *Fors Clavigera*.

But having buried his father in March 1864, Ruskin stepped up his attempt to perfect his own life and use his possessions to 'exercise the widest possible influence on others'. At the same time, the volume and tone of his attacks on those who were not following his prescription became louder and more intemperate.

The following month, for example, he was in Bradford Town Hall, attacking local industrialists and politicians in a splendidly thunderous lecture published later as 'Traffic' (as in trade), and accusing them of idolising 'the "Goddess of Getting-on," or "Britannia of the Market."'

The locals had invited him to advise on the design of their new wool exchange, but he disabused them of the idea that he was there to offer some diplomatic counsel in the opening words of the lecture: 'You asked me down here among your hills that I might talk to you about this Exchange you are going to build, but... I am going to do nothing of the kind,' he said. Then he rocked them back on their well-padded behinds with this: 'I do not care about this Exchange, – because *you* don't; and because you know perfectly well I cannot make you.'[3]

Echoing passages from *Unto This Last*, he explained that 'it does not follow, because you are general of an army, that you are to take all the treasure, or land, it wins...; neither, because you are king of a nation, that you are to consume all the profits of the nation's work'. The *Bradford Observer*, in a lengthy review, reported – in what may have been an understatement – that 'the lot of much of the audience was that of having expected much and having got more'.

Ruskin did not oppose the making of money, but he deemed it 'physically impossible' for a 'well-educated, intellectual or brave man' to make it his sole aim, as he pointed out in his lecture 'Work' a year later. 'All healthy people like their dinners, but their dinner is not the main object of their lives. So all healthy-minded people like making money – ought to like it, and enjoy the sensation of winning it; but the main object of their life is not money, it is something better than money.'[4]

Ruskin defined wealth by reference to its dark side 'illth'. It may be the most useful word never to have found a permanent place in our vocabulary. Most rich people, he pointed out in *Unto This Last*, were 'no more wealthy than the locks of their own strong boxes' and operated as 'pools of dead water and eddies in a stream'. Rather than providing for the nation (my first Ruskinian lesson for modern merchants), the illthy cause 'various devastation and trouble' with their misused riches.

Modern examples of illth abound: retailer Sir Philip Green's third yacht (and quite probably the first two as well[5]), money gleaned from socially useless finance, returns from landscape-defacing property, polluting factories, illegal drug shipments, and arms sales. All these would have attracted Ruskin's ire.

Illth has continued to expand – in the misselling of financial products, for instance, global growth at the expenses of social welfare, tax evasion and mere self-enrichment. Some modern businesses have started to distinguish between wealth and illth. At the time that I came across *Unto This Last*, for instance, Jeffrey Immelt, then chief executive of General Electric – one of the world's largest industrial and financial holding companies – warned about the 'terrible traits' of 'meanness and greed' that infected the previous generation of business leaders. Rewards for executives, he said, 'became perverted', widening the gap between rich and poor in America. Much good his sermonising did: excessive executive pay remains largely uncurbed and is still one fundamental reason for the lack of trust in business around the world; Immelt stepped down in 2017, under fire for his strategy but with a pension worth an estimated $84 million.

To reduce the risk of illth creeping into his own affairs, Ruskin's first move after inheriting his father's fortune was to start giving money away, handing chunks to relatives. They included his cousin Joan, who as the later co-habitant of Brantwood, with her not-so-diligent husband Arthur Severn and large family, kept a very close eye on how far Ruskin went with his personal finances. One biographer has estimated that within ten years of John James's death, he had given away or spent much of the legacy. By 1884, he was nearly out of money.

In part, this was because of the way in which he chose to deploy his 'possessions'. In 1871 Ruskin used an edition of *Fors Clavigera* to announce he was going to start a fund and put into it a tenth of his remaining fortune not already 'engaged in maintaining art-workmen' or other useful causes. He invited others to do the same.

This was the St George's Fund, which later became the Guild of St George, which still exists today – and of which I am a 'Companion', to the perplexity of friends. They think it sounds like a dodgy patriotic brotherhood. They are half-right. Ruskin's image of St George was underpinned by his own patriotism. It is no coincidence that chose George, patron saint of England, as his guild's symbol, also picking up a strong connection with Venice.

Carpaccio's painting of St George slaying the dragon bowled Ruskin over when he saw it in Venice. The painting – and the rest of the cycle Carpaccio painted – can still be admired in the tiny Scuola di San Giorgio degli Schiavoni. The building is not far off the tourist trail, but easily missed. Inside, in what Ruskin described as 'a little room about the size of the commercial parlour in an old-fashioned English inn', the left-hand wall is dominated by the dimly lit painting.

Ruskin's attention to the detail of the paintings was, as always, acute: in describing them, he advises the use of opera glasses to avoid missing anything. A determined blond George, of saintly beauty, mounted on horseback, has lanced the beast through the jaws and out of the back of its head, ending the ordeal of the town seen in the distance. This is graphically recalled by the gory scattering of the dismembered and rotting bodies of previously sacrificed maidens. Ruskin pointed out that the golden-haired George rode without a helmet, because 'the real difficulty in dragon-fights…is not so much to kill your dragon, as to *see* him in time, it being too probable that he will see you first'.[6] (For Ruskin's copies after Carpaccio see colour plates 16, 17 and 18.)

Ruskin's encounter with Carpaccio's work in Venice, with

which he first seriously engaged in 1869, became entwined with both his philanthropy and his fragile emotional state. George and the dragon became for Ruskin symbolic of his own Christian quest against the reptilian, fiery threat of unfettered industrial capitalism. The Guild was his lance.

It was, and to some extent remains, an unconventional philanthropic enterprise. Ruskin had enormously ambitious plans for it, though in some cases he seemed to be merely playing with ideas that were never likely to be practicable.

Letter 58 of *Fors Clavigera*, written in 1875, proposes a detailed scheme for a St George's coinage, from gold ducats (with the archangel Michael on one side and an Alpine rose – guess why – on the other) to pennies with a St George's shield and an English daisy on the reverse. As for getting hold of the bullion for these coins, this would not pose a problem, he wrote: 'The Englishman, as he is at present educated, takes pride in eating out of a silver plate; and in helping, out of a silver tureen, the richest swindler he can ask to dinner'. Ruskin here was mainly having fun at the expense of the illthy. As he pointed out, the good and generous companions of St George would drink from pewter mugs and eat off china and 'will have no knaves for guests, though often beggars'.

Nearly 150 years later, Ruskin did get a currency of his own, or at least a banknote. His bearded portrait peered out from the 'LD£20' note – commemorating 'Love for the Landscape' – in a special Lake District currency launched as part of a visitor campaign in 2018. The project had a Ruskinian tinge. The notes could be exchanged, one on one, for sterling, but the hope was that tourists would either spend them with local businesses or take them home as souvenirs, with any profit funding local charities. 'A new way of looking at the world; a drive to protect and conserve,' read the legend under Ruskin's name.

Ruskin promised (and fulfilled his promise) to be utterly transparent about his, and its, accounts. He wrote that companions should have 'glass pockets' – quite a good injunction for executives and directors of any organisation.[7] He appointed independent overseers, including Egbert Ryding, the idealistic weaver who owned the Laxey woollen mill in the Isle of Man, and published his own finances in *Fors*.

So radical was the idea of crowdfunding this experiment with a medieval tithe, that it took time to establish. Ruskin's own glorious vision for the fund, which became the Guild in 1877 after much legal wrangling, may have put a few people off. He envisaged myriad helpers 'entirely devoted... first to the manual labour of cultivating pure land, and guiding of pure streams and rain to the places where they are needed; and secondly, together with this manual labour...they are to carry on the thoughtful labour of true education, in themselves, and of others'.[8]

What he imagined was an ambitious omni-charity that spanned – like his own career – everything from sustainable living and environmentalism, to poverty relief, to inspirational arts-based social ventures.

In another early description, in 1871, what was to become the Guild sounds like a combination of the Arts Council, the National Trust, Save the Children and Friends of the Earth. It is no exaggeration to say all of them owe something to his early idealism. He called the fund 'a frank and simple gift to the British people', none of which would yield a return to the giver, and which would be spent 'in dressing the earth and keeping it, – in feeding human lips, – in clothing human bodies, – in kindling human souls'.[9]

Rose La Touche was, by this point, close to becoming a human soul beyond kindling. In 1872, Ruskin was in Venice studying Carpaccio's Saint Ursula, asleep in her lofty 15th-century four-poster bed, and the painter's valiant St George. Rose herself was in England, becoming increasingly desperate, tormented by rumours – ill-explained by various go-betweens – about Ruskin's disastrous marriage to Effie, and unable to reconcile any of them with her own religious fervour. Ruskin noted in his diary a series of Rose-related sicknesses and depressions. In the end, he cut short his Italian visit and hastened back to see her.

Both Rose and Ruskin seemed to be experiencing the extreme highs and lows of their different mental disorders. Finally, Rose cracked, berating Ruskin before heading home to Ireland, where she almost immediately fell seriously ill. Ruskin described 7 September 1872 as 'The Ending Day' in his diary and channelled his agitation into Rose-inspired imagery in contributions to *Fors*, lectures and letters. In one such letter, to the *Pall Mall Gazette*, he took the extraordinary step of declaring that 'one of my best friends has just gone mad; and all the rest say I am mad myself'.[10]

By 1874, Rose was a peripatetic invalid, staying in resorts and nursing homes around England, including Norwood – virtually within sight of Ruskin's London base in Herne Hill. Travelling in Italy again, Ruskin was making bizarre, and sexually frustrated associations between pictures he studied and Rose herself: Botticelli's 'Spring' and Zipporah – Moses' first wife – in the fresco *Youth of Moses* in the Sistine Chapel; Carpaccio's Ursula; and the immortal sculpture of Ilaria di Caretto in Lucca cathedral.

Despite the apparently definitive rupture of 1872, though, Ruskin and Rose were to meet again. In late 1874, he returned to London, where Rose was staying and they passed time together, the terminally ill 27-year-old, and the 55-year-old professor. Outwardly, Ruskin was at the very pinnacle of his powers and magnetism. This was the period when Oxford undergraduates, including Oscar Wilde, were flocking to join their idol's Hinksey road-building crew. Inwardly, he was in despair, sustained only by this odd, melancholic relationship with a dying young woman.

There was one set of final encounters, in early 1875, when Rose returned to England for treatment. From the fact that Ruskin did not keep visiting her, it seems clear she must have become incoherent by this point. He wrote to a friend in late February: 'Poor Rose is entirely broken – like her lover, and what good there may be for either of us must be where Heaven is.'[11]

Within two months, Rose was back in Ireland. She died on 25 May. In a letter, Ruskin wrote, in a typically floral association with the woman he had worshipped for nearly fifteen years, 'I've just heard that my poor little Rose is gone where the hawthorn blossoms go.'[12]

2

The shock and grief of this bereavement were, in time, to un-hinge Ruskin completely. In the short term, and in private, he turned to spiritualism, abandoning his earlier scepticism about séances, in the hope of communicating with Rose. ('Surely I may have my little ghost?', he pleaded with Joan Severn, as he tried to persuade himself that intermediaries had made contact with the dead woman.[13]) In public, he poured his energy into the St George's Fund, whose erratic evolution he described in his *Fors* letters.

He had cultivated Queen's gardens for Rose while she was alive. Now Ruskin was shaping the Guild as an idealised utopia after her death.[14]

His quixotic schemes using the initial St George's Fund were cheerful failures as commercial enterprises. In letter 48, from 1874, he admits that their results 'for the present, are not altogether encouraging'. Agricultural operations were generating three-pounds-ten of hay from a field rented for six pounds. A kitchen garden was likely to yield a dish of strawberries every three years. An attempt to clean a freshwater spring at Carshalton required constant upkeep and vexing communication with the local authority. The road-cleaning experiment near the British Museum had petered out (despite, again, the intervention of loyal 'Downsie', the gardener). Any profit after salaries at a Ruskin-and-St George-funded, and Rose La Touche-inspired tea-shop in Paddington Street, Marylebone, was sucked away in rent and taxes.

It took another three years before the Guild could be properly constituted, at which point Ruskin was known as 'the Master' and addressed as such by his companions. Frankly, you would not have given it much of a chance of survival beyond the first Master's death. The Guild's finances may have been transparent, but they were never strong, and while Ruskin had plenty of followers, they were starting to branch out with their own projects. Few wanted to tie themselves to the idiosyncratic fancies of the elderly genius. Most of his Hinksey road builders from Oxford decided not to join. Ruskin was reduced to trying to press-gang his devoted secretary Collingwood, presenting him with the Guild equivalent of the 'king's shilling' in a half-serious attempt to trick him into Companionship. Collingwood declined.

Even so, the Guild, while an unashamedly visionary project, is still Ruskin's longest lasting social network, binding projects as diverse as Ruskin Land and Sheffield's Ruskin gallery. Ruskin himself used to shrug off the increasingly frequent jibe that he was a utopian. He advised people to 'cut the word out of your dictionary altogether... Things are either possible or impossible,' he wrote. 'If the thing is impossible, you need not trouble yourselves about it; if possible, try for it.' The Guild is active in the modern world and remains full of possibility.

I went to Sidney Sussex College, Cambridge, to visit the current Master, Clive Wilmer, a Ruskin expert and the man responsible for pulling me into the interconnected world of Ruskin devotees. Wilmer is an affable professor of English, and a tireless promoter of Ruskin around the world, with a penchant for fedora and panama hats. He wrote the foreword to the Penguin edition of *Unto This Last* that I bought at Brantwood in 2009 and was my first call when I was exploring some of the ideas for a column about Ruskin's relevance. It is a mark of Wilmer's deft touch in the arcane-sounding role that he quickly invited me to be a companion, binding me into an eclectic network of craftspeople, academics, politicians, poets, activists, writers, farmers and environmentalists.

'John Ruskin's purpose was to make England a happier place,' he told me over coffee in the college's senior common room. 'It was a large statement that couldn't ever have been fulfilled, but what I admired about him was that [he said] that if you have a job in front of your eyes, then just do that. Good work is exemplary.'

This refreshing perspective allows the Guild to ignore or discard the least achievable, or least palatable, parts of what John Ruskin would have wanted from future masters and their companions. The fact that there is no longer a formal tithe – combined with the current master's enthusiastic recruitment policy – may be one reason why the number of companions had grown to 278 by 2018, more than in its entire history, including members from as far afield as Japan, Russia and Australia. 'If you quite literally

Clive Wilmer, Master of the Guild of St George

tried to change England, it would be a disaster or some sort of revolution,' Wilmer said candidly. 'What's much more interesting is to behave in a different way from what we are expected to.'

It does not sound as spectacular as George putting the dragon to death, but there are ways in which Wilmer's Guild is living up to Ruskin's ideals. One is in using rather than hoarding its funds: 'I want to be in charge of an organisation that's interested in spending money, not saving money,' he told me. After he took over as master in 2009, Wilmer booked a hotel room in Sheffield and went to find out what ordinary Sheffield people felt about the collection. Ruskin in his time did the same. He went to meet Henry Swan, his old student from the Working Men's College, in Sheffield, gathering inspiration from local working people for what would become the Museum of St George in Walkley. Wilmer, too, found immense loyalty in the city to Ruskin and the collection. He told me: 'I thought if we started to think more about Sheffield and less about Ruskin, it might be more productive.'

It is easy to miss the collection, now housed in the Millennium gallery, a few minutes' uphill walk from the city's station. But then, it is as impossible to display it all as it was when Swan was around. The cycling vegetarian complained how hard it was to accommodate the varied objects that Ruskin kept sending – plaster casts of architectural details, new canvases, geological and botanical specimens – not to mention his own family who lived on the site. Ruskin argued that there was a power in stuffing the place full of inspirational things, but that was easy to say from the relative spaciousness of Brantwood or Herne Hill.

These days, the greatest virtue of the small Ruskin gallery is that it allows a more intense scrutiny of the objects put on display there. On a tiny scale, it is a version of the fantasy Ruskin outlined in his 1851 pamphlet on Pre-Raphaelitism, according to which 'armies' of artists would chronicle and record the world's natural and human history for public display and use. On the Saturday of Sheffield's Big Draw festival in 2017, children and their parents were engrossed in drawing selected objects from the collection, just as Ruskin envisaged they should.

What is more, he and Swan always saw the museum as being part of its surroundings. Even its original location in Walkley, overlooking the city was supposed to elevate and open the minds of workers usually confined in the polluted industrial centre. The area still offers a good view across the valley, when glimpsed between the suburb's terraced houses. When it snows you might squint and even believe Ruskin's typically exaggerated opinion that it was comparable to the sublime Alpine landscapes he knew.

One of Swan's heirs is Ruth Nutter, the enthusiastic producer of the lively Ruskin-in-Sheffield arts programme. She echoed the same sentiment as Wilmer when I asked her whether eyes ever rolled at the mention of the sage's name in the city. 'I haven't had a single eye roll in four years,' she told me. But at the same time, she pointed out, the events she organises are deliberately not 'all Ruskin all of the time'. They include site-specific art, pop-up museums, walks, and performances. Gerry's Bakery, a few streets away from the original museum site in Walkley, has baked a sourdough 'Ruskin loaf'. You can still buy one if you get there early enough.

Nutter's own background in theatre did not expose her to Ruskin. But in another example of how Ruskinite interconnections can be forged unexpectedly, she was led to his work via Jonathon Porritt, the environmentalist, and a reference to Ruskin's lecture 'The Work of Iron'.

In this great tour de force from 1858, Ruskin explained to a fashionable crowd in Tunbridge Wells how the iron in the water of their local spa literally brought colour to the world. The lecture was a triumph of interconnection. Ruskin, then at the midpoint of his career, linked his wide-ranging love of science, nature and art with his growing concerns about social injustice and heedless accumulation of wealth. 'The definite result of all our modern haste to be rich is assuredly, and constantly, the murder of a certain number of persons by our hands every year,' Ruskin said. 'Therefore, the choice given to every man born into this world is, simply, whether he will be a labourer or an assassin; and that whosoever has not his hand on the Stilt of the plough, has it on the Hilt of the dagger.'[15] Whether or not this pointed metaphor hit its target, a local reporter said Ruskin's talk was received with 'continued and protracted cheering'.[16]

For Nutter, 150 years on, the lecture 'just chimed'. 'I could really see and feel myself the disconnect that Ruskin recognised in Victorian times: the disconnect from work, nature, craftsmanship;

Ruth Nutter

people avoiding the word "beauty".' She realised that a hunger to reconnect with these themes was 'just under the surface'.

As a result, she has tried to take Ruskinian ideas out of the museum and build on a 'latent interest' in the man and his work. She discovered 'there were a lot of people with a similar world view and outlook', that could be underpinned by knowledge of the deep history of Ruskin's involvement in the area. Ruskin's own words, even extracted from their heavy Biblical context, can have a crushing weight these days. Hence the risk of eye-rolling. But Nutter found that 'once you said "This is the way John Ruskin inspired and educated workers in Sheffield", it enriched what they were doing.'

⤚ 3 ⤙

Ruskin's stitching together of wealth and welfare also motivated many of his Oxford road builders. Undergraduate builder Arnold Toynbee is the link to the second stretch of the winding road from Hinksey to the welfare state, paved in 1884.

Toynbee (not to be confused with his nephew of the same name, also an historian) had died suddenly at the age of 30. But he was a charismatic and persuasive young man, who had already poured much energy into efforts to improve living conditions in east London's slums. Inspired, his Oxford friends and other pioneers such as Samuel and Henrietta Barnett pushed ahead with a plan to establish university settlements in deprived city centres, where the ivory towers would meet the slums, for mutual benefit. Toynbee Hall was set up in Whitechapel in Arnold's name.

Here, the interconnections that Ruskin had inspired and encouraged start to become too numerous to count.[17] The Barnetts, for instance, were also leading lights in the establishment of Hampstead Garden Suburb, part of the garden cities movement.[18]

The university settlements, of which Toynbee Hall was one of the first and most enduring, also took inspiration from the determined Octavia Hill, who sparred with Ruskin throughout her career. Hill – another co-founder of the National Trust – had received funding from Ruskin that paid for cottages in Marylebone that Hill rented to the poor. In due course, she also ended up owning the commercially unsuccessful Guild-funded tea-shop nearby. Hill herself took a close interest in the well-being and moral character of the tenants, and by 1877 she was collecting rent from an empire of 3,500 properties.[19] If you are visiting the expensive foodie stalls at Borough Market, just west of London Bridge, break off from selecting organic carrots, walk five minutes south east and you can still see Red Cross Cottages, designed in a Tudor revivalist style for Hill in 1887. They are among 5,000 properties run by Octavia, the not-for-profit affordable housing organisation that runs in a direct line from Ruskin's original philanthropic donation.

Meanwhile, in Manchester, a few minutes' stroll east from the City Art Gallery's collection of pre-Raphaelite paintings – including Ford Madox Brown's *Work* – you can still glimpse, between the new luxury flats and converted warehouse and factory developments, the unpromising foundations of another Ruskin-inspired project in old Ancoats. Cross the busy ring road and on the edge of what was one of Manchester's most notorious Victorian slums, flanked by trendy new coffee bars, smart take-aways, and a shop selling upmarket furniture and furnishings, is a surviving Victorian shop. It has been rebranded The Horsfall in tribute to one of Ruskin's most dedicated followers, Thomas Horsfall, philanthropist and founder of the Ancoats Art Museum, which, like its Walkley equivalent, sought to offer an artistic education and inspiration to working people.

Julie McCarthy was until 2018 creative producer at 42nd Street, a charity that provides therapeutic support for the mental health and wellbeing of local 11- to 25-year-olds, of which The Horsfall is a part. While the charity was wondering what to do with the Victorian property next door to its modernist headquarters, she uncovered the Horsfall connection. Despite knowing little about Horsfall and Ruskin, 'the more I read, the more I realised [the museum] was a very early venture in the arts and health,' she told me.

Just as Ruskin had seen the promise of art and education as an antidote to the dirt and deprivation of Sheffield, Horsfall formed a vision of a similar approach to social reform in Ancoats. Horsfall and the older Ruskin seemed well-matched. They were both sons of wealthy merchants (Horsfall's father was a successful cotton manufacturer), who did not have to work for a living. Both had strong Christian backgrounds, and both had artistic and philanthropic leanings. Ruskin knew Manchester. He had lectured there often and his 1864 talk 'Of Queens' Gardens', was given in aid of a fund for schools in Ancoats.[20]

But there was a drawback. Ruskin hated the city, many times declaring it irredeemable. It was the crucible for the laissez-faire ideas that Ruskin had excoriated in *Unto This Last*. The Free Trade Hall – now a posh hotel – was built in the 1850s on the very site of the Peterloo Massacre in the year of Ruskin's birth, when cavalry charged a rally about parliamentary reform inflicting many casualties. Manchester was also a vast industrial metropolis displaying all the worst byproducts of rapid mechanised expansion. The city 'can produce no good art and no good literature,' Ruskin declared in a typically polemical letter in *Fors*.

Ruskin's antipathy towards the city did not deter Horsfall, who started a long and fruitful correspondence with Ruskin. With the older man's grudging support, and plenty of his own funds, Horsfall developed and then championed a museum in the smoggy heart of Ancoats, half a mile away from the Victorian store that since 2017 has borne his name and kept his – and Ruskin's – ethos alive.

Julie McCarthy explained to me that the Ancoats museum was 'working with local people to give them access to arts and nature to improve their wellbeing'. Similarly, she and 42nd Street wanted to open artistic therapy to young people. In one partnership project, young people from the area were encouraged to create objects that were, informed by Ruskin's concept of 'useful and beautiful': bath 'melts', silk scarves, fridge-magnet plant holders were sold from a vintage caravan in a pop-up gift shop. In another programme, young people worked with an artist on 'creative mindfulness', painting, looking at objects and simply 'mark-making' – like the learners at today's Working Men's College, or Ruskin's worker-students from the 1850s.

Like so many modern projects informed by Ruskin, including the Guild of St George under Clive Wilmer, The Horsfall is selective of the successful experiments of the Victorian past. 'What I've focused on,' said McCarthy, 'is very much that [Thomas] Horsfall was very practical: he took Ruskin's ideas and put them into practice. He himself ignored a lot of what Ruskin said, particularly about Manchester. What he did take was the idea that art and nature could be a force for good for people who were living in the most dire and awful circumstances.'

In Ruskin's day, building a route to social welfare involved hacking through an undergrowth of embryonic public programmes and funding, usually provided locally, and private philanthropy. Thomas Horsfall and his followers plunged into municipal life in the quest to realise their vision but suffered through endless negotiations with the local corporation. Octavia Hill was suspicious of government intervention, and the committees and politicking that it involved, preferring to rely on enthusiastic personal commitment.

A straighter path to the welfare state was found by William Beveridge, a young man with a strong grounding in Ruskin's work and a particular respect for his practical good works and devotion to working people's education. Beveridge arrived at Toynbee Hall in 1903, aged 23, to study the 'causes and cures of poverty'. What he learnt there, particularly about the unintended consequence of the patchwork of welfare schemes at the time, fed into his thinking for the Beveridge report of 1942 and thence to the comprehensive insurance of the welfare state.

It looks a stretch to put Ruskin's name on the roll of honour alongside Beveridge, Attlee and other architects of the welfare state. There is no John Ruskin Memorial Hospital (though King's College Hospital in Denmark Hill, London, has a Ruskin wing). His inspiration is too distant to merit a mention in a recent chunky and exhaustive recent 'biography' of the health service.[21] Without Ruskin, the welfare state would probably still exist. The direction of reform was already set when Ruskin died, and the First and Second World Wars added weight to the campaign for a more secure, state-provided social safety net. Even the Guild's Master, Clive Wilmer, told me Ruskin did not 'say enough to be counted as a founder of the NHS'.

Scholar Stuart Eagles' description of Ruskin as 'a motivator, a starting point, a signpost' hits the mark, however.[22] The evidence is strong that Ruskin's ideas – and even his way of expressing them – inspired and gave impetus and direction to Beveridge and others of similar mind, including the fledgling Labour movement. These politicians and public servants then had the difficult task of translating his emotional appeals into hard practice. This was usually where the idealistic Ruskin stumbled, but his own impracticality did not prevent others fuelling genuine political reform with raw materials he had unearthed.

I have already mentioned that the first intake of Labour MPs valued Ruskin's works, notably *Unto This Last*. The Scottish MP Keir Hardie, first leader of the party, was a self-educated self-improver – the sort who might have attended Ruskin's classes at the Working Men's College. Instead, he studied Ruskin, Carlyle and Morris privately. After Ruskin died, he commented: 'Thus disappeared from earthly view the last of the giants who make the modern British socialist movement possible.'[23]

Clement Attlee, the post-war Labour prime minister who

ultimately enacted Beveridge's proposals – and had himself been secretary at Toynbee Hall – also picked up threads of Ruskin's ideas. Attlee's brother Tom, an aspiring architect, was turned into a socialist by his reading of 'The Nature of Gothic' and his subsequent interest in Morris's work. Tom introduced his younger brother to the texts that, in the words of Attlee's biographer, 'left a lasting imprint on his political lexicon'.[24]

In his maiden speech as a member of parliament in November 1922, Attlee told the Commons: 'We do want an economy campaign, but it must be a true economy campaign – economy in mankind, economy in flesh and blood, economy in the true wealth for the State and of the community, namely, its citizens. That can only be brought about by deliberately taking hold of the purchasing power of the nation, by directing the energies of the nation into the production of necessities for life, and not merely into the production of luxuries or necessities for profit.'

If he had said 'choose wealth, not illth', the echo of Ruskin could not have been much louder.

Ruskin's views may have helped inspire Attlee and other, who found ways to apply Ruskin and Morris's ideas in the real world. But they are virtually invisible in the modern parliamentary Labour party, which is odd. Parts of Ruskin's 'violent Toryism' will never sit well with the harder socialism of Jeremy Corbyn's leadership. Ruskin's horror at the free-market excesses of the early economists, however, his distress at rampant inequality, and his desire to vanquish capitalism, St George-style, might, however, attract the Labour leader and his avowedly Marxist shadow chancellor John McDonnell.

David Drew, Labour member for Stroud, was led to Ruskin's work after completing a PhD on New Labour's rural policy. The assumption that Labour is an urban metropolitan party

David Drew

clearly vexes him. 'I come from a belief that the Labour party was formed as much out of rural socialism as industrial,' he told me at Portcullis House, the parliamentary offices down the road from the Palace of Westminster. 'The worry I always have is that the needs of the urban areas drown out the considerable needs in rural areas,' he said.

Drew later found some ideological underpinning for his views in the work of Ruskin, as a philosopher who 'celebrated the skills, crafts and unique identity of a rural way of life'.[25] Ruskin was important, he told me, for providing 'some of the thinking of what a Labour party might do', such as backing 'the welfare state, dealing with acute poverty, and understanding that the economy wasn't just about profit.' Such goals overlap with the views of long-standing Labour MP Frank Field, now an independent, who is a companion of the Guild.

Even so, Ruskin's name is rarely invoked in Parliament these days. Labour peer Chris Smith – former secretary of state for culture, now master of Pembroke College, Cambridge – discovered

Ruskin's social criticism, like me, when he picked up a copy of *Unto This Last* during a visit to Brantwood. He took away the strong message about the importance of the wealthy and privileged contributing 'to the capital of society, rather than just to the enrichment of individuals'. Yet, he told me, over his decades in parliament he did not recall ever having heard Ruskin's name cited on the floor of the House of Commons or the House of Lords, 'where there are probably more people who've read him'. That, together with the neglect of other thinkers of the democratic left is, he says, is a matter of huge regret.

An online search of Hansard, the official parliamentary record, reveals that Ruskin does occasionally get quoted. (Interestingly, the parliamentarian with the readiest line in Ruskin quotations in recent years is a Conservative: John Hayes, a backbencher who previously served as government minister in departments including energy, education and transport.)

Smith and Drew pointed out, though, that when Ruskin's name is heard, it is usually – again – as one voice in an ill-matched duet with William Morris. And even then, said Drew, 'Ruskin, Morris and [Ruskin follower and early socialist George Bernard] Shaw seem to be historical figures now'. Of the Ruskin-Morris duo, he added, Ruskin did not have 'the same afterglow' as Morris. That is quite a comedown. Shaw himself once wrote that 'extremely revolutionary characters' he had known usually cited Ruskin as more influential than Marx – whose afterglow, radioactive or illuminating depending on your point of view, certainly outshines most 19th-century political thinkers.[26]

Chris Smith points to a wider, lamentable ignorance within Labour of the party's intellectual hinterland. 'There are very clear relevances in Ruskin's writing to some of the major economic and social issues of the day,' he told me, but 'in the modern

Labour party – and this isn't just a Corbyn thing, it's been the case for quite some time – there's too little knowledge of, understanding of, and tribute to the long-standing thinkers of the progressive left, which includes Ruskin'.

Ruskin would not have regretted his absence from the rough and tumble of parliamentary politics, though. For all his ideological outpourings on political and economic questions, his public polemics about economic equality, and his unlikely sympathy for working people, he was no democrat.

In 1852, he proposed a system of universal suffrage in a series of letters to *The Times* that his ultra-Tory father decided should be withheld, to protect his son's reputation. The idea, as outlined by the young critic, was progressive, but a long way from one person, one vote. Explaining to his conservative father that they were not so far apart on the question of universal suffrage, Ruskin made clear his system would involve votes based on property and education, so that 'one man of parts and rank would outweigh in voting a whole shoal of the mob'.[27] On this, unlike on many other points, Ruskin was – depressingly for his modern fans – consistent. 'So far from wishing to give votes to women, I would fain take them away from most men,' he wrote in 1870.[28] Praising Ruskin's overall inspirational influence on economic ideas in a pamphlet issued on the centenary of his birth in 1919, suffragette Edith Morley advised ignoring his 'somewhat perverse attitude on the subject of a fully democratic suffrage'.[29]

Ruskin also had a lofty disdain for party politicians, which bordered on outright disgust for the machinations of those working in the extravagant Gothic surroundings of Charles Barry and Augustus Pugin's Houses of Parliament (the building he wanted demolished). They triggered some of his richest vituperative prose.

In the first letter of *Fors Clavigera*, Ruskin wrote that 'men only associate in parties by sacrificing their opinions, or by having none worth sacrificing; and the effect of party government is always to develop hostilities and hypocrisies, and to extinguish ideas'.[30] In a later letter, he wittily amended Milton's description of Satan as 'darkness visible' in *Paradise Lost* to describe 'parliamentary talk' as 'darkness voluble'.[31] And when asked by a student group to stand for the position of Lord Rector of Glasgow University, he responded, on the issue of party politics, that he cared 'no more [either] for Mr. D'Israeli or Mr Gladstone than for two old bagpipes with the drones going by steam, but that I hate all Liberalism as I do Beelzebub, and that, with Carlyle, I stand, we two alone now in England, for God and the Queen'.[32]

⅏ 5 ⅏

By the late 1870s, overwork was starting to drive Ruskin to the edge of sanity. Sir John Simon, a surgeon and old family friend, wrote to Charles Norton expressing his wonder that Ruskin had 'not broken down long ago'. He warned of 'the utterly spendthrift way in which (with imagination less and less controlled by judgment) he has for these last years been at work with a dozen different irons in the fire – each enough to engage one average man's mind. And his emotions all the while as hard-worked as his intellect – they always blowing the bellows for its furnace'. (In a coincidental forewarning, Ruskin had written to his mother a few years earlier that he had 'a little too many irons in the fire'.)

Ruskin's first phase as Slade Professor had lasted nine years, but in 1877, the great art critic of the 1840s and 1850s, stumbled badly – and with retrospect, inexplicably – when he launched a fierce criticism of the work of James Abbott McNeill Whistler.

He was infuriated by what he saw as the slapdash technique of Whistler's *Nocturne in Black and Gold: Falling Rocket*, a flamboyant depiction of a London firework display against a night sky. Writing in *Fors*, Ruskin called the American painter a 'coxcomb' who had asked 'two hundred guineas for flinging a pot of paint in the public's face'. The publicity-hungry painter sued.

A younger Ruskin would surely have spotted that Whistler, even though he shunned precise truth to nature, was heir to Turner's impressionistic landscapes and Millais' rebellious streak. Ruskin based his disdain for the Whistler painting less on his assessment of the painting's aesthetic qualities than on anger at the lack of work the painter had put into it. His criticism was rooted in the same reasoning that had led him to praise the Pre-Raphaelites two decades earlier. Their habit of 'working everything, down to the most minute detail' seemed to be contradicted by Whistler's wild splatters, which also stood in stark contrast to the highly polished work of Ruskin's old friend Edward Burne-Jones hanging alongside the *Nocturne* in the same exhibition.

'The ancient code of the Artist's honour,' Ruskin wrote in preparation for the trial, is 'that no piece of work should leave his hands, which his diligence could further complete, or his reflection further improve [and the Artist's] fame should be founded on what he had given, not on what he had received.' Whistler had transgressed the code.

Ruskin at first boasted to Burne-Jones that he was looking forward to a public fight. 'It's mere nuts and nectar to me,' he wrote to the artist. By late 1878, though, after the major breakdown Sir John Simon had predicted, he was deemed too ill to attend the libel trial. Letters to Ruskin's doctor, only uncovered a century later, suggest that he was by this point, looking for an excuse to escape the limelight. He asked, in effect, for a doctor's note that would say 'that you think it definitely dangerous for me to face the excitement of a public trial'. The likelihood is that Ruskin had grown dependent on opium – which he called 'tonic'. The letters, suppressed until the 1980s, read like exchanges between an addict and his dealer. 'I miss my tonic dreadfully,' Ruskin wrote, in one 'cold turkey' phase.[33]

The doctor played along, writing to the court that Ruskin was 'altogether unable to take part in any serious business as even slight irritation, annoyance, or excitement upsets him very much'. Whistler, on the other hand, was never going to miss the opportunity for self-promotion. Cross-examined in court about the price-tag of the notorious painting, he admitted the picture had taken him a couple of days to paint. He added the famous line that 'he did not ask 200 guineas for two days' work; he asked it for the knowledge he had gained in the work of a lifetime'.

Whistler won but received derisory damages of a farthing. This was a moral victory to Ruskin, but it was no consolation to the man to whom the whole London art world once bowed. His reputation – his great eye for art – had been impugned. In November 1878, he gave up the Oxford role, telling Henry Liddell, by then dean of Christ Church, that the 'professorship is a farce, if it has no right to condemn as well as to praise'.

Whether you care for Whistler's work or not, with hindsight it is possible to see that it was part of the next wave of painting. This was a wave that Ruskin, albeit inadvertently, had helped launch. Though the critic could not have known this, the pointillist Georges Seurat had read *The Elements of Drawing*, and Claude Monet was reported in 1911 as having said that the manual contained 90 per cent of the theory of impressionist painting.

A more debilitating burden for Ruskin was his growing sense that his ideas had been ignored in the real world, when in fact they were beginning to take root among the young men and women he had inspired, directly or indirectly.

Communities founded by him, or based on his ideas, were springing up – and in some cases thriving. There was Ruskin Land itself. There was Cloughton, near Scarborough, where a plot of land was bought for a Ruskin disciple who refused to work with steam-driven machines. Long gone is Mulberry Cottage in Wavertree, Liverpool, established as a mini-community of self-sufficient Ruskinians. But you can still climb up to the cottages at Dinas Oleu, in Barmouth, which somewhat appalled Ruskin with their ill repair when he paid a visit in 1876. (They were among the first National Trust properties, donated by a Ruskin follower.) You can also see eight Guild properties at Westmill, a lovely Hertfordshire village, and have tea and cake in a Guild-owned tea-shop that appears to be far more commercially successful than the Marylebone version Ruskin oversaw in the 1870s.

But all this time the great thinker's mind was increasingly deranged by memories of, and grief for, Rose, channelled through bizarre imaginings and Rose-tinted inventions.

In 1880, two years after the first bout of insanity, Ruskin self-diagnosed a case of thwarted ambition. He rebuked the doctors for saying he had gone mad through overwork. Not true, he wrote in *Fors*: 'I went mad because nothing came of my work,' a fate he described as a 'humiliation' and an 'enduring calamity'.[34]

His depression is understandable. Despite his limitations as a practical man, Ruskin set great store by the practical achievement of his ambitious goals. Being a 'stimulating power, a disturber of... vulgar modern complacency, an awakener of ideals', in the suffragette Edith Morley's words, would not have satisfied him as a legacy.

It is a fact that what followers such as Octavia Hill had in spades – strong, hands-on management skills – Ruskin himself lacked. It was Hill who pointed out the deficiency, after Ruskin accused her publicly of disparaging his running of the Guild and then chose to wreck a two-decade-long fruitful association with the younger philanthropist by publishing the subsequent exchange of letters in 1877-78. The bickering was the most extreme and most disappointing instance of Ruskin's odd and repeated habit of falling out with sympathetic associates and friends.[35]

Hill wrote, with admirable self-restraint, that she had noticed 'an incapacity in you for management of great practical work, – due, in my opinion, partly to an ideal standard of perfection, which finds it hard to accept *any* limitations in perfection, even temporarily'.[36]

She was right. Ruskin relished imperfection in carving, but he could not stand deviation from his political prescriptions. Her assessment explains why, at least in his lifetime, his ideals were not applied in the practice of governing nations, running economies, or managing organisations.

Meanwhile, the deaths of contemporaries started to crowd in on Ruskin, who had always been especially affected by the passing of friends.

Though his mentor Carlyle was nearly quarter of a century older than Ruskin, his death at 85 in 1881 provoked a typical reaction: Ruskin drew a cross or crucifix in his diary and started to slide towards further mental breakdown at Brantwood.

Joan Severn and Ruskin's assistants began a month-long vigil to prevent his harming himself or others. His behaviour included smashing panes of glass, swearing and issuing absurd and contradictory orders, throwing his food, and entertaining delusions about Rose, Catholic cardinals and the Queen. For close associates used to dealing with Ruskin at his most gentle, generous and intellectually acute, this must have been appalling. Even as his behaviour mellowed, Ruskin remained painfully absent from the real world. 'It almost breaks my heart,' Joan wrote in one letter: 'I'd rather hear him jabbering nonsense – than *seeming* so much himself, & yet so insane.'[37]

What is so evident in hindsight – that Ruskin was beginning to spiral towards his last decade of infantilization and near-silence – was far from obvious at the time even to those inside the exclusion zone that Joan increasingly dominated at Brantwood.

For those outside, he appeared as active as ever. He continued to write letters for *Fors*. The remarkable late-flourishing of the autobiography *Præterita*, written between 1885 and 1889, was yet to come.

So in 1882, after taking a far from restful convalescent tour with his secretary Collingwood to the continent, Ruskin asked to resume his post as Slade professor at Oxford, to start the following year.

This was unwise, to say the least. While Ruskin was still capable of conjuring remarkable insights for his audience, he was also out of touch, out of date and nearly out of his mind.

Not surprisingly, after he had resigned the professorship, his immediate successor had found it impossible to introduce a more modern curriculum at the drawing school without transgressing Ruskin's idiosyncratic principles that there should be no life drawing and no oil painting. The contents of the teaching collection – Standard, Reference, Educational and Rudimentary – had always been somewhat moveable, given the Slade professor's tendency to circulate items between displays at Sheffield and at Whitelands teacher training college in London. In his absence, the collection had disintegrated.

By 1883, when he returned to Oxford, Ruskin cut an eccentric figure even in the tolerant surroundings of eccentric academia. He still sported his old-fashioned frock-coat and blue neck-tie and he had odd habits, such as occasionally riding around the city on the roof of his own carriage. Oxford colleges were opening for women, following Ruskin's encouragement, Oxford students, such as Toynbee, were pursuing the public service that Ruskin's earlier period at the university had helped inspire, and the university was pressing ahead with the endowment of chairs in medicine. The younger Ruskin would have been overjoyed; the older man was less tolerant of such advances.

As the reception to his 'Storm-Cloud' lecture in 1884 suggests, Ruskin was increasingly a show in his own right, and his curious behaviour simply added to the attraction. His lectures were intermittent – he spent long periods in 1883 and 1884 out of Oxford, either at Brantwood, or staying in hotels in London – but they were always packed. Students scrambled onto window-ledges and cupboards to see the university's best-known professor in action. Ruskin had to give some of the talks twice to meet demand.

His popularity had a dangerous double-effect on Ruskin. It gave him licence to say what he wanted about anything. He was a bit like a celebrated film director – Woody Allen, say – given an unlimited budget and total artistic freedom to direct a series of duds. He under-prepared for some of the series, trusting to his improvisational skills, which were on the wane. While he found room to talk about Tintoretto and other favourites in his lectures, he also introduced references to artists he had recently encountered such as Francesca Alexander, Kate Greenaway and Lilias Trotter. His championing of women in the arts was creditable and ahead of its time, but, for all their merits, they were slighter painters than Turner or Tintoretto. The importance he gave to these artists and illustrators seemed to underline how the older Ruskin had lost his critical edge.

The volatile popular reception his lectures excited, also excited the lecturer himself. This led to notorious episodes such as the occasion he danced around the stage flapping his gown to illustrate birds in flight. Even as he struggled to re-establish order over his drawing schools, he was attracting ridicule for his public performances, and not just within Oxford, because the London press made a point of turning up to review and report on the Ruskin show. Sympathetic observers such as Ruskin's future editor Cook, who was reporting for the *Pall Mall Gazette* saw many glimmers of the inspiring, generous, thought-provoking professor of old. He smoothed over some of the oddities and absurdities when reporting on these talks. Plenty of other critics were less forgiving.

In private, Ruskin was a man still tortured, as he would be for the rest of his life, by his grief over Rose. He slept poorly, if at all. By the end of autumn 1884, he was describing himself as 'off the rails altogether'. In March 1885, citing as his reason his fervent opposition to the granting of a licence to the new professor of medicine to experiment on animals, Ruskin angrily resigned the Slade professorship for a second and final time.

The narrowing of Ruskin's life to a close and often closed coterie in Brantwood now accelerated. He was increasingly, and somewhat pathetically, dependent on Joan Severn, who handled his finances (and those of the St George's Fund), ran the household, which was also her own family's home, and even cut his hair.

Ruskin wrote many letters to her – nearly 3,000, and those are just the ones that have been found. From the late 1860s on, he often wrote in a sort of baby-talk. She was 'Doanie', 'mamie' or 'di wee ma'; he was 'Donie', 'Di Pa' or sometimes 'St C', a reminder of the 'St Crumpet' nickname Rose had given to him. Taken out of context, these letters seem an embarrassment, and they may not even be the most awkward ones, since the over-protective Joan destroyed some of the correspondence to protect her ageing cousin's reputation. But the correspondence was also a vivid signal of Ruskin's vulnerability, not only in his weakened final decade and a half, but in the prime of his professional fame and importance.

By confiding some of his concerns to the person closest to him, Ruskin offset the stress of his lofty, formal, public position. In the early part of his first period as a professor at Oxford, for instance, he wrote to Joan in the persona of a nervous, stammering beginner: 'Poo Donie must go to p- p- pro – fess, tings at Oxford – Pease, mamie dee – tell wee Donie, what peepies mean by – pro-fess –? Donie ike <u>doin</u> tings –: he don't know how to pro-fess tings.'[38] Later, the baby-talk became a way to cede control to Joan, as Ruskin slipped into a final childishness.

Like any close family member, Joan and her family also bore the brunt of Ruskin's rages. She was, in the words of academic Rachel Dickinson, both Ruskin's abuser and helper.[39] In 1887-88, he spent a disturbing and disturbed ten months largely alone in Folkestone and nearby Sandgate, staying in guest houses, wandering the beaches, and contributing chapters to *Præterita* by post, because she had in effect banished him from his own home in Brantwood.

As he recovered his health, though, the Severns planned a recuperative trip to the continent. In 1888, under strict orders from Joan not to spend too much money, Ruskin and her husband Arthur, together with the valet Peter Baxter, took the Folkestone-Boulogne ferry. It was to be Ruskin's 35th trip abroad – and his last.

Ruskin set off on the familiar south-easterly route towards Venice, encountering on the way new friends. Detmar Blow, a twenty-something architect-craftsman who went on to design in the Arts and Crafts style, met him in Abbeville and accompanied him as far as Italy on what must have been an odd road trip, and a disturbing one for Blow. Ruskin was clearly unwell. Collingwood, in his biography, skips the detail of the trip but even his generous appraisal describes the thinker's 'best hours' as 'hours of feebleness and depression'. They were marked by increasingly distressed letters to Joan in Brantwood, and fantastical love letters to Kathleen Olander, a young painter he had met in the National Gallery the year before. (In a faint echo of the scandal over Ruskin's proposal to Rose, he had suggested marriage; the borderline-insane correspondence from the continent prompted Kathleen's parents to ban Kathleen from contacting him.)

When the party arrived in Venice, the great, meticulous chronicler of the paradise of cities was unable even to explain to Blow which buildings were which. Others who met him found not the acute, angry critic but a vague old man, 'aged and bent', curiously unmoved by attacks on the city he would previously have condemned. 'He is a strange creature!' archæologist Sir Austen Layard wrote after meeting Ruskin on this final visit to Venice. 'Instead, as I expected, of denouncing Venice and all its works, he says that penny steamers are in no way objectionable, that the restorations of St Mark's have been lovingly and carefully done, that the new capitals of the columns supporting the ducal Palace are so admirably executed that you could not tell them from the old etc. etc.' [40]

Ruskin was racked with delusions of love for Kathleen, deeply troubled by guilt about his mistreatment of Joan, and still haunted by Rose, about whom he had been writing in some of the most

troubled chapters of *Præterita*, drafted during this trip. As his condition deteriorated on the return leg of the journey, Baxter and
Blow (Arthur Severn had already given up and returned home)
rushed Ruskin from Switzerland back to the Hotel Meurice in
Paris, a favourite haunt. Joan, summoned to collect him, found her
cousin trembling and hallucinatory – a broken man who would,
from that point to his death in 1900, never truly be mended.

Joan brought Ruskin home to Brantwood – though in
truth, the expansion both of her family and the property itself,
combined with Ruskin's own confusion, meant it was not like
the 'home' he remembered. Still, somewhat recovered and with
Joan as his amanuensis, he pressed on with what would be the
final chapter of his autobiography. They include a last passage
that alone stakes a claim for John Ruskin as one of the great 19th-
century writers. In it, he looks back to a visit to Siena in 1870,
when he and Charles Norton, his literary executor, walked in the
hills above the city's most famous fountain, the Fontebranda:

> Fonte Branda I last saw with Charles Norton, under the
> same arches where Dante saw it. We drank of it togeth-
> er, and walked together that evening on the hills above,
> where the fireflies among the scented thickets shone fitful-
> ly in the still undarkened air. How they shone! moving like
> fine-broken starlight through the purple leaves. How they
> shone! through the sunset that faded into thunderous night
> as I entered Siena three days before, the white edges of the
> mountainous clouds still lighted from the west, and the
> openly golden sky calm behind the Gate of Siena's heart,
> with its still golden words, "Cor magis tibi Sena pandit,"
> and the fireflies everywhere in sky and cloud rising and
> falling, mixed with the lightning, and more intense than
> the stars.[41]

He dated the chapter, 'Brantwood, June 19, 1889', and called it – in tribute to Joan – 'Joanna's Care'. John Ruskin still had just over ten more years to live, but these were among the very last of his nine million written words.

Chapter X

Finish

No true disciple of mine will ever be a 'Ruskinian'! –
he will follow, not me, but the instincts of his own soul,
and the guidance of its Creator.
(St Mark's Rest)

⟩𝕣⟨ I ⟩𝕣⟨

Somebody has vandalised his upper lip – roughly at the spot where a black Newfoundland dog called Lion nipped him when he was five, leaving a scar. But the side-burned image is still unmistakably that of John Ruskin: an 18-foot tall version of his first self-portrait from 1861.

'It is very sulky but has some qualities about it better than [a] photograph', the 42-year-old writer wrote of the original pencil-and-watercolour image.[1] Stern, and slightly suspicious, in dark grey tie and high collar, this 21st-century picture of the Victorian seer gazes out sidelong from a mural on the old Clark's Furniture building onto a sun-scorched empty parking lot, near the main road through Ruskin, Florida.

'Better than a photograph' sums it up well. This giant-size Ruskin, painted to celebrate the Gulf coast community's centenary in 2008, is so lifelike that if you try to sneak up on the painting using Google's Street View, you will find that the over-zealous pixellators from the technology company have blurred the writer's portrait to guard his privacy and that of the moustachioed men depicted alongside him.

It is an unnecessary precaution. If you did not know the mural was there, you might not find it anyway, even on foot. The painting is hidden from drivers passing through on Route 41, part of the old 'Tamiami Trail' that links Tampa to the north, to Miami, 250 miles south east.

Most travellers do pass through. In fact, I may be the only foreign tourist to have chosen to fly south one November weekend with the sole aim of exploring Ruskin from a room at the 'Caribbean-influenced' Inn at Little Harbor, facing onto Tampa Bay and west across the Gulf towards Mexico.

 2

Ruskin, the place, and Ruskin, the man, never met. Yet at the same time, echoes of John Ruskin and his thinking are everywhere. Ruskin, Florida, is not Venice, or Coniston, or even Herne Hill. None of those places has a drive-in movie theatre with Ruskin's name on it. But Ruskin, Florida, has as much of a claim to be part of Ruskinland as communities with a more direct connection to the prophetic Victorian.

The nearest city is Tampa, with its big-city cultural, sporting and industrial history, ambitions and pride. (Locals like to remind visitors that Centcom, the US military's central command, responsible for US interests in the Middle East and central Asia is housed at nearby MacDill Air Force Base.) Orlando lures tourists to its theme parks a couple of hours north-east. Ruskin is not a city and not really a town, but an 'unincorporated census-designated place', home to just over 17,000 people, some 40 per cent Latino or Hispanic. That percentage may be higher by now. I was told the local elementary school is 90 per cent Hispanic, most eligible for free lunch programmes. In many cases, their parents, grandparents and great-grandparents arrived in the middle of the 20th century to farm the tomatoes for which Ruskin became famous.

The homes here span the full range: from large, detached 'McMansions' and condominium developments, heavily advertised along Route 41, via low-rise, clapboard homes that Gustav Stickley might have recognised, to the occasional mobile home park.

The most desirable real estate fronts the beach or overlooks Ruskin Inlet or the Little Manatee River. The river flows soupily into Tampa Bay near Shell Point, where it meets the inlet. Here in 1539, at what was then the village of Uzita, the conquistador Hernando De Soto is believed to have first made camp in the New World, bringing disease and discord to the indigenous population. Around the same time, a 21-year-old artist called Jacopo Robusti – nicknamed 'the little dyer', or Tintoretto, after his father's job – was making a name for himself in Venice, to be rediscovered by John Ruskin three centuries later.

In the first years of the 20th century, a mixture of the features that attracted the Hispanic explorer and more recent immigrants also appealed to a pioneer and educator called George McAnelly Miller. He is one of the moustachioed faces on the 2008 mural. He was also the man who brought Ruskin's ideals to what was to become Ruskin, Florida. For Miller, this was third time lucky. He bore the scars of ill-fated attempts to establish Ruskinite communities and colleges in Missouri and Illinois. He knew that if you set up too close to a big city, your idealistic goals risked being diluted or destroyed by competition. Set up too far away, or on unpromising land, and the community would wither and die, often in acrimonious circumstances, as had recently happened to Ruskinite settlements in Tennessee and Georgia, brought down by litigation and arson.[2]

This tract of unpromising, relatively isolated, land was a day-long boat-voyage away from Tampa and previously farmed by convicts for turpentine and timber. It seemed to the idealistic but pragmatic Miller to offer the right balance. He and three brothers-in-law, the Dickmans, traded their Missouri holdings for 12,000 acres, complete with scrub palms, cockroachs and rattle-snakes. They established a co-operative 'commongood' society, and in 1908 founded Ruskin, and a new free Ruskin College, subsidised by sale of commongood land. Its students, taught an eclectic curriculum, divided their days equally between work, study and relaxation, and aimed to achieve a happy combination of 'head, heart and hand'. Just over 50 years after Ruskin himself had promoted this triad of intellectual, moral and vocational education in a lecture in drizzly Manchester, it somehow took root next to the mangroves and manatees of Florida.

⤙ 3 ⤚

One devoted British follower of John Ruskin was so animated by his diatribes against railways that he refused to use the postal service in case his letters found their way onto a landscape-despoiling steam train. Instead, this man spent a large part of his life 'tramping about the country delivering letters in person'. But when he finally met Ruskin, the great man told him off, pointing out that he personally preferred 'to abuse railways, but meanwhile to use them'. 'It was grievous to discover that the Master himself was no true Ruskinian,' the chastened disciple recalled.[3]

Few if any people would now claim to be 'true Ruskinians', and if they did, it would be hard to know how to define what being a true Ruskinian involves. Apart from dressing up, donning side-burns and a sky-blue stock, and putting on an entirely historical Ruskin one-man show, it is difficult to see how anyone could swallow and regurgitate the ideals, contradictions and ambitions of Ruskin whole.

The image John Ruskin projects onto the 21st century is still one of forbidding oddness. The popular reaction is best summed up by 'The William Morris Years', an episode of *Peep Show*, the sitcom about a dysfunctional friendship between Mark (played by David Mitchell) and Jez (Robert Webb), in which even nerdy Mark baulks at watching a Ruskin documentary.

Ruskinland itself can seem a strange place, populated by academics and the occasional oddball. Yet it exists – a network of influences and interests linking people, places and practices – and it flourishes. In areas as diverse as furniture design, mental health therapy, conservation and ecology, many people, some unknowingly, are energetically taking forward ideas that owe a lot to what Ruskin thought, wrote and did.

And then there are the practices and policies – the living wage, pay ratios, the future of the National Health Service, pensions, purposeful and meaningful work – where the distance from the source has erased Ruskin, but the roots can still be traced back to ideas of which he was one of the first and most prominent and vocal advocates.

Some of the connections and influences of Ruskin stretch the mind. A bibliography compiled by the Ruskin Library is 112 pages long and includes articles about Ruskin's influence on, among others, black art and culture, the London Underground and Pierre de Coubertin, founder of the modern Olympic games.[4] One modern scholar warns against the temptation, in searching for influence, of finding 'the shadow of your subject lurking in every doorway'.[5] I plead guilty. It is true that Ruskin wrote so much, and ranged across so much territory, that it is easy to presume that modern thinking that correlates with his ideas was somehow caused by them. But once I started to read more by and about him, I found myself adjusting my own approach to exploring the shadows.

I started to look up, rather than down – taking in the architectural style of buildings. Look at the first floor of the town centre, where the chance of being distracted by the ever-changing, attention-grabbling shop fronts is less. Then even higher, at the shape of mountains and clouds. I picked up a pencil and sketchpad for the first time in years, inspired by Ruskin's abundant but sometimes extraordinarily demanding rules on draughtsmanship, in an effort to understand better what I was looking at by trying to draw it.

I may well have invented a few sightings of Ruskin, and, again, I am certainly guilty of the 'journalistic' sin of expressing his importance 'in terms of "influence" and "relevance"'.[6] Finding modern parallels with the predictions of dead prophets can do no harm, though as Ruth Nutter of the Ruskin-in-Sheffield programme pointed out to me, a connection with the past may even help people realise that they are not alone as they explore radical solutions to important contemporary problems.

There are plenty of risks in allowing yourself to be led too closely by Ruskin. As an avid reader of the Molesworth books, set in the terrible prep school St Custard's, I can see something of the unworldly parts of Ruskin in Basil Fotherington-Thomas, the effete sissy that Molesworth detests, skipping to lessons singing 'Hullo clouds, hullo sky!'

One friend, who underwent an epiphany as a young man on reading Kenneth Clark's *Ruskin Today* – a selection of Ruskin's writing that is still one of the best out there – warned me before I started the project that it might drive me mad. Halfway through writing the book, I met him again for a coffee. He verified that I had not gone insane. Then he recalled how sticking too closely to the preachy perfectionism of his idol had led him into a phase where he now realises he was priggishly unbearable. It is how Ruskin himself must have sometimes come across to those who didn't know him. It is certainly how his most superior lectures now appear to the modern reader. That contemporary newspaper reviewer's description of reading *Unto This Last* – being 'preached to death by a mad governess' – still sums up many people's first reaction to his work. It was mine, too. When I was asked to turn my thoughts about *Unto This Last*'s modern relevance into an introduction to the Pallas Athene edition of the book, the publisher pointed out that my first draft said nothing about what I thought of the prose itself.

'For almost fifty years, to read Ruskin was accepted as proof of the possession of a soul,' Clark wrote in his rousing introduction to *Ruskin Today*. Reading Ruskin introduced Clark to the Gothic, to Turner, and to art criticism in general, but, more importantly, Ruskin's example made him realise just how vital it was to spread ideas of art and beauty beyond the kind of elite into which he had been born. His magisterial television documentary series *Civilisation* – which starts with the words 'Ruskin said…' – was the highest expression of this conviction, transferred to the most popular and widely consumed form of modern entertainment.[7]

Clark was also, however, a Ruskin sceptic. He would not have referred to himself as a disciple. He may have lamented the decline in Ruskin's reputation – 'No other writer, perhaps, has suffered so great a fall' – but he understood why it had happened. A little like Ruskin himself, who began his lofty claims for the Pre-Raphaelite school with some sharp criticism of their work, Clark points out that his hero's Biblical quotations and allusions are now 'embarrassing and incredible' and his 'inability to concentrate… reduces his reader to a kind of hysterical despair'. He also attributes the discarding of Ruskin in the first half of the 20th century to a 'mistrust of eloquence', too often used to justify the unjustifiable. 'Personally I believe that posterity will continue to find a great many of these 39 volumes unreadable,' he says, referring to the collected works, edited by Cook and Wedderburn. With friends like that…

As the story about the mail-shunning, train-hating follower suggests, even Ruskin himself was suspicious about disciples who turned their devotion into hero-worship. From his prose style to his missionary zeal, Ruskin makes for an awkward and demanding role model. Even where Ruskin's name is above the door, his legacy is often partial, selective and occasionally non-existent. His fierce conviction that his ideas had to be combined with his high Anglican spiritual beliefs is only the most obvious example of how he would have hated some of the modern echoes of his voice.

In an odd way, Ruskin's legacy became a victim of his own success in raising awareness of the worst excesses of the industrial revolution. Within a few years of his death, reformers had tackled many of the most significant abuses that he addressed in stentorian fashion from the middle of the 19th century. On the centenary of his birth in 1919, his most devoted follower John Howard

Whitehouse listed policies Ruskin had already influenced. They included areas relating to land reforms, slum management, tax, unemployment, sweatshops, care of the aged poor, working hours and conditions, educational reform and city planning.

It was also clear by 1919, though, that the First World War had blasted an uncrossable chasm between the ideas that inspired the parents of those soldiers who perished or were traumatised by the conflict and their offspring. The children of the early 20th century saw in Ruskin and his peers only smug hypocrisy and blindness to impending disaster. Then, by the middle of the century, the revulsion at some of Ruskin's views, for example on the role of women – mixed with the over-reaction to his sexual (in)activity – had helped apply an off-putting sticky layer to his best work. As the bicentenary of his birth approached, his racial prejudices added further to reasons not to try even to touch his legacy.

Ruskin was, though, as one wit has described him, 'an encyclopedia with sideburns'.[8] The sideburns should not deter us from choosing the best ideas from the treasury housed between them. He was also a person who sought to engage with others – and still can, as a glance at recent comments in Brantwood's visitors' book suggests: 'A wonderful caring man – an inspiration to us all', 'Ruskin speaks [to] today's capitalism…. His message is for today too'; 'Loved the visit. Made me think of my own life'; 'Room for a Ruskinista movement!'

 4

Arthur 'Mac' Miller, grandson of George McAnelly Miller, is an emeritus professor of literature, now in his eighties. Over a long

The author and Mac

life lived in the Florida sunshine, he has developed a deep, freck-led tan and an immunity to the late-season mosquitoes that seem to regard me as a juicy target.

Mac lives in the house built by the third man celebrated in the mural – Ruskin's other founder, 'Captain' A. P. Dickman. It is one of a few architectural remnants of the original Ruskinite set-tlement. A short drive away is the house of AP's sister, and Mac's grandmother Adaline. Built in 1912, and home to the Ruskin Woman's Club since 1940, it is modelled – incongruously for this part of the world – on a picture of a Swiss chalet that Ruskin admired and wrote about in his first published article, *The Poetry of Architecture*.

The Millers were in some senses typical of the diaspora of Ruskinites who fanned out across Britain and the US in the late 19th century. George McAnelly Miller was a Chicago lawyer, first called on to help extricate Ruskinite utopians in Tennessee from their legal problems.

As far as anybody knows, the Millers never corresponded with Ruskin, but they did try to reach him after his death – in séances that Mac's father attended as a teenager in the Miller house. Mac tried to show me the 'Quiet Room', where the family once wielded a Ouija board, but it is now a bathroom for a rental unit and was off-limits. In any case, the attempts to communicate with the shade of the man who inspired the Ruskinites appear to have been no more successful than the spiritualist sessions that Ruskin himself took part in when he was trying to make contact with Rose La Touche in the 1870s.

Ruskin's teachings provide a useful framework on which to hang educational ambitions. Ruskin College, Oxford, established as Ruskin Hall in 1899, is probably the best known of the institutions that still carries Ruskin's name. It was certainly named after John Ruskin and still carries on a noble Ruskinian tradition of educating adults with few or no qualifications. But its founders have more direct links to its Floridian namesake, and its Missouri and Illinois predecessors. Walter Vrooman, one of Ruskin Hall's founders, at first backed Missouri's Ruskin College, and provided some funding.

In Florida, the First World War, a devastating fire in 1918, and the death of George himself the next year, ultimately did for the Millers' third Ruskin College experiment. The Commongood Society, however, continued until 1967 when descendants of the Dickmans and Millers ceded their 'common' lands to the county and local entrepreneurs, who dredged the inlet and a swath of Tampa Bay littoral land to build new mansions on the waterfront. The entrepreneurial instincts of the Dickmans – in real estate and agribusiness, two areas that Ruskin himself deplored – were both the making and unmaking of Ruskin, Florida.

These days, it is hard to tell which direction the community is going. It sits in an uncertain middle ground. Development is advancing, but so is inequality. As a non-incorporated community, there is no obvious limit to the number of new blocks of land that can be put up for sale for homes for commuters and retired people. 'We grew tomatoes and became the "Salad Bowl of America",' says Mac, ruefully, on a visit to the local cemetery, where Dickmans and Millers lie side by side. 'Now we grow sub-divisions.'

Ruskin himself – that 'violent Tory of the old school' – has a strange and distorted reputation here. In *South County*, a short 2013 film about the area, Major Ronald Hartley, Hillsborough County sheriff, now retired, sums it up: 'Ruskin was basically a socialist and this was going to be a utopia here and everybody was going to all get along and sing "Kumbaya" and hang around, eat s'mores by the fire and stuff. That's how Ruskin got started.'[9]

To many, communal equals 'communist', explains Melody Jameson, a local journalist and writer. Another resident tells me she believes the 2008 mural was defaced because the writer was a left-winger.

'If you took a hundred people and asked them if they knew about the history of the community or had read a biography of John Ruskin, two would say yes,' says Jameson, over a grilled fish sandwich with me and Mac at The Dog House open-air barbeque stop near the Commongood Park. Even that could be an exaggeration.

But you do not have to dig far to find some useful echoes of Ruskin, the thinker, in Ruskin the place.

There is still a Carlyle Road on the north bank of Ruskin Inlet (opposite a Dickman Drive to the south). Until recently, a large billboard south of the town advertised Ruskin as a 'Progressive Community'.

Mac describes Ruskin in its early days as a 'dynamic melding' of commongood aspirations and the realities of private ownership; later, in a tussle between capitalism and co-operative ownership, he says capitalism came out on top. In his public presentations, he illustrates the idea of an 'intentional community' by referring to today's gated communities or condominium developments, with their mutually agreed rules and guidelines on behaviour.

Jameson adds: 'People here appreciate the value of work; they have some appreciation of the agrarian lifestyle; there's an appreciation at least in philosophy of higher formal education. There would be a cross-match with local appreciation of neighbour helping neighbour.' She says that 'across the population there's little recognition of the value of art.'

There is some, though. Bruce Marsh is a California-born artist who settled in the area. In his work, he indulges a Ruskin-like obsession with cloud formations and a distinctly unRuskinian taste for painting deserted traffic intersections in oils. Without referencing the man, Marsh says that his work is about 'moving people to relook at the world… to think again about their perceptual processes – about the way they see'.[10]

In 2008, the centenary of Ruskin's foundation, Marsh helped coordinate the local version of the Big Draw Festival, staged out of Firehouse Cultural Center, just off the Tamiami Trail and next to the local library and pawnshop. In the repurposed fire station, where a small portrait of Ruskin hangs ('If you go to the bathroom, you see it,' grumbles Mac Miller), locals are working on ways to build a bigger cultural community, with plans to expand the campus and perhaps even link the library via a bridge over Ruskin Inlet.

From the Firehouse car park, you can see the edge of the 2008 mural in the distance. The stocky, muscular Boston-raised artist

Mike Parker

who rallied a group of about twenty volunteers to work on the project is Mike Parker. He also teaches two classes at the community college and discussed his work with me in a workshop full of customised bicycles reclaimed for his next project.

Parker did not know much about Ruskin himself, but as he started researching the mural, 'just the fact that [Miller and Dickman] started a community based on someone they had never met – that blew me away [and] the type of community we live in now is a direct result of their foresight'.

There are echoes here in the warm Florida sunshine of the spirit that drove Ruskin to teach at the Working Men's College, to launch the Hinksey road-building project, to popularise drawing as a way of understanding the world better, and to campaign for improvements in working conditions. The interconnections, when you start to look, are everywhere.

Parker confirms that Ruskin is a place in flux. Behind the Dollar General discount store, he says, migrants live in a tractor-trailer, and this place on the old Tamiami Trail is also a stop on a long journey from Mexico to Ruskin and, if things don't work out for the fruit- and vegetable-pickers, back again. 'This community has changed drastically,' he says. 'There's just an influx of kids and there's nothing to do here.' As for the theory that the John Ruskin in the mural lost his upper lip to locals suspicious of his lefty leanings, Parker dismisses it: 'It was probably just kids making mischief.'

What is certain is that if John Ruskin did unexpectedly roll into Ruskin, Florida, in his double brougham, he would shun the illthy residents in their waterfront McMansions. As Melody Jameson, puts it, 'if he came to Ruskin today, he might say "Let's organise the tomato-pickers".'

🙖 5 🙖

Ruskin – who was a great admirer of 'finish' in a painting – admitted he was bad at finishing things himself: drawings, books, and, ultimately, his over-ambitious plans to reform England and the world.

Partly, this was because Ruskin's mind bubbled over with so many ideas that it would have required several lifetimes – even the workaholic lifetimes of Ruskin in his prime – to achieve, or even begin, all of them.

Biographer Tim Hilton laments the absence of what Ruskin called his 'unwritten books in my brain', which the prolific sage planned or hoped to write but never got round to. They would have covered such subjects as 'agates and basalts, Apolline myths,... Carlyle's descriptions of people... clouds,...seagulls and... the proper education of working girls' as well as biographies of Scott, Pope and David, a *Stones of Verona*, 'examinations of French and Swiss landscape' and an 'interpretation of the Homeric poems'.[11]

I have occasionally wished – for all the pleasure of dipping into Ruskin's voluminous output – that he had slowed down. I often wish, too, for signs of an editor who could have challenged his worst excesses, or at least cut them short, as the novelist Thackeray did in keeping *Unto This Last* to a manageable length.

Instead, Ruskin developed, at the end of his writing life, the epistolary form that lent itself to endless publication. *Fors Clavigera* could have lasted as long as he, or his funds, did. Ruskin did start planning an index, suggesting that he was also thinking of how to end it, but this was probably because he recognised he was growing short of energy rather than that he was short of ideas.

The writing and content of his idiosyncratic memoir *Præterita* overlapped with *Fors*. He repeated some of the early public letters more or less verbatim in its opening chapters. It too appeared episode by episode, and petered out in 1889, rather than concluding neatly, as Ruskin had anticipated. The old man could probably have continued dictating it, if only he had found an amanuensis more tolerant than his ward-turned-nurse Joan Severn.

Within five or six years, though, after a series of strokes and more, largely unchronicled, episodes of mental illness, Ruskin – once the great 19th-century master of the paragraph-long, semi-coloned sentence, polished for publication – was struggling to string a few coherent words together. 'Alas! He had nothing but monosyllables,' said one person who met him a few years before his death.[12]

Sometimes, as I stumbled through the foothills of Ruskin scholarship, meeting en route scores of fascinating, different people who, like me, were moved, inspired, infuriated or, occasionally, appalled by Ruskin's work, I wondered what I had begun and how I would finish.

As he grew older, Ruskin became increasingly frustrated that his words were not being heeded, even as he realised that his work would never be done. Ruskin's inability to finish is rather apt, though.

Nobody needs Ruskin to tell them what to do any longer. But as Brantwood's Howard Hull told me, if an idea 'has a vitality of its own, it will continue to travel and that may mean it loses touch with the person from whom it came'.

In any case, rather than fixating on the stereotypical bewhiskered sage it is more interesting to look for ways in which John Ruskin differs from the popular image of 'some dreary old hasbeen with a beard'.

Academic Marcus Waithe said that in the early 2000s his students tended to criticise Ruskin for romanticising manual labour ('What about the burger flippers?' was a typical question – to which I suppose Ruskin's answer would have been that in his ideal society, nobody would want to eat burgers). Now, they have a more positive attitude – focusing on the writer's version of ethical capitalism but misunderstanding the conservative Ruskin as a leftie. In other words, the students make the same mistake the ex-sheriff of Hillsborough County in Florida did, except coming from the other direction.

David Peacock was obliged to take a crash course in Ruskin's legacy, and its relevance, in 1985, when he took over as principal of Whitelands College, the teacher training school that Ruskin endorsed in the 1870s. He sums it up like this: 'There's a name that's known but what does he stand for and where is his influence? No doubt it's there, in the National Trust, in the environment, in the welfare state, in his æsthetics. But it's a substratum.'

Yet the challenges Ruskin addressed keep recurring, and, as they do, it is essential to bring to the surface the sorts of solutions that lie in that substratum, a good geological term for the legacy

of a natural-born geologist, and to explore the deep connections that link Ruskinland, from Venice's Grand Canal to Florida's
Little Manatee River. It does not matter that people pick 'their'
Ruskin from the many contradictory models available. As each
generation comes to Ruskin fresh, selecting those parts of his
output that seem most appropriate to fuel or guide their own
projects and ideas, it becomes ever clearer that the work he began
is never-ending and endlessly relevant.

Wearily wrapping up the fifth volume of *Modern Painters* in
1860, Ruskin wrote this: 'Looking back over what I have written,
I find that I have only now the power of ending this work, – it
being time that it should end, but not of concluding it; for it has
led me into fields of infinite inquiry where it is only possible to
break off with such imperfect result as may, at any given moment,
have been attained.'

Acknowledgments

Dozens of people devoted time to speaking to me for this book. Many are cited in the preceding pages, but a few deserve special additional mention here.

Clive Wilmer helped me flesh out the first *Financial Times* column I wrote about Ruskin's social and economic thinking in 2009 and drew me into the Ruskin world with his enthusiasm. Stuart Eagles and Stephen Wildman were generous with their help and ideas at the outset of my research for the book, when I knew even less than I know now. Robert Hewison has offered wise advice throughout the project and agreed to read and critique a draft of the book, as did David Barrie, who has been a genial source of support and wise counsel. Clive Hayward, David Bodanis, Justin Hunt and Isabel Berwick also read drafts and offered invaluable suggestions for improvement. Any errors of fact or tone are mine, of course.

I have benefited immensely from membership of the loose network of Ruskin supporters who gather under the umbrella of Ruskin To-Day, as Companions of the Guild of St George, or as trustees of the Ruskin Foundation, under its tireless chair Jacqueline Whiteside. Howard and Pamela Hull shared their warm enthusiasm for, and knowledge of, Ruskin and Brantwood. Jim Dearden, Jim Spates, Rachel Dickinson, Sara Atwood, Paul Dawson, Nicholas Friend and Sarah Quill all shared ideas from their own research.

At Lancaster University, Sandra Kemp brought new perspective to my thinking on Ruskin, as did Ian Gregory, Andy Tate and Alan Davis, while Diane Tyler, Jen Shepherd and the team at the Ruskin Library helped direct my delving into the vast collection there. Martin Hewitt at Anglia Ruskin University, Gilly King at Whitelands College, Maria Rosenthal at the Working Men's College, Eleanor Sier at Toynbee Hall, and Alistair Burtenshaw at the Watts Gallery helped fill gaps in my knowledge.

The constructive criticism of Arvon Foundation tutors Lois Pryce and Ian Marchant (my 'ideal reader') was invaluable at a key moment in the writing of the book, as was the warm and continuing support of the other writers on the same tutored retreat at The Hurst in Shropshire. David Waller and Tim Harford provided useful advice on next steps as I tried to bring the book towards publication, while my FT colleagues showed unfailing interest in my eccentric sideline.

In Florida, Georgia Vahue, executive director of Ruskin's Firehouse Cultural Center, her husband Milt, and their friends made me welcome. Arthur 'Mac' Miller was an engaging guide and a rich source of historical knowledge, while Mike Parker provided the cover image and further encouragement as I sought to make the connection between Ruskin the man and Ruskin the place.

I should also mention John Alford and Phil Woolley who taught me art and art history when I was at Shrewsbury School and led the school trip to Florence and Venice in 1982w that provided my first direct experience of some of the extraordinary works of art and architecture that excited Ruskin.

At Peters Fraser Dunlop, my agent Caroline Michel first expressed interest in the seed of an idea of a book exploring Ruskin's influence on the modern world, and persisted until I produced a proposal, which was shaped into the solid foundation of this book with the help of Tim Binding. At Pallas Athene, Alexander Fyjis-Walker endured the occasional nagging of a journalist more used to short lead times and instant publication, patiently but swiftly shaping the text and illustrations, with able support from Anaïs Métais and Patrick Davies.

Finally, I owe my mother, Judy, a huge debt of gratitude for so many things, but in particular for indirectly sparking my interest in Ruskin through her enthusiasm for Arts and Crafts, as well as for helping me frame my thoughts about Ruskin's life and influence in many enjoyable conversations. I could not have achieved what I have achieved without her support and that of my late father, Tim, and my brother Jeremy.

Unlike John Ruskin, I hold down a paid job, so I had to carry out most of the work on this book in my spare time. Inevitably, that meant borrowing from holidays, weekends and other time that I should really have spent with my family. My first and last thanks must go to my wife Jimena, and children Tomás and Ana, for their patience, love and encouragement.

Further reading

Only 2,062 copies of the 39-volume Cook and Wedderburn Library Edition of John Ruskin's *Complete Works* were produced, issued between 1903 and 1912, when the 689-page index appeared ('A, the letter, ornamental Greek, to be copied' to 'Zwingli, friar Samson repulsed by'). A complete set on the shelves may be the sign of a reader who is a 'true Ruskinian', or of his or her perplexed descendants, but I have found the online edition, hosted by Lancaster University's Ruskin Library, a useful and searchable short-cut: www.lancaster.ac.uk/ruskin-library/the-complete-works-of-john-ruskin.

In the Notes that follow, I have referred to the Library Edition of the *Complete Works* as LE, followed by the volume and page number, adding the name of the lecture and/or collection of lectures for any reader who wants to track down a separate published edition.

The Ruskin Library's website also features a meticulously annotated electronic edition of the first volume of *Modern Painters* and a facsimile and transcript of Ruskin's Venice notebooks from 1849-50.

From my Ruskin bookshelf, I have also referred to the following published works by Ruskin:

Complete Works (ebook, Delphi Classics, 2014) – this version is unfortunately marred by the way Ruskin's sometimes lengthy footnotes appear in the main text.

The Crown of Wild Olive (George Allen & Sons, 1909)

The Elements of Drawing (Dover Publications, 1909)

Præterita, ed. Francis O'Gorman (Oxford World's Classics, 2012)

Selected Writings, ed. Dinah Birch (Oxford World's Classics, 2009)

Unto This Last and Other Writings, ed. Clive Wilmer (Penguin Classics, 1985)

Unto This Last, introduction by Andrew Hill (Pallas Athene, 2010)

EXHIBITION CATALOGUES

Tim Barringer, Jason Rosenfeld, Alison Smith, *Pre-Raphaelites: Victorian Avant-Garde* (Tate Publishing, 2012)

Christopher Newall and others, *John Ruskin: Artist and Observer* (Paul Holberton Publishing, 2014 – the excellent catalogue of the fine 2014 exhibition of Ruskin's work)

LIVES OF RUSKIN

If you can be bothered, reading the introductions to the 39 volumes in Cook and Wedderburn's edition will give you a detailed insight into Ruskin's life. It is coloured by the editors' advocacy for the man and was written within a decade of his death, before much other material had been researched or even read.

Of more recent biographies, I have particularly relied on Tim Hilton's huge and very fine *John Ruskin* (Yale University Press), now available in one volume, though I cite from the two titles, published 15 years apart, *The Early Years* (1985) and *The Later Years* (2000) – 'Hilton I' and 'Hilton II' in the Notes.

I also reference John Batchelor's *John Ruskin: No Wealth But*

Life (Chatto & Windus, 2000), Kevin Jackson's *The Worlds of John Ruskin* (Pallas Athene, 2009), the best-illustrated recent life of Ruskin, and James Dearden's endlessly fascinating *John Ruskin: A Life in Pictures* (Sheffield Academic Press, 1999), which traces Ruskin's life through the many paintings, caricatures and photographs of the writer.

I have also enjoyed Robert Hewison's short Life for the Dictionary of National Biography, available as an ebook, *John Ruskin*, in Oxford University Press's *Very Interesting People* series (2007).

Ruskin's first biographer was W. G. Collingwood. His *Life of John Ruskin* is included in the Delphi Classics ebook of Ruskin's *Complete Works*.

A SELECTION OF BOOKS ABOUT RUSKIN

Robert Brownell, *Marriage of Inconvenience* (Pallas Athene, 2013)

Suzanne Fagence Cooper, *Effie Gray: The Passionate Lives of Effie Gray, Ruskin and Millais* (Gerald Duckworth, 2012)

Stuart Eagles, *After Ruskin: The Social and Political Legacies of a Victorian Prophet, 1870–1920* (Oxford University Press, 2011)

Sara E. Haslam, *John Ruskin and the Lakeland Arts Revival, 1880–1920* (Merton Priory Press, 2004)

Robert Hewison (ed.), *'There is No Wealth but Life': Ruskin in the 21st Century* (Ruskin Foundation, 2006)

Kevin Jackson and Hunt Emerson, *Bloke's Progress* (Knockabout, 2018)

Francis O'Gorman (ed.), *The Cambridge Companion to John Ruskin* (Cambridge University Press, 2015)

Sarah Quill, *Ruskin's Venice: The Stones Revisited* (Lund Humpries, 2018) – a wonderful selection from *The Stones of Venice* with Quill's photographs

Scholar Jim Spates has built a rich, ever-expanding online introduction to Ruskin, including a vast treasury of quotations, as well as reflections on Ruskin's place in the modern world, called *Why Ruskin?* at https://whyruskin.wordpress.com/. Enthusiasts can subscribe for updates via email.

Beyond further reading, there is plenty to see and explore at Brantwood – the best place to gain a sense of how Ruskin lived, particularly in his later years – and in Coniston itself, at the Ruskin Museum, the village's permanent memorial to the writer. Elements of the Ruskin collection brought together initially by John Howard Whitehouse are usually on display at Brantwood or at the Ruskin Library at Lancaster University. Treasures from the Guild of St George's collection, supplied by Ruskin himself to St George's Museum in Walkley, are always on display at Sheffield's Millennium Gallery.

Illustrations

and pen and ink over graphite on wove paper, with some scratching out. Ashmolean Museum

Plate 6: *Rocks in Unrest*, c. 1857, 18.5 x 30.8 cm, watercolour, point of brush, scratching out, over pencil. Inscribed 'Drawn from my favourite St. Gothard, for Mod. Painters 4th vol. J. Ruskin Brantwood. 23rd Aug. 86.' Morgan Library and Museum

Plate 7: *Trees in a Lane*, 1847, 44.7 x 57.5 cm, pen and ink on paper. Ruskin Foundation/Google Arts

Plate 8: *St Sauveur, Caen*, 1848, 50 x 36 cm, pencil and wash. Ruskin Foundation/Google Arts

Plate 9: *Ca d'Oro*, 1845, 33 x 47.6 cm, pencil, watercolour and bodycolour. Ruskin Foundation/Google Arts

Plate 10: Architectural Notebook, 'Door Book', 1849/1850, 19.5 x 12.4 cm (closed), pencil, black ink and watercolour. Ruskin Foundation/Google Arts

Plate 11: *Doge's Palace, Venice: 36th Capital*, 1849/1852, 22.3 x 23.5 cm, pencil, black ink and ink wash. Ruskin Foundation/Google Arts

Plate 12: *The Chateau des Rubins at Sallanches, with the Aiguille des Varens Beyond*, 1860, 21.5 x 19.3 cm, watercolour and gouache, over an underdrawing in pencil, on faded blue paper. Sothebys.com

Plate 13: *Vineyard Walk, Lucca*, 1874, 35.5 x 42.3 cm, watercolour, bodycolour and pencil. Ruskin Foundation/Google Arts

Plate 14: *A Seed of the Common Rush*, 1872, 18.5 x 13 cm, pen and brown ink and watercolour over pencil, heightened with bodycolour. Sothebys.com

Plate 15: *Dawn, Coniston*, 1873, 23.2 x 35.7 cm, watercolour, Abbot Hall Art Gallery and Museum/ Google Arts

Plate 16: *Cloud effect over Coniston Old Man*, c. 1880, 24.9 x 39.1 cm, pencil and watercolour on paper. Ruskin Foundation/Google Arts

Plate 17: 'The Dream of St Ursula', after Carpaccio, 1876, 29.4 x 27.7 cm, watercolour and bodycolour over graphite on wove paper; retouched photograph by David Gould, c. 1890, Collection of the Guild of St George, Museums Sheffield

Plate 18: 'St George and the Dragon', after Carpaccio, 1872, 18.2 x 46.2 cm, sepia, pencil and ink with white highlights on paper, Collection of the Guild of St George, Museums Sheffield

Plate 19: 'Upper Part of the Figure of St George', after Carpaccio, 1872, 34 x 48.6 cm, watercolour and body-colour on paper, Collection of the Guild of St George, Museums Sheffield

Plate 20: *Northwest porch and corner of St. Mark's*, 1877, 64.8 x 77 cm, pencil, watercolour and bodycolour, Ruskin Foundation/Google Arts

Notes

ABBREVIATIONS USED IN THE NOTES

LE: *The Library Edition of The Complete Works of John Ruskin*, ed. Edward Tyas Cook and Alexander Wedderburn (39 vols., George Allen, 1903-1912). The following numbers refer to volume and page.

Batchelor: John Batchelor, John Ruskin, *No Wealth But Life* (Chatto & Windus, 2000)

Brownell: Robert Brownell, *Marriage of Inconvenience* (Pallas Athene, 2013)

CC: Francis O'Gorman (ed.), *The Cambridge Companion to John Ruskin* (Cambridge University Press, 2015)

Dearden: James Dearden, *John Ruskin: A Life in Pictures* (Sheffield Academic Press, 1999)

Eagles: Stuart Eagles, *After Ruskin: The Social and Political Legacies of a Victorian Prophet 1870-1920* (Oxford University Press, 2011)

Haslam: Sara E. Haslam, *John Ruskin and the Lakeland Arts Revival, 1880-1920* (Merton Priory Press, 2004)

Hilton I: Tim Hilton, *John Ruskin: The Early Years* (Yale University Press, 1985)

Hilton II: Tim Hilton, *John Ruskin: The Later Years* (Yale University Press, 2000)

Jackson: Kevin Jackson, *The Worlds of John Ruskin* (Pallas Athene, 2nd ed., 2018)

Newall: Christopher Newall, *John Ruskin: Artist and Observer* (Paul Holberton Publishing, 2014)

Quill: Sarah Quill, *Ruskin's Venice: The Stones Revisited* (2nd ed., Lund Humphries Publishers, 2018)

SW: John Ruskin, *Selected Writings* (Oxford University Press, 2009)

ABOUT THIS BOOK

1 LE 19:xlvii

CELEBRITY

1 Jackson, p. 143
2 Haslam, p. 82
3 *The Illustrated London News*, No. 910, Vol. XXXII
4 Dearden, p. 178
5 Between the wars, the range, marketed with an image of the bearded sage, became one of the company's most popular products; Paul Dawson, *Perceptions of Ruskin* (Oxenbridge Press, 2017). ?

6 Dearden, p. 194
7 Dearden, p. 198
8 L. Du Garde Peach, 'An Anniversary Broadcast'. Transcript reprinted in *The Companion*, Guild of St George, No. 17 (2017)

RUSKINLAND

1 Hilton II, p. 74
2 Footnote to 'Of the Pathetic Fallacy', from *Modern Painters*, LE 5:206, cited in SW (p. 71)
3 Cambridge School of Art Inaugural Address, 1858, LE 16:187; SW, p. 100

SEEING

1 *Præterita*, LE 35:48. Peter Sellers's satir-
  ical sketch 'Balham – Gateway to the
  South', in which his American narrator
  describes how visitors can enter the suburb 'through the verdant grasslands of
  Battersea Park', springs to mind.
2 *Præterita*, LE 35:619
3 *The Stones of Venice*, LE 10:97
4 Dearden, p. 5
5 *Præterita*, LE 35:78
6 Dearden, p. 6
7 As Francis O'Gorman has written,
  there is 'something uncanny' about the
  way Ruskin's life story is built round
  properties, including the south London
  houses, that are no more; Introduction to
  Præterita (Oxford University Press, 2012).
8 *Præterita*, LE 35:40
9 *Modern Painters*, LE 6:368
10 *The Elements of Drawing*, LE 15:50
11 *Inaugural Lecture*, LE 16:181
12 Nichola Johnson, 'Sight', in Robert
  Hewison (ed.), *'There Is No Wealth but
  Life': Ruskin in the 21st Century* (Ruskin
  Foundation, 2006)
13 Letter to his father, cited in Stephen
  Wildman, *John Ruskin, Photographer &
  Draughtsman* (Watts Gallery, 2014), p. 15
14 Letter to Cameron, cited in Wildman, op.
  cit., p. 17
15 'A guide to the most Instagram-worthy
  places in the UK', *The Citizen*, 18 June
  2018
16 Alister McGrath, 'Does Science Rob
  Nature of Its Mystery and Beauty?',
  Gresham College Lecture, 4 October 2016,
  https://www.gresham.ac.uk/lectures-
  and-events/does-science-rob-nature-of-
  its-mystery-and-beauty
17 *The Stones of Venice*, LE 11:49
18 Kenneth Clark, *Ruskin Today* (1967), cited in Newall, p. 24
19 *The Seven Lamps of Architecture*, LE 8:159
20 *Præterita*, LE 35:109
21 *Præterita*, LE 35:119
22 John Murray, *A Handbook for Travellers in
  Switzerland*, cited in John Hayman, *John
  Ruskin and Switzerland* (Wilfrid Laurier
  University Press, 1990)
23 *Præterita*, LE 35:115

DRAWING AND PAINTING

1 *Præterita*, LE 35:179
2 Cited in Hilton I, p. 48
3 Hilton I, p. 44
4 *Præterita*, LE 35:75
5 *Præterita*, LE 35:311
6 *Modern Painters*, LE 3:624
7 *Letters*, LE 37:566, cited in Newall, p. 25
8 Cited in Newall, p. 26
9 *Præterita*, LE 35:419
10 Rachel Spence, '*John Ruskin: Artist and
  Observer*, Scottish National Portrait
  Gallery, Edinburgh – review', *Financial
  Times*, 24 August 2014
11 Letter to his father, 1852, cited in Newall,
  p. 20
12 *Præterita*, LE 35:356
13 Newall, p. 240
14 Cited in Dearden, p. 41
15 *Inaugural Lecture*, LE 36:184
16 *The Laws of Fesole*, LE 15:354
17 *Præterita*, LE 35:368
18 *Modern Painters*, LE 6:79
19 *Præterita*, LE 35:305
20 Cited in Theresa M. Kelley, *Reinventing
  Allegory* (Cambridge University Press,
  2010), p. 211
21 Cited in Hilton I, p. 70
22 Obituary syndicated in several US newspapers from 21 January 1900
23 *Modern Painters*, LE 3:254
24 Franny Moyle, *Turner: The Extraordinary
  Life and Momentous Times of JMW Turner*
  (Penguin, 2017), ch. 1
25 Reporting on Ruskin's appearance and
  lecture style, the *Edinburgh Gazette* in
  1853 wrote, 'Mr Ruskin's elocution is
  peculiar; he has difficulty in sounding
  the letter "R"' (cited in Dearden, 17).
  Tim Hilton describes Ruskin's 'burring
  way of pronouncing his "r"'s', perhaps
  acquired because of his father's Scottish
  accent (Hilton I, p. 41)
26 'Pre-Raphaelitism' (1853), LE 12:157
27 'Pre-Raphaelitism' (1851), LE 12:349
28 Cited in Louise Pullen, *Genius and Hell's
  Broth: A Tale of Two Guild Artists – Frank
  Randal and William Hackstoun* (Guild of
  St George, 2017). Randal and Hackstoun
  worked for the Guild, receiving a characteristic mixture of constructive criticism
  and autocratic commands from Ruskin,

until his ill health led to a severing of the relationship.

BUILDINGS

1 *The Stones of Venice*, LE 10:4
2 W. G. Collingwood, *Ruskin Relics* (1903), cited in Hilton II, p. 282
3 *The Stones of Venice*, LE 10:82
4 Cited in Quill, p. 74
5 Obituary syndicated in several US newspapers from 21 January 1900
6 Cited in Brownell, p. 110
7 Brownell lists a number of admirers and speculates that 'comments about the nature of the marriage [including George Gray's financial affairs] must have been made to John after he arrived in Perth for the wedding: perhaps even by one of [Effie's] former suitors... The marriage would therefore have been fatally undermined even before it began'.
8 Mary Lutyens, *Effie in Venice* (Pallas Athene, 1999), p. 20
9 Tim Barringer, *Men at Work: Art and Labour in Victorian Britain* (Paul Mellon Centre/Yale University Press, 2005), p. 74. For more on Ford Madox Brown's great painting *Work*, see Chapter 7, 'Work and Education'
10 *Fors Clavigera*, LE 27:61
11 Batchelor, p. 86
12 Letter to George Richmond, 1846, LE 36:63
13 'Architecture, Memory & Metaphor: The Ruskin Library', Richard MacCormac, MJP Architects, 1 December 1996. http://mjparchitects.co.uk/about/publications/architecture-memory-metaphor-the-ruskin-library/
14 Ken Jacobson describes the sale in *Carrying Off the Palaces* (Bernard Quaritch, 2015), the beautiful catalogue written with his wife Jenny. The book reproduces Ruskin's 'lost' daguerreotypes, rediscovered and purchased by the Jacobsons. 'One account mentions a box being opened by a porter in the sale room tradition of "showing" the bidders its contents just prior to them being auctioned – a sudden burst of wind swept the documents, possibly precious letters

or manuscripts, high into the air. The horrified storyteller... saw them blow into nearly Coniston Water and then watched as they sank into the lake.' The Whitehouse collection is now kept safe from gusty squalls in the Ruskin Library at Lancaster University.

15 Lars Spuybroek, *The Sympathy of Things: Ruskin and the Ecology of Design* (Bloomsbury, 2016), p. 2
16 Passports of the time were nothing like the booklets we now carry. Brantwood has one of Ruskin's later versions, from 1866, which is more like a large letter authorising the writer's safe passage, as well as that of his travelling companions and servant, signed by Lord Clarendon, then foreign secretary.
17 This is the same letter (May 1859, cited in LE 9:xxviii) that I quoted earlier about Ruskin's favourite place.
18 Robert Hewison has pointed out to me that the Giudecca at the time was an industrial and working-class district of Venice.
19 *Le Pietre di Venezia*, exhibition, Palazzo Ducale, 2018
20 'John Ruskin e le pietre di Venezia. Il video della mostra', *Artribune*, http://www.artribune.com/television/2018/05/video-john-ruskin-e-le-pietre-di-venezia-mostra/
21 *Fors Clavigera*, letter 20, SW, p. 210
22 The inaugural Premio Letterario La Calcina John Ruskin was won by Elisa Pilia for 'Urban ruins. Memorial value and contemporary role' http://premioletterario-lacalcina-johnruskin.com/?p=793
23 *The Stones of Venice*, LE 11:235
24 Batchelor, p. 76
25 *The Seven Lamps of Architecture*, LE 7:218
26 Batchelor, p. 109
27 *The Seven Lamps of Architecture*, LE 7:244; SW, p. 25
28 Cited in 'Introducing the Carlo Scarpa monograph', Phaidon, http://uk.phaidon.com/agenda/architecture/articles/2013/june/26/introducing-the-carlo-scarpa-monograph/
29 *The Seven Lamps of Architecture*, LE 7:160
30 For more about his lecture 'Traffic' and Ruskin's resounding attack on the

industrialists' idolatrous worship of the 'Goddess of Getting-On', see Chapter 9, 'Wealth and Welfare'.

31 Cited in Blair J. Gilbert, 'Puncturing an Oxford Myth: the Truth about the "Infamous" O'Sheas and the Oxford University Museum', *Oxoniensia*, 74 (2009), p. 90

32 Batchelor, p. 148

33 Gilbert, op. cit., p. 89

34 LE 22:525

35 Quoted in Geoffrey Tyack, 'Architecture', in CC, p. 109

36 Lars Spuybroek memorably describes Alfred Waterhouse's extravagantly decorated Manchester Town Hall (begun 1868), with its myriad turrets, bow windows and gables, as a 'megacottage', linking it back to Ruskin's first writings on architecture in the 1830s, where he praised picturesque small rural dwellings in England, France, Italy and Switzerland (Spuybroek, op. cit., p. 168).

37 David Spurr, *Architecture and Modern Literature* (University of Michigan Press, 2012), open access on JSTOR: www.jstor.org/stable/j.ctt1qv5nb5.9. See chapter on 'Figures of Ruin and Restoration', pp. 142-161

38 *Fors Clavigera*, LE 28:688, cited in Michael Lang, *Designing Utopia* (Black Rose Books, 1999), p. 36

39 LE 29:264, cited in Hilton II, p. 150

40 Both Wright and Gustav Stickley, whose plans for Craftsman homes offered a Ruskinian domestic existence, realised that it was possible to apply mass production methods to Arts and Crafts principles and spread those principles at a scale that William Morris and his British counterparts never achieved. See Chapter 8, 'Craft'.

41 *The Seven Lamps of Architecture*, LE 7:225; SW, p. 18

42 Edwin Heathcote, 'A Shrine to Ornament', *Financial Times*, 21 November 2015

43 See '*A House for Essex*', https://www.living-architecture.co.uk/the-houses/a-house-for-essex/overview/

44 Frank Lloyd Wright, 'The Art and Craft of the Machine', *Brush and Pencil*, 8/2 (May 1901), 77-90 (p. 87)

45 Recounted in the opening chapters of

46 Franny Moyle, *Turner: The Extraordinary Life and Momentous Times of JMW Turner* (Penguin, 2017)

46 Hilton I, p. 173

47 *The Stones of Venice*, LE 10:193

48 Cited in Brownell, p. 423

49 This is Brownell's theory in *Marriage of Inconvenience*.

50 *Præterita*, LE 35:415

51 Suzanne Fagence Cooper's fine and balanced biography, *Effie: The Passionate Lives of Effie Gray, John Ruskin and John Everett Millais* (Gerald Duckworth & Co., 2012), maps her whole life and describes how Effie, later Lady Millais, suffered from Queen Victoria's long refusal to receive her at court.

52 John Howard Whitehouse, *Vindication of Ruskin* (1950), cited in Eagles, p. 257

LANDSCAPE AND NATURE

1 Cited in LE 7:xxii

2 Cited in Alan Davis, 'Shedding Light on the "dark clue": Ruskin, Turner, Sex and Death', *Turner Society News*, 119 (2013), 10-14

3 See Ian Warrell, *Turner's Secret Sketches* (Tate Publishing, 2012)

4 Cited in 'Arts – Ruskin's view of Turner', *Financial Times*, 1 April 1995, a review of the Tate exhibition *Through Switzerland with Turner: Ruskin's First Selection from the Turner Bequest*

5 Letter cited in LE 7:xxxvii

6 'Notes on the Turin Gallery', cited in LE 7:xl

7 *Fors Clavigera*, LE 29:89

8 *Præterita*, LE 35:496

9 *Præterita*, LE 35, Vol. III, Ch. 1, cited in Jackson, p. 78

10 *Modern Painters*, LE 7:205

11 *Præterita*, LE 35:441

12 https://tourdumontblanc.holiday/fitness/

13 *Sesame and Lilies* (1864), LE 18:90, cited in Simon Schama, *Landscape and Memory* (Alfred A. Knopf, 1995) p. 506

14 Terry Gifford, *Reconnecting with John Muir* (University of Georgia Press, 2006), p. 83

15 *The Eagle's Nest*, LE 22:153 cited in Hilton II, p. 225.

16 Francis Darwin (ed.), *Life and Letters of*

Charles Darwin (1887), cited in LE 29:xlv

17 Sara Atwood, '"The secret of sympathy":
Ruskin and the Language of Nature',
lecture to The Guild of St George and
Campaign to Protect Rural England,
London, 14 July 2016, https://youtu.be/
AOI_Ko5HMu8

18 Lars Spuybroek, *The Sympathy of Things:
Ruskin and the Ecology of Design* (Bloomsbury, 2016), p. 56

19 *Fors Clavigera*, LE 27:86

20 Cited in Alan Davis, 'Technology', in
CC, p. 170

21 Cited in Batchelor, p. 161-2.

22 Alan Davis, 'Technology', in CC, p. 171

23 Potter's interests, from the drawing of
animals and natural phenomena, through
close observation, to conservation and
a love of the Lake District, overlapped
with Ruskin's, but she apparently had
little time for him. She once described
the critic, whom she had spotted at the
Royal Academy in the 1880s, as 'one of
the most ridiculous figures I have seen...
hump-backed, not particularly clean
looking'. John Everett Millais was a close
friend of Potter's father, so it is possible, I
suppose, that word of Ruskin's behaviour
towards Effie Millais, when they were
married, had seeped down to young
Beatrix.

24 Nomination Dossier, Section 2.b,'History
and Development', p. 210, http://www.
lakedistrict.gov.uk/caringfor/projects/
whs/lake-district-nomination

25 Dearden, p. 127

26 For an explicit example of 'Ruskin inside' branding, see Chapter 8, 'Craft',
about Ruskin Design, a company that is
putting John Ruskin inside Land Rover
Defenders.

27 *Fors Clavigera*, letter 80, LE 29:171, cited in Neil Sinden, 'Ruskin Land: The
Evolving Story' (2017), ruskinland.org.uk

28 *Fors Clavigera*, LE 27:96

29 Edith Hope Scott, cited by Sinden, op. cit.

30 *The Two Paths*, LE 16:339

31 Cited in Michael Lang, *Designing Utopia*
(Black Rose Books, 1999), pp. 35-6

32 LE 18:184. The passage came from a lecture called 'The Mystery of Life and Its
Arts' that Ruskin delivered in Dublin in
1868.

33 The Prince of Wales is certainly aware of
Ruskin – perhaps inheriting his appreciation from his great-great-great uncle
Prince Leopold, Ruskin's student and
occasional chess rival. In a speech in 1990
to the American Institute of Architects, in
Washington DC, he referred to *Unto This
Last* and 'The Poetry of Architecture'.
He praised their Gold Medallist Fay
Jones, a disciple of Frank Lloyd Wright,
and urged architects to 'regain the art
and the craft [of their profession] and
then combine them with the science'.
(https://www.princeofwales.gov.uk/
speech/speech-hrh-prince-wales-titled-
accent-architecture-american-insttute-
architects-gala-dinner)

34 I'm grateful to Sara Atwood for pointing
this out to me.

35 James Stewart, 'Postcard... from Florida',
Financial Times, 18 May 2018. https://
www.ft.com/content/4388ce14-5530-
11e8-84f4-43d65af59d43

36 'The Mystery of Life and Arts', cited in
Lang, op. cit., p. 41

37 Cited in the Introduction to LE 34

38 *Atlantic Monthly*, September 1904, cited
in Dearden, p. 147

39 Dearden, p. 148

40 *The Storm-Cloud of the Nineteenth Century*,
LE 34:40

41 Later that year, Barrett staged an innovative production of *Hamlet*, which Ruskin
– as well as luminaries such as Gladstone
and Matthew Arnold – attended. Ruskin,
a keen theatre-goer, said Barrett's productions were 'educational examples for the
elevation of English taste' (James Thomas,
'Wilson Barrett's Hamlet', *Theatre Journal*,
31/4, 1979). Jeffrey Richards referred
to Barrett's involvement in 'Storm-
Cloud' at the Ruskin Seminar, Lancaster
University, 10 May 2018.

42 Hilton II, p. 281

43 *London Evening Standard*, 6 February
1884

44 Jackson, p. 133

45 LE 28:136

46 'Analysis: UK carbon emissions in 2017
fell to levels last seen in 1890', *Carbon Brief*,
https://www.carbonbrief.org/analysis-
uk-carbon-emissions-in-2017-fell-to-
levels-last-seen-in-1890

47 Jonathon Porritt, 'Nature', in Hewison (ed.), *'There Is No Wealth But Life': Ruskin in the 21st Century* (Ruskin Foundation, 2006). I analyse the significance of *Unto This Last* in Chapter 7, 'Work and Education'.

48 Ruskin quoted this letter in *Storm-Cloud of the Nineteenth Century*, adding that 'dead men's souls' had been intended in part to allude to the destructive Franco-Prussian war being waged in 1871. I describe the breakdown more fully in Chapter 8, 'Craft'

49 *Landscapes After Ruskin*, exhibition at Grey Art Gallery, New York, 17 April-7 July, 2018 https://greyartgallery.nyu.edu /exhibition/landscapes-ruskin-redefining-sublime/sec/images/

50 Sara Atwood, '"The secret of sympathy": Ruskin and the Language of Nature', lecture given to the Guild of St George and Campaign for the Protection of Rural England, 14 July 2016

51 Joseph Ryan, *The Ruskin Art Club: A History* (Ruskin Art Club, c. 1997), p. 3

52 https://www.theguardian.com/uk-news /2018/jan/07/campaigners-zip-wire-lake-district-environmental-thirlmere-reservoir-attraction

53 Fiona Reynolds, *The Fight for Beauty* (OneWorld Publications, 2016)

54 Robert Hewison in 'The Elements of Ruskin: Ruskin Now', paper for the Ashmolean Study Day on *The Elements of Drawing* (3 June 2011) http://ruskin. ashmolean.org/media/_file/doc/ elements_of_ruskin_robert_hewison_ 1.pdf

WORK AND EDUCATION

1 *Unto This Last*, LE 17:25

2 Ruskin's reading of Adam Smith was deliberately one-sided. In *Fors Clavigera*, he returns repeatedly to what he calls Smith's 'gospel of covetousness' and attacks his selfishness. As Jesse Norman has pointed out in *Adam Smith: What He Thought and Why It Matters* (Allen Lane, 2018), Smith was neither an advocate of laissez-faire, nor of selfishness, and would have opposed 'modern market fundamentalism' (Jesse Norman, 'In search of the real Adam Smith', *Financial Times*, 22 June 2018, https:// www.ft.com/content/64ee4a34-7600-11e8-b326-75a27d27ea5f).

3 Cited in Eagles, p. 208

4 Jonathan Glancey, 'Of Skeletons and Souls', *The Guardian*, 19 June 2009

5 Andrew Hill, 'Ruskin Offers a Moral Code on Just Rewards', *Financial Times*, 21 August 2009

6 Cited in Sorensen, 'Ruskin and Carlyle', in CC, p. 194

7 Letter to his mother, 25 May 1868, LE 36:550

8 From a letter to Charles Norton, paraphrased LE 24:xlii

9 Batchelor, 77

10 Cited in Tim Barringer, *Men at Work: Art and Labour in Victorian Britain* (Paul Mellon Centre/Yale University Press, 2005), p. 143

11 *Fors Clavigera*, LE 27:183

12 Quoted in Hilton I, p. 204-5

13 *The Elements of Drawing*, LE 15:97

14 *In Our Time*, 31 March 2005, BBC Radio

15 John Ruskin, letter to Effie, cited in Brownell, p. 195

16 *Præterita*, LE 35:525

17 For context, Robert Brownell reminds readers the age of consent was raised during Ruskin's time – from 12 to 13

18 Cited in Hilton II, p. 87

19 *Sesame and Lilies*, LE 18:121

20 Kate Millett, *Sexual Politics* (1970; repr. Virago, 1977), p. 89

21 Samira Ahmed, *John Ruskin's Eurythmic Girls*, BBC Radio 3, February 2017; and 'The Making of *John Ruskin's Eurythmic Girls*', samiraahmed.co.uk, 21 February 2017, http://www.samiraahmed.co.uk/ the-making-of-john-ruskins-euryth mic-girls/

22 *Fors Clavigera*, LE 29:484

23 *Fors Clavigera*, LE 29:503, cited in Sara Atwood, 'John Ruskin on Education', in *The Encyclopaedia of Informal Education* (2008), http://infed.org/mobi/john-ruskin-on-education/

24 *The Crown of Wild Olive*, LE 18:503

25 *Ruskin, Bembridge and Brantwood* (Edinburgh University Press, 1994), by the great Ruskinian James Dearden (an Old

Bembridgian himself), cited in Eagles, p. 251

26 According to an article in *The Westminster Budget* (10 March 1899), the school was heated and ventilated by a 'propulsion system, which means that the air in the rooms is renewed seven times every hour, that there is no dust, and' – implausibly – 'that the schoolrooms at the end of the day are as fresh as they were at the commencement of lessons'. The teachers and students reported that 'this purified air makes them uncommonly hungry'.

27 'The Croydon Archives: Clive Whitehead investigates the origins of John Ruskin Grammar School', http://www.mel-lambert.com/Ruskin/

28 At least three other ex-pupils of John Ruskin Grammar School went on to senior roles in football management, including at Crystal Palace, the club where Hodgson was appointed manager in 2017 (https://www.independent.co.uk/sport/football/premier-league/crystal-palace-appoint-roy-hodgson-new-manager-frank-de-boer-sacked-a7941596.html). Crystal Palace is, of course, named after the 1851 Great Exhibition building, which was relocated to south London three years after Effie visited it (and Ruskin disparaged it). See Chapter 8, 'Craft'.

29 *Lectures on Architecture and Painting*, LE 12:67

30 Strangely, this seems to be a slight misquotation. The original from Ruskin's lecture 'The Relation of Art to Morals' is 'life without industry is guilt, and industry without art is brutality' (LE 20:93).

31 Luke Leitch, 'The Philosopher King', *1843 Magazine*, April/May 2017, www.1843magazine.com/style/the-philosopher-king

32 Rachel Sanderson, 'King of Cashmere Cucinelli Finds Trend for Menswear Is Right Fit', *Financial Times*, 19 January 2014

33 Andrew Hill, 'Work 2.0', *Financial Times*, 21 September 2012. http://ig-legacy.ft.com/content/4f5b4b30-02b7-11e2-9e53-00144feabdc0

34 Adair Turner, then the UK's financial regulator, remarked in 2009 that the banking sector had become 'swollen beyond its socially useful size' (*Prospect*, 27 August 2009), an echo of Ruskin that I referenced in columns for the *Financial Times* and in my introduction to a new edition of *Unto This Last* (Pallas Athene, 2010)

35 *The Crown of Wild Olive*, LE 18:405

36 *A World of Work*, Brantwood, March–September 2018. The cartoon 'Work' features in a graphic book about Ruskin's ideas, *Bloke's Progress* (Knockabout Ltd/ The Ruskin Foundation, 2018), by Kevin Jackson and cartoonist Hunt Emerson, with Howard Hull and Emma Bartlet, the latest in a series of 'Ruskin Comics'.

CRAFT

1 *The Stones of Venice*, LE 10:196

2 Cited in Hilton I, p. 235

3 Hilton II, p. 535

4 Fiona MacCarthy, *William Morris: A Life for Our Time* (Faber & Faber, 2010), cited in Peter Faulker, 'Ruskin and Morris', *Journal of the William Morris Society*, 14/1 (Autumn 2000), p. 15

5 Cited in Faulkner, op. cit., p. 14

6 This is itself a third-hand account. Pre-Raphaelite painter Henry Holiday was recalling, years later, Gladstone's recollection of Ruskin's comments (cited in Hilton II, p. 369)

7 *Black and British: A Forgotten History*, BBC, season 1, episode 3, 2008

8 A contemporary account by John Tallis, cited in Tim Barringer, *Men at Work: Art and Labour in Victorian Britain* (Paul Mellon Centre/Yale University Press, 2005), p. 243

9 Cited in Barringer, op. cit., p. 260

10 Ruskin also expressed doubts about Japanese art and civilisation, though he accepted some examples of Japanese cloisonné work for the Guild's Sheffield museum and at one point, surprisingly, dropped a note to a correspondent, thanking him for a book of Japanese landscapes and saying he would like to live in Japan. Ruskin enjoys some continued fame in Japan thanks to Ryuzo

Mikimoto, scion of the 19th-century tycoon who founded the Mikimoto pearl empire. Mikimoto studied Ruskin, collected his work and translated some of his writing into Japanese in the first part of the 20th century. He assembled a Ruskin Library in Tokyo that was revived in the 1980s. A Mikimoto Ruskin Memorial Lecture is still given every year at Lancaster University.

11 *The Two Paths*, LE 16:260

12 Cited in Adam Hochschild, *King Leopold's Ghost: A Story of Greed, Terror and Heroism in Colonial Africa* (Picador, 2011), loc. 1460 in Kindle edition

13 Dearden, p. 84. The Rhodes connection has also given rise to an extreme conspiracy theory, easily uncovered by a quick internet search, that casts Ruskin as the inspiration of a British 'secret elite' that provoked and then prolonged the First World War in a bid for world domination.

14 *Lectures on Art*, LE 20:42

15 http://ruskin.ashmolean.org/collection/8990/9168/9269

16 Selwyn Image, cited in Dearden, p. 82

17 No. 100 in James Dearden's excellent collection of images of Ruskin (Dearden, p. 81)

18 Paul Dawson, *Perceptions of Ruskin* (The Oxenbridge Press, 2017), p. 33

19 Hilton II, 250-251

20 Letter to Joan Severn, cited in LE 22:xxi

21 *Pall Mall Gazette*, cited in Hilton II, p. 465.

22 *Præterita*, LE 35:427

23 Marcus Waithe, 'Ruskin and Craftsmanship', Annual Guild of St George Lecture, November 2015. https://www.youtube.com/watch?v=LvPx9TPekRQ

24 Dearden, p. 18

25 Cited in Haslam, p. 24

26 Haslam, p. 42

27 H. D. Rawnsley, *Ruskin and the English Lakes* (James Maclehose, 1902), cited in Haslam, p. 87

28 Haslam, p. 130. As Clive Hayward has pointed out to me, this is often the pattern for programmes in rural communities in developing countries, led by women.

29 Haslam, p. 99

30 More in Chapter 9, 'Wealth and Welfare'

31 http://www.victorianweb.org/authors/ruskin/quotation.html

32 'Pre-Raphaelitism' (1851), LE 12:344-5

33 Letter 27, LE 27:497

34 Jeff VanderMeer with S. J. Chambers, *The Steampunk Bible: An Illustrated Guide to the World of Imaginary Airships, Corsets and Goggles, Mad Scientists, and Strange Literature* (Abrams, 2011), p. 103

35 LE 17:336

36 'Author Lists His Favourite Books', Oxford Mail, http://www.oxfordmail.co.uk/news/2436468.Author_lists_his_favourite_books_/

37 Cited in VanderMeer with Chambers, op. cit., p. 103

38 The original line comes from *Put Yourself in His Place,* an improving dramatic novel by Charles Reade (1870).

39 Jeff VanderMeer, '60 in 60: #15 – Ruskin's On Art and Life (Penguin Great Ideas)', 29 December 2008, http://www.jeffvandermeer.com/2008/12/29/60-in-60-15-ruskins-on-art-and-life-penguins-great-ideas/. In this blogpost, VanderMeer analyses in detail this Penguin edition that combines two Ruskin works, 'The Nature of Gothic' and 'The Work of Iron'.

40 Cited in Andrew Hill, 'Why I Hope Etsy Survives Flotation with Its Soul Intact', *Financial Times*, 19 March 2015

41 Matthew Crawford, *The Case for Working with Your Hands or Why Office Work Is Bad for Us and Fixing Things Feels Good* (Viking, 2010), p. 197. I prefer the title of the original US edition: *Shopclass as Soulcraft.*

42 LE 8:47

43 LE 9:52

44 Walter Isaacson, *Steve Jobs* (Simon & Schuster, 2011), cited in 'Steve Jobs' obsession with quality of the things unseen', *The Next Web*, https://thenextweb.com/apple/2011/10/24/steve-jobs-obsession-with-the-quality-of-the-things-unseen/

45 Andrew Hunt and David Thomas, *The Pragmatic Programmer* (1999), cited at Chad Dickerson, 'Code as Craft', 10 February 2010, https://codeascraft.com/2010/02/10/code-as-craft/

46 Cited Hilton I, p. 219. This was the same pamphlet that contained Ruskin's proposal to form an association of monument-watchers in every town to help preserve old buildings – the outline of what became, 23 years later under William Morris's leadership, the Society for the Protection of Ancient Buildings.

47 Hilton II, p. 436

48 Cited in Eagles, p. 101. Stuart Eagles makes a persuasive case that the Hinksey road-builders were 'digging the foundations of reform', as he entitles the chapter about the project and its participants.

WEALTH AND WELFARE

1 I drew five: 'Provide for the nation', collaborate, be honest, lead (wisely), create wealth (Andrew Hill, 'Ruskin's Message for the Modern Merchant', *Financial Times*, 3 February 2011, https://www.ft.com/content/fac23c82-10fb-11df-9a9e-00144feab49a).

2 Hilton II, p. 66

3 *The Crown of Wild Olive*, LE 18:433

4 *The Crown of Wild Olive*, LE 18:412

5 For the British pavilion at the Venice Biennale of 2013, Jeremy Deller painted a mural showing William Morris tipping oligarch Roman Abramovich's brash superyacht Luna into the Venetian lagoon – an image Ruskin would certainly have appreciated.

6 LE 27:476, cited at ruskinatwalkley.org

7 *Fors Clavigera*, letter 8, LE 27:132

8 Letter from 1875, cited Hilton II, 307

9 *Fors Clavigera*, LE 27:142

10 Cited in Hilton II, p. 250

11 Cited in Hilton II, p. 302

12 Hilton II, p. 304

13 Letter to Joan Severn, cited in Hilton II, p. 328

14 Tim Hilton suggests that 'we might also consider the Guild of St George as a utopia in which Rose, alive or dead, might find a spiritual home' (Hilton II, p. 295).

15 *The Two Paths*, LE 16:406

16 Cited in LE 16:lx

17 If you want to start counting them, let me recommend *After Ruskin* (Oxford University Press, 2011), Stuart Eagles's

meticulous analysis of the way the roots of Ruskin's ideas grew into social and political movements and institutions.

18 See Chapter 5, 'Buildings'

19 Eagles, p. 120

20 See Chapter 7, 'Work and Education'

21 Nicholas Timmins, *The Five Giants: A Biography of the Welfare State* (new edition, William Collins, 2017)

22 Eagles, p. 228

23 Caroline Benn, *Keir Hardie: A Biography*, (Hutchinson, 1992), p. 146. I am grateful to David Barrie for tracking down the reference.

24 John Bew, *Citizen Clem: A Biography of Attlee* (riverrun, 2016), p. 61

25 David Drew, 'How Labour Can Reconnect with Rural Voters Left Behind by Relentless Austerity', *Huffington Post*, 27 March 2018, https://www.huffingtonpost.co.uk/entry/labour-rural-voters_uk_5ab90a89e4b0decad04c4715. Drew's doctoral thesis for the University of Western England is entitled '*New Labour in Power in the English Countryside 1997-2010: A Social Democratic Moment Forgone?*' (http://eprints.uwe.ac.uk/29502/14/Thesis%20-%20Draft%203.pdf)

26 Bernard Shaw, *Ruskin's Politics* (1921), cited in Eagles, p. 204, where Eagles provides comprehensive evidence of how Ruskin gave working men at the turn of the 20th century 'a new language and grammar of political economy with which they could do battle with the injustices of industrial capitalism'.

27 LE 12:lxxxii

28 LE 34:499

29 Edith J. Morley, *John Ruskin and Social Ethics* (Fabian Society, 1917), p. 23, available at https://digital.library.lse.ac.uk

30 *Fors Clavigera*, LE 27:15

31 *Fors Clavigera*, LE 27:18

32 LE 34:547, cited in Eagles, p. 27

33 There is an excellent account on the website of Ambleside's Armitt Museum, in the Lake District, which holds this cache of once highly sensitive confidential correspondence with the doctor, George Parsons: http://armitt.com/armitt_website/john-ruskin-armitt-museum-art-gallery-and-library/

34 *Fors Clavigera*, LE 29:386

35 Ruskin later recognised that he had misjudged Hill – he said he was 'choked with humble pie' (Hilton II, p. 550) – though, tragically, they never truly made up.

36 Cited in Batchelor, p. 284

37 Cited in Hilton II, p. 424

38 Cited in Rachel Dickinson, *John Ruskin's Correspondence with Joan Severn: Sense and Nonsense Letters* (Routledge, 2009), p. 2. Dickinson's exhaustive, generous analysis of the letters paints a picture of interdependence between Ruskin and Joan Severn that is an antidote to the more critical view of her as a thick, provincial money-grubber.

39 Dickinson, op. cit., p. 6

40 Dearden, p. 165

41 'More than her gates, Siena opens her heart to you.'

42 John Ruskin, *Præterita*, LE 35:562

FINISH

1 Letter to his father, cited in Dearden, p. 61.

2 Much of the detail of the history of Ruskin, Florida, and its links to other Ruskinite communities is drawn from 'John Ruskin's American Utopias', Arthur McA. Miller, unpublished paper, https://hccfl.digital.flvc.org/islandora/object/hccfl%3A1731

3 LE 27:xxviii, cited in Michael Wheeler (ed.), *Ruskin and Environment: The Storm-Cloud of the Nineteenth Century* (Manchester University Press, 1995), p. 142

4 De Coubertin, in a further interconnection of Ruskin's legacies, once stayed at Toynbee Hall on a visit to London.

5 Eagles, p. 17

6 Francis O'Gorman in his Introduction to CC, p. 1.

7 Clark's narration begins, 'Ruskin said: "Great nations write their autobiographies in three manuscripts;–the book of their deeds, the book of their words, and the book of their art. Not one of these books can be understood unless we read the two others; but of the three, the only quite trustworthy one is the last." On the whole, I think this is true.' ('The Skin of Our Teeth', *Civilisation*, episode 1, BBC, 1969). Clark is quoting from the Preface to *St Mark's Rest*, Ruskin's late return to analysis of Venice and its history. His cautious 'on the whole' is a clue to the admirably objective way in which he approached Ruskin, and the way we should, too.

8 Anthony Lane, 'Art for Love's Sake', *The New Yorker*, 14 August 2000

9 *South County*, QA Productions, 2013

10 Ibid.

11 Hilton II, p. ix. Tim Hilton published *John Ruskin: The Early Years*, which covers the thinker's first 40 years to 1859, in 1985; it runs to 301 pages. The second 'half' appeared 15 years later and is more than twice as long. Hilton points out that for the second volume he had to analyse 'more abundant and complex' materials and assess previously unexplored 'records of many of Ruskin's intimate concerns'. He does it brilliantly and touchingly.

12 Walter Crane, cited in Dearden, p. 189

Index

INDEX

INDEX

INDEX

Parker, Barry, 136
Parker, Mike, 272, 273
parliamentary politics, Ruskin's detestation
  of, 246
pathetic fallacy, 17, 141
Peace – Burial at Sea (JMW Turner), 66
Peacock, David, 166, 275
Peak District, 126, 127
Peden, Paul, 173
Peep Show (TV sitcom), 263
Perera, Sumi, 75
perfection and imperfection, 180, 215-19
Perry, Grayson, 110
Peterloo Massacre, 240
photography, 30, 45, 46, 76
Pisa, 61, 134, 135
pizza, 99
Poetry of Architecture, The (John Ruskin),
  268
Porritt, Jonathon, 142-3, 236
Potter, Beatrix, 129
PowerPoint, Ruskin's visual aids compared,
  158
Praeterita (John Ruskin), 36, 52, 120, 252,
  255, 257, 274, 279, 290
Pragmatic Programmer, The (Andy Hunt and
  Dave Thomas), 218
Pre-Raphaelite Brotherhood, 6, 22, 27, 60,
  61, 65, 70-3, 114, 143, 181, 186-7, 193
  Ruskin's defence of, 71, 152, 155, 199,
    248, 266
  Young British Artists compared, 70
'Pre-Raphaelitism', lecture (1853, John
  Ruskin), 71, 73
'Pre-Raphaelitism', pamphlet (1851, John
  Ruskin), 71-72, 175, 211, 235
Primavera (Sandro Botticelli), 196, 230
Proust, Marcel, 23
provenance, 31, 109, 214, 216-17
pubic hair, 166, *see also* Ruskin, John:
  marriage to Effie Gray
Pugin, Augustus, 102-3, 110, 246
Pullman, Philip, 214
purpose in business, 28, 100-1, 131, 175,
  see also work, meaning of

Queenswood School, 166
Quercia, Jacopo della, 82
Quill, Sarah, 98

railways, 21
  Ruskin's opposition to, 19, 36, 49, 98, 104,
    128

Ramzan, Mohammed, 170, 171
Randal, Frank, 75
Raphael, 72, 84
Rawnsley, Edith, 205
Rawnsley, Hardwicke, 19, 22, 146, 147, 205,
  221
Redentore (Venice), Church of, 96, 99
restoration, 84, 92, 97-8, 103, 177, 189
Reynolds, Fiona, 148
Rhodes, Cecil, inspired by Ruskin, 194
Ricardo, David, 152
Richardson, Mary, 53
road-building, Ruskin's experiment, 222,
  231-2, 237
robots and robotics, *see* automation
Rochdale, 134
Roehampton, University of, 166
Rogers, Samuel, 51, 95
Rossetti, Dante Gabriel, 70, 157
Royal Academy (London), 70, 122, 152, 158,
  197
Royal College of Art, 77
Royal Institute of British Architects, 123
Roycroft, 208
RUSKIN (bags), 208, 210, 217
Ruskin (Florida), 259-62, 267-73
Ruskin Art Club (Los Angeles), 7, 144-5,
  217
Ruskin Centre for Art Appreciation (Venice),
  171
Ruskin collection (Sheffield), 23, 43, 147,
  176, 177, 234, 237, *see also* Guild of
  St George; Sheffield
Ruskin College (Florida), 269
Ruskin College (Missouri), 269
Ruskin College (Oxford), 27, 269
Ruskin Design, 210, 211, 213, 214
Ruskin Hall, *see* Ruskin College (Oxford)
Ruskin House, *see* John Lewis Partnership
Ruskinite settlements and communities,
  see also Ruskin Land
  Barmouth, 250
  Cloughton (Scarborough), 250
  Florida, 259-62, 267-73
  Georgia, 262
  Illinois, 261
  Liverpool, 250
  Missouri, 261, 269
  Tennessee, 23, 268
  Wavertree (Liverpool), 250
Ruskin-in-Sheffield, 235, *see also* Guild of
  St George; Ruskin collection (Sheffield)

INDEX

INDEX

Published by Pallas Athene (Publishers) Ltd,
Studio 11A, Archway Studios
25-27 Bickerton Road, London N19 5JT
For further information on our books please visit
www.pallasathene.co.uk

First edition 2019
Reprinted 2019

 pallasathenebooks   PallasAtheneBooks

 Pallas_books   Pallasathene0

ISBN 978 1 84368 175 5

Printed in England